D0043834

PRAISE FOR

RUNNING AGAINST THE DEVIL

"Packed with the same punchy, straight-to-the-jugular humour that has made [Rick Wilson] a sought-after television guest and columnist in the Trump era . . . Wilson explains it all. Chapter by chapter, he debunks the myths, wishes, and pipe dreams which have led previous Democratic presidential nominees down the garden path to the runner-up's position in November."

—*The Independent*

"*Running Against the Devil* is pugnacious and profane . . . blunt and funny . . . relentlessly irreverent and breathtakingly brutal."

—*The Guardian*

"A caustically funny, outraged, and deadly serious analysis . . . Political consultant Wilson . . . intensifies his strident excoriation of Trump with a hard-hitting assessment of Democrats' chances of winning the next presidential election—a victory that is crucial for saving the country."

—*Kirkus Reviews* (starred)

"Democrats . . . would do well to consider the book's fundamental warning that winning in 2020 will require 'put[ting] electoral realities ahead of progressive fantasies.'"

—*Publishers Weekly*

"If you believe America's future depends on Donald Trump's political machine being crushed at the polls next year, then Rick Wilson's *Running Against the Devil* is a must-read. Wilson brilliantly explains how Democrats could lose to Trump's 'racist and blisteringly stupid' campaign message yet again unless they change course now. Drawing upon Wilson's insights, Americans can take back their government and send the reality TV host back to Mar-a-Lago once and for all."

—Joe Scarborough, MSNBC

"Rick Wilson is one of the best political strategists of our times. He knows the calculus of how to win better than a mathematician. This book is going to give some old-school Democrats a little heartburn. But if we want to win in 2020, Wilson's analysis is a full stop. Period. Read and get to work."

—Donna Brazile, former interim chair, Democratic National Committee

"Florida Man Chooses Country Over Party! It appears the Democratic Party's 2020 Election briefing book has been written by a lifelong Republican strategist, and you're looking at it."

—Brian Williams, MSNBC

"No one understands the nature of Trumpism better than Rick Wilson. He also knows how the Democrats can blow this election. This may be a hard book for some of them to read, but it is a message they absolutely need to hear if they want to beat Donald Trump."

—Charles Sykes, author of *How the Right Lost Its Mind*

RUNNING AGAINST THE DEVIL

RUNNING AGAINST THE DEVIL

A PLOT TO SAVE AMERICA
FROM TRUMP—AND
DEMOCRATS FROM THEMSELVES

RICK WILSON

CROWN
FORUM

NEW YORK

2020 Crown Forum Trade Paperback Edition

Copyright © 2020 by Rick Wilson

All rights reserved.

Published in the United States by Crown Forum, an imprint of Random House, a division of Penguin Random House LLC, New York.

CROWN FORUM with colophon is a registered trademark of Penguin Random House LLC.

Originally published, in slightly different form, in hardcover in the United States by Crown Forum, an imprint of Random House, a division of Penguin Random House LLC, in 2020.

Library of Congress Cataloging-in-Publication Data

Names: Wilson, Rick, author. Title: Running against the devil / Rick Wilson. Description: First Edition. | New York : Crown Forum, 2020. | Includes index. Identifiers: LCCN 2019042005 (print) | LCCN 2019042006 (ebook) | ISBN 9780593137581 (Hardcover) | ISBN 9780593137604 (Paperback) | ISBN 9780593137598 (eBook) Subjects: LCSH: Trump, Donald, 1946—Influence. | Presidents—United States—Election—2020. | United States—Politics and government—2017—Classification: LCC E915 .W55 2020 (print) | LCC E915 (ebook) | DDC 973.933092—dc23
LC record available at https://lccn.loc.gov/2019042005
LC ebook record available at https://lccn.loc.gov/2019042006

Printed in the United States of America on acid-free paper

crownforum.com

9 8 7 6 5 4 3 2 1

To the men and women inside government who have confronted enormous risk and danger to their careers, reputations, and personal safety to tell the truth about this White House and this president. In the face of the hatred and abuse that hits anyone Trump designates as an enemy, they have demonstrated something truly rare in today's Washington: honor. Every authoritarian regime in history depends on silence, either coerced or purchased, and every whistle-blower and truth-teller who raises their hand, swears to speak the truth, and takes fire is deserving of our appreciation.

CONTENTS

PART I
THE CASE AGAINST TRUMP, OR FOUR MORE YEARS IN HELL   19

A NOTE TO READERS

When I wrote *Everything Trump Touches Dies,* I had no idea the slightly flippant title would become an iron law of American politics, but here we are. The reaction to *ETTD* was beyond my wildest expectations, and I am honored that folks have found it a source of encouragement and inspiration. Every day, the damage mounts and Trump's curse adds to the political body count.

ETTD changed my life. In it I found a voice I didn't know I had, and *Running Against the Devil* is the next step on a very unexpected journey.

Running Against the Devil isn't simply a sequel; it's also a warning to take the 2020 election with the deadly seriousness it merits. As we understand more clearly each day the dangers Trump poses for America's future, everything legal should be on the table. (And if you do something illegal, don't tell me. I'm in enough trouble already.) This book is a window into how I fought and won campaigns for decades, and if sometimes the tough love seems a little more tough than love, I hope you'll understand that's exactly why. This is the fight of our lives, and we can't afford to fuck it up.

The creation of *ETTD* took place in late 2017 and early 2018, and then as now the belief that any book would be overcome by events drove me to write faster. If anything, the sense of rising danger from Donald Trump made the writing of *Running Against the Devil* even more urgent. Books take time, and by the time this is in the hands of readers, a thousand new crazy moments that would have been unthinkable a decade ago, or a month ago, mean that new information and new realities will intrude into even my best-laid plans. Stick with me, though. There's a quiz at the end.

A FEW NOTES FROM THE SUMMER OF 2020

When the hardcover version of *Running Against the Devil* went on sale in January 2020, it shot to number 4 on the *New York Times* bestseller list. I was immersed in the usual tasks of promoting the book—traveling, doing signings and interviews, and hitting the TV circuit with my usual vigor. My new posse, the Lincoln Project—a band of ex-Republican strategists, consultants, and heavy hitters opposed to Trump—was off the ground and plotting to make the next ten months as long and painful as possible for Donald Trump.

Considering the umber shitlord in the White House, life was, on the whole, pretty good. I was on the road at the end of February when the world took a sharp turn off the exit ramp to COVID.

The COVID-19 pandemic is a titanic force that has altered the trajectory of the country, the Trump presidency, and the 2020 election. But there was another force that had an enormous impact on the country and our politics: the breakdown of the Trump campaign's massive investment in making Bernie Sanders the Democratic presidential nominee. From the moment Sanders entered the race in February 2019, the Trump campaign worked tirelessly to push him into the lead, from presidential tweets to the campaign's paid social-media efforts seeking to make Sanders the pick. By December, it looked like Bernie was building a head of steam, and he began to be seen as inevitably sliding toward victory in the Democratic primary. It is only by some unknown providence that the Trump campaign failed.

In retrospect, the brief window in December 2019 and early January 2020 when Bernie Sanders seemed to be on track to take the Democratic nomination was the best moment of the entire presidency for the Trump team. Mitch McConnell had done what Mitch does; by breaking the will and souls of enough Republican senators, he had stopped the Ukraine impeachment trial in its tracks. The Federal Reserve kept pumping liquidity into the system to keep the markets booming. The campaign and its grifter archipelago of MAGA super PACs was sucking up the Social Security payments of boomer rubes like an industrial vacuum. Hell, Brad Parscale even leveraged his role as campaign manager into a $2.5 million waterfront home in Ft. Lauderdale, two condos worth almost a million each, a new Ferrari, and a new Range Rover.

Life for Team Trump was also good.

I can't overstate the degree to which Trump world was salivating over the prospect of running against the Vermont socialist. With visions of Bernie as the nominee dancing in their heads, Team Trump was busily planning for a second term, scheming to poison their rivals (looking at you, Ivanka), planning new internment camps (well, at least Stephen Miller was, but then again, isn't he *always*?), and preparing the Trump dynasty for decades of power and grift.

The subtitle of *Running Against the Devil*—"A Plot to Save America from Trump—and Democrats from Themselves"—got a little blowback from Democrats when the book was released. "We've *got* this," they said. "Bernie has the *passion* and the *energy* and just you wait for the revolution, kulak!" Meanwhile, the anti-anti-Trump brigade (I know it's awkward, but honestly, so are they) were giggling furiously, confronting people like me with, "You're really going to vote for a *communist* over Trump? For *Bernie*?"

Then, to the disappointment of the triumvirate of intolerables comprising the Bernie bros, the Trumpers, and anti-anti-Trump boys, the Democratic primary gradually played out, with various flavors-of-the-moment falling away and Joe Biden rising to the top of the field. The bruising primary I described in this book got a major twist when Mike Bloomberg jumped into the race and spent the GDP of Belgium only to see his lane blocked and his political fortunes sunk. Bloomberg was the first real proof case that even unlimited money can't give a candidate those elusive gifts, luck and charisma. He did buy Biden some space and time, and gave Warren and Sanders, the hardest progressives in the race, a different focus for their ire.

Joe Biden's campaign was rescued in large measure by forces that are relevant in every Democratic primary race: older voters, African Americans, and the luck that comes from both political persistence and blocking-and-tackling.

In late February, South Carolina representative Jim Clyburn made what may have been the most important political endorsement in modern electoral history. Ahead of his state's Democratic primary, the respected spokesman for the African American community—whose vote would be critical for a Biden win after bruising losses in Iowa and New Hampshire—made a passionate case for the former vice president. From that moment, the Sanders predicate was dead in the water. There was no surge of young progressives at the polls. There was no powerful force of far-left AOC-flavored activists. The Bernie bros were revealed to be an online circle jerk, sound and fury signifying trolling. There was no hidden socialist cadre waiting in the Midwest cornfields for the revolution to begin.

The Democrats resisted their worst impulses. Almost heroically, they turned their gaze from Bernie and decided that electable and centrist Biden was better than a Thousand-Year Trump Reich. I like to think my humble little book had something to do with that, and I'm grateful for the folks from Biden's campaign who let me know they'd read it and internalized it.

In late February, Biden's inevitability was coming into focus, and I was in Happy Warrior mode. This campaign was going to be a referendum on Trump (which I mentioned enough times in the hardcover edition of this book to make readers want to throw it—and me—against the wall), not a debate over socialism and the workers controlling the means of production.

Inside the Trump camp, the massive fundraising hauls—just under a half-billion dollars in 2019 for the Trump campaign, the RNC, and the affiliated Trump super PACs—were offset by two grim realities. First, no matter how much money the Trump campaign money launderer (pardon me, campaign manager) Brad Parscale dumped into the Facebook maw or other advertising efforts, Trump's approval numbers stayed stuck in a narrow band: never much under 41 percent and never much over 45. For me, a guy who for thirty years has eaten and slept polling, the danger signs flashing in that circumstance were clear: Trump didn't have room to grow, and too many of his base voters were in already deep-red states.

In late January, in the midst of all this, a story started to flicker on the edges of the news cycle. A new infectious disease had swept through the Chinese city of Wuhan. The novel coronavirus was spreading, as viruses do in our modern interconnected world, and had already reached our shores. In late February, the United States marked what were at the time believed to be the first deaths in the country from COVID-19, the disease caused by the virus.

As a guy who loves politics, aviation, and cooking, on top of my full-time job as political savant, you'd think my hobby list would already be pretty full. But in fact I happen to have another interest, and that's a fascination with infectious diseases. Naturally, the coronavirus was right up my alley. I wondered if *this* was the thing that would finally disrupt a complacent Washington that had accustomed itself to Trump's terrible leadership, or even herald the zombie apocalypse. *Finally.*

The prospect of Donald Trump facing an actual crisis—not the usual problems, like "Why is my Filet-O-Fish cold?" or "Why can't I find gloves in a men's extra-twee?"—had worried me ever since his candidacy. I always had my money on "hot war in Iran due to Trumpian fuckup," but in an actual pandemic, it was obvious that Trump would be overmatched instantly. Managing that kind of crisis takes intellectual rigor, discipline, foresight, candor, and selflessness. Sound much like Donald Trump?

By early March, it was clear the toll of COVID-19 would border on the unimaginable, and the world was about to take a very grim turn. In the weeks that followed, I was pleasantly surprised by the rapid, transparent, science-based reaction of the White House as the administration ordered immediate distribution of supplies, put medical need before politics, and prepared the American people for the economic and human toll of the virus.

Oh. Wait.

That was in the *other* timeline, where Jeb Bush was president.

No, here on Earth 1, we had the bloated, boasting, mentally insufficient manbaby in charge. So of course he fucked it up just as fully and painfully as you might have expected from a man who had "governed" only in the loosest sense and whose three-year track record of abject failure, corruption, idiocy, management by tweeted rage-fits, and short-attention-span fuckery had already locked him in to first place as America's worst president.

It was inevitable that Trump would face a crisis immune to his particular brand of mendacity and incompetence. It was inevitable he'd face someone or something that didn't respond to juvenile tweets or stupid memes or insulting nicknames.

Tragically, with a virus as contagious and deadly as the coronavirus, it was also inevitable that Donald Trump's failures would lead to untold deaths and misery. With God as my witness, when I titled my first book *Everything Trump Touches Dies* I didn't mean it literally.

ETTD was a simple rule, a shorthand for the damage Trump does to everyone and everything around him. Sure, over the preceding three years, it had become an iron law of American politics, an invariable and inevitable process as regular as the president's daily jones for adulation and fast food, but I didn't think it would extend to *everyone in the country*. I didn't think even his team of risible morons would allow him to mismanage a crisis this profoundly.

There will be volumes written about Trump's bungling of this crisis, and this brief chapter is not that history. But here we are. As I write this, more than 100,000 Americans have died. Our economy is reeling, and unemployment is at Great Depression levels.

For months, Trump's handling of the coronavirus has zigzagged between tragicomic and insidious. He has downplayed, denied, and deceived. He owns this crisis no matter how much he wishes to push it out and blame the governors, the Chinese, or the Never Trump movement.

As a man who has studied Donald Trump too closely for too long, I feel like an anthropologist in hell, doomed to watch for some sign of conscience or insight or awareness to flicker in his beady eyes, or for some emotion other than pissiness to cross his jowly face. Instead, in response to a crisis that dwarfs every event in our history save the Civil War and World War II, there's . . . nothing. No compassion for the death toll. No moment of leadership and dignity. Nothing but a constant stream of excuses.

He has, of course, demanded praise and recognition for his "perfect handling" and his "very big brain." He has tried desperately to change the subject over, and over, and over. He even boasted that his run of daily Castro-style press briefings had "great ratings." In the midst of a crisis that was killing thousands of Americans every day, he boasted of his "number one" status on Facebook.

Through all of this, as the death toll mounted and the army of heroic doctors, nurses, and EMTs worked tirelessly in viral war zones, the Trumpenvolk complained. About the lockdowns ordered to contain the virus, they whined, "The cure is worse than the disease." This was Trumpspeak for, "Let granny die for the Dow Jones, but we've got to get NASCAR, World Wrestling, and the local Applebee's running because I miss those jalapeño poppers," and "Shut up, cucks, we're reopening the economy."

But with every lie about testing kits, personal protective equipment, miracle cures, economic resurgences, and his understanding of the science behind epidemics, viruses, and the healthcare system, Trump has broken the faith of Americans a little more.

Every day that passes compounds his errors from the day before. Every time he promises miracles and produces little but chaos, he leaves the states on the front line of this battle a little less able to face the rising curve of the coronavirus crisis and the downward slope of our economic fortunes.

It's time to use Donald Trump's terrible failure to boot his ass from office.

"But, Rick," you ask, "would that mean exploiting a terrible pandemic for political gain, merely to defeat Donald Trump?"

You bet your ass it would.

This tragedy, with its unspeakable damage to our people and our economy, has a political upside, and if you don't think I'm going to tell you how to leverage that, you haven't been paying attention.

COVID AND 2020

I wrote in the hardcover edition of this book that every reelection is a referendum on the incumbent, and it's true. Typically those referenda span a variety of the decisions and actions made by the incumbent: the quality of his leadership, the security of the country, the strength of the economy, and a host of smaller factors.

If COVID had not entered the scene, the 2020 race would have been a referendum on Donald Trump's corruption and failed leadership. Now that it has, the election of 2020 is about one thing, and one thing only. It is about Donald Trump's mishandling of this crisis and the terrible toll of his foolishness, weakness, vanity, and corruption. It isn't a question of whether we want four more years of Trump, but rather whether we can *survive* four more years of Trump.

The election was never about policy, and it still isn't. It is only about who can lead from the place in which Donald Trump's failures have stranded this nation. Joe Biden is an imperfect nominee but possessed of several attributes that are letter-perfect for the moment and the mission at hand.

Joe Biden can be goofy. Joe Biden can be a little handsy. Joe Biden can go off script.

We get it.

But the man spent forty years in public service, and it never really changed him. He didn't come out of his time in the Senate or in the vice presidency as a billionaire or a lobbyist. His imperfections are owned and obvious. The Trump campaign keeps trying to push various attacks that smack of projection, not credibility, including the Tara Reade claims, which quickly flashed to public attention and just as quickly disappeared.

I can tell you one thing: Joe Biden likes people. He likes to talk. He likes to bullshit. He likes to laugh. Unlike Trump, he doesn't take every criticism as a personal affront.

Biden is a man full of compassion. His empathy is front and center, as we saw in his response to the COVID-19 crisis and his words of reconciliation in the wake of the police murder of George Floyd in Minneapolis. It didn't look like that would matter in 2020, but now by God, it sure as hell matters. We are in the middle of a crisis for which a president who gives a damn about the lives and loss in this tragedy could make a difference. The ramifications of this pandemic will continue to play out in American life not for a year or a single presidential term or a decade but for a generation. Biden may be a transitional figure, but someone willing to show humanity and to feel the loss of so many is the leader we need, right now.

To win the White House, Biden doesn't need to reach soaring heights of rhetorical perfection. He doesn't need libraries of policy papers and briefing books full of Elizabeth Warren–esque geekery. He needs to fall back on the characteristics that Americans expect from a president.

Donald Trump once famously said to Americans, "What have you got to lose?" as he asked them to place the reins of the most powerful office in the world into his pudgy little paws.

The answer, it turns out, is everything.

The Biden campaign and its allies need to bring the debate back, time and again, to Trump's handling of this crisis. Remind American voters over and over that Donald Trump has, at every turn, put his own political fortunes before their lives, their safety, and their economic well-being. We are suffering from his calculation that he could bullshit his way past a virus, and tweet away an economic depression caused by his incompetence.

In the face of the worst mass casualty event in American history, the question of this election is simple: Who is to blame and who can fix it? We know both answers, but it is incumbent on the Biden campaign not to fall for the distractions, not to play into Trump's hands. The campaign must neither be lulled into complacency or outfoxed by Trump's trickery.

Stay on target. All day. Every day. This is a referendum. It's Biden or four more years of the Trump Death Circus.

A STRATEGIC RESET

When it comes to the way the 2020 election campaign will be waged and won, COVID has reset the battlefield: In fact, this is a strategic reset the likes of which we've never seen in a modern presidential election.

This won't be a season of conventions, rallies, and big events. Gone are the moments that would have provided a big earned-media lift. We won't see bus tours in swing states, or hands-on events.

Everything is digital now. Everything is virtual. The tyranny of Zoom is everywhere. Everything is both more isolated and more intimate. This matters, because the Biden campaign is not, to put it mildly, composed of digital natives. They'd better learn fast and hire fast to reset the advocacy mechanisms that will work in the 2020 race.

I loathe saying this, but Biden needs to up his Facebook game, and he needs to do it yesterday. Trump's campaign, for all its flaws, has Facebook very clearly on their side; Mark Zuckerberg has consistently acted in Trump's favor, refusing to block even his most ludicrous lies and incendiary provocations.

Why? Who can see into Mark Zuckerberg's android heart? Is it a desire to avoid regulatory oversight, or to destroy the planet in a sea of nuclear flame? He's not telling. But the ludicrous amplification mechanism of Facebook, like nature, abhors a vacuum. Trump and Russian online propaganda (*but I repeat myself*) are still in place on Facebook, turning the social network into a hive of conspiracy-theory whackadoodles and their millions of friends. Biden has to buy, borrow, or steal a group of Facebook ad experts and content developers. The site is a hellhole, but it's also a hellhole where older voters are exposed to this campaign, particularly in the era of COVID.

The essence of this campaign, its very core, will be a battle for attention and devotion in the digital space. In 2008, Republicans understood that Barack Obama had stolen the mark on them and advanced beyond the old micro targeting of the Bush era. Obama's team took it to another level; they leveraged the first true digital campaign into a turnout mechanism that produced a crushing electoral victory. In 2012, owing to a variety of competing factors, they spanked us on digital *again*.

That shit is over now, and the faster Democrats understand that they're dealing with people who are both amoral and fully submerged in every single technique of digital voter contact, the better. They're not bound by the truth or, you know, little things like laws. Democrats must not fool themselves with antique ideas like door-knocking unless and until they have their digital shit together.

In the spring of 2020, Republicans also announced they were investing $20 million in an army of attorneys to fight "voter fraud." (In related news, I'm spending $20 million on the prevention of leprechaun incursions.) They are signaling that they will go balls-to-the-wall on any kind of voting irregularities, push to have polls closed early, and fight to the death on every precinct across the country.

Instead of weeping inconsolably, my Democratic friends should go out and build a war chest for a similar army of election lawyers ready to litigate poll closings, ballot counts, bogus ID checks, and other Republican nitpicking. The GOP will use these lawyers to increase the political friction of the campaign, and the only response is to make a giant pile of money and burn it as an offering to the legal gods. You're going to need it. Don't bring whiny complaints about voter suppression when you haven't built an equally aggressive army of your own. Did you learn nothing from how badly we rolled you in 2000?

Get your vote in as soon as humanly possible. I know there are fifty state-level Democratic organizations, and that the DNC can barely order Uber Eats, but this election will be decided six weeks in advance. And that's a problem, because a lot of the Democratic voter base doesn't like to vote by mail. Older voters and African Americans have a preference for in-person voting. I get it. I like it also. But in 2020 we can't afford not to bank votes early.

The traditional campaign model builds excitement until the very end, surging in a one-day sale of the ultimate political startup company. Now, the sale window is about six weeks.

By August, the Democratic parties and the Biden effort should have been pounding voters to sign up for early or absentee voting and educating them on the mechanics of it. They should start banking those votes as quickly as possible.

The Trump campaign will work its hardest to produce an October surprise of such scope and volume that it turns down Democratic enthusiasm on Election Day. Never, ever underestimate how low they'll sink to generate a last-minute shocker and roundly fuck the Democratic nominee. The earlier the Biden campaign and the Democrats roll in votes by mail, the safer they are.

Donald Trump and his media minions are screeching that vote-by-mail is inherently fraudulent and that the Democrats only want it so they can cheat. Horseshit. Republicans have been using vote-by-mail tactics for years to bank their vote early. The Trump campaign, the RNC, and the state Republican parties will all engage in a hyper-aggressive, supertargeted early- and absentee-ballot campaign, and don't you for a moment think otherwise.

Experts in epidemiology and virology expect that, as the fall approaches, the second wave of the coronavirus will hit. Don't count on voters feeling safe on Election Day if the scenario is as grim as some scientists predict. Donald Trump will be banking votes as early as he can as insurance against it. If the Democrats aren't doing the same, they deserve to lose.

BIDEN'S EXPANDING ELECTORAL MAP

Joe Biden's electoral map has been consistently expanding. Since the release of *Running Against the Devil*, he has shown solid leads in many of the swing states, including Michigan, Wisconsin, Pennsylvania, and Florida. His resources may have to be spread a little thinner to cash in on that support, but this is, as they say, a good problem to have. For Biden there are many paths toward the 270-plus Electoral College votes he needs to win, and many fewer for Trump.

When I wrote this book, Florida and Ohio seemed out of reach for Joe Biden both financially and politically. That ground has shifted. Florida has shown a drift away from Trump—inside most polling margins, to be sure, but the pattern seems consistent. This is, of course, no excuse for taking anything in my home state for granted. The Democrats have often polled 7 to 10 points up and still lost, not because of voter fraud or shenanigans but because the Republican Party in Florida is full of young hustlers who know how to work their asses off.

In other vital Electoral College states—Pennsylvania, Michigan, Wisconsin, and Minnesota—Biden's cultural fit is also coming into clear focus. Biden lacks the East Coast elite cultural signifiers that surrounded Hillary Clinton (through no fault of her own), and he's much more of a "have a beer" guy than Trump. The toll that COVID and Trump's trade war has taken on the Upper Midwest states cannot be overstated, and the battlegrounds there look different from what Team Trump expected.

Biden even has shown a competitive position in places like Georgia and North Carolina, which was an unthinkable scenario a year ago. There's many a slip twixt the cup and the lip, but, at the time of this writing, as a candidate you'd much rather be holding Biden's cards than Trump's.

THE REPUBLICAN WALL IS CRACKING

The 2020 election has always been a game of small numbers.

This battle will be waged and won in the Electoral College, just as it was in 2016—which means Biden and his outside allies aren't looking for a massive swing in every battleground state. Would a crushing wave election be nice? Of course. However, even with all Trump's deficits, he'll still hold a core of red states, which makes a wipeout less likely. A solid double wins this game.

Biden has to move just enough votes in just enough places to swing the campaign. By the early summer of 2020 Trump's numbers had slipped badly in state-level polls in Florida, Michigan, Ohio, Pennsylvania, Wisconsin, and Arizona. His slippage even within the GOP is real. It was telling that at that point Trump's advertising wasn't in swing states and counties but rather in some of the most conservative areas of the country. As I send this book to the publisher, Donald

Trump is up on television in Grand Rapids, Michigan, and in the panhandle of Florida, trying to get his base solidified again. If he's worried there, he's bleeding to death elsewhere. Blocking Trump's path is increasingly both doable and affordable.

Another bellwether of the possible wave election in 2020 is the collapse of Republican Senate prospects. Because Mitch McConnell is very, very good at what he does, those numbers may still turn around for the GOP. But Colorado and Arizona in particular look increasingly like lost causes. The Georgia Senate race is beset with scandal. North Carolina is a mess, with Senator Thom Tillis polling behind and Senator Richard Burr having been forced to step down from his position as the Senate Intelligence Committee chair because of an insider-trading investigation. Susan Collins of Maine is still furrowing her brow.

Thus far, the only bright spot on the Republican Senate map appears to be Alabama, where, without noted child-dating aficionado and overall creep Roy Moore on the Republican ballot, Jeff Sessions might regain his Senate seat.

As this goes to print, a few Republicans are creeping toward sorta kinda maybe thinking about being slightly, elliptically critical of Donald Trump, and one such, Nebraska senator Ben Sasse, has actually done it. More will follow, but for almost all of them, it's too late. Even if Arizona senator Martha McSally had a last-minute conversion and started blasting Trump, she has the same problem that every Republican not named Mitt Romney has: She's gone full Trump, and you never go full Trump.

The disconnect between the needs of the American people at this moment and Donald Trump's Republican Party is absolutely astounding. In the Senate races, Democrats should take advantage of this—not to push their ideological wish list, but simply to draw a contrast, making the Senate races the same referendum as the race for the White House. "We do give a shit about people. We're going to help you. We need to do this right, and together."

Republicans at the grassroots level are starting to break free. The female and educated Republican voters who broke from Trump in 2016 and 2018 are largely out of the GOP now, and more will split away as the campaign rolls on. Trump's base-only strategy repels many of them, and for Biden they're absolutely gettable. Steve Bannon himself acknowledged that if groups like the Lincoln Project split off 3 to 4 percent of the Republican vote, Trump can't win.[1]

The GOP base is no longer monolithic. Yes, Trump will still win a large majority of their votes. He will still win many, many red states. Yes, he can still fill a rally hall at the Petri Dish Sportatorium like no other political figure.

But remember, it's a game of small numbers. I speak this simple truth over and over: Donald Trump won three states by 77,000 votes. His margin in Florida was 150,000 votes.

Part of the slow but measurable drift away from Trump comes down to his incompetence. If anyone still believed the reality-TV-star shtick, his deadly and disastrous handling of COVID washed away that illusion once and for all. Many of the hardest-hit places were in red states that would have been solidly GOP but for Trump's handling of the virus. Ohio, Pennsylvania, Michigan, and Wisconsin have suffered a heavy blow.

In a time of peace and prosperity, the great Trump Show was a wild, transgressive, fuck-you to the hated establishment. It was a luxury political good, fun and funny. Republicans loved the chaos and name calling, but now the sense is just of weariness. Polling shows that even the qualified defense of Trump that one heard from supporters before—"I don't like his tweets, but I love the judges and tax cuts"—has started to fade in power. The voters who stuck with Trump through three years of scandal are simply exhausted. He's the raucous party guest who won't leave at 2 A.M. because he insists on telling one more story only he finds hilarious. He's the office loudmouth, always right on every issue, but never smart enough not to press the point.

In December 2019, I cofounded a group called the Lincoln Project, a band of former Republican consultants, operatives, and campaign officials who had burned our boats with Trump's GOP. We weren't interested in some quixotic effort, like going the third-party route or finding a long shot of an independent candidate. That wouldn't do it, so we went all-in for Biden and started hitting Trump, harder than even the toughest Democratic super PACS.

We've been going right at Trump and Trumpism, and with the happy gusto of pirates, leading him to online and in-person temper tantrums focused on us, while Biden and his allies are able to keep working. Distracting Donald Trump and serving as a harassing force is perfectly in our wheelhouse; we're agile, vicious, and unbound by a party or the rules of normal campaigning.

You're *welcome*, Democrats.

WHAT TO EXPECT FROM TRUMP

This is going to get *ugly*. I'm talking wrath-of-God stuff. The living will envy the dead. Every previous campaign viewed through the lens of this exercise will look like a mild intramural dispute, or the battle over who would be the assistant treasurer of the Oxford Mississippi Ladies' Auxiliary, circa 1952. And that's just inside the Trump campaign itself.

In the Trump campaign we will see reflected back at us the very worst impulses of our politics.

You can already see the outlines in the summer of 2020. In May, Trump's large adult son, Don Jr., insinuated on Instagram that Joe Biden was a pedophile. The idea that accusing your opponent of being a pedophile isn't the *worst* thing that can happen in the 2020 election should clarify for you the territory in which we now reside. There will be no moment when the better angels of Trump's nature emerge. This is an existential battle for the Trump family, his campaign team, his campaign donors, his Washington enablers, and the Trumpian right-wing media complex that has monetized him to the hilt.

Victory means an eternity of grift, a dynastic money machine vomiting its ill-gotten gains into the maw of this vulgar tribe of grasping shitbirds. Defeat means actual investigations into their behavior, audits of their businesses, examinations of their taxes, a slow, torturous peeling away of the bullshit façade of success to reveal the corrupt, petty scams and scammers at the heart of every Trump enterprise. If he loses, Congress and law enforcement will be investigating this carnival of corruption for decades. (If the idea of Prisoner

45692721, Trump, Donald J., isn't enough to get you out of bed in the morning, we can't be friends.)

When I tell you that Donald Trump has to win or go to prison I'm not trying to be sensational. Losing may very well come down to that outcome, so he will fight the dirtiest, sleaziest election operation you have ever seen.

No one and nothing will be off limits. They will dig through every moment of Joe Biden's life, including the most agonizing tragedies. They will lie and mock the times he lost loved ones in order to manipulate his campaign. They will spew out unsourced stories of alleged victims of alleged assaults. The Tara Reade boomlet of April 2020 was just a warmup act.

Part of this strategy is to exhaust Americans morally and mentally, to convince them that the horrors being displayed before them make staying home on Election Day a perfectly rational option, a decent choice, a vacation from the hell on their televisions and tablet screens 24/7.

This is a burden on Americans, and a painful one. A regrettable one. Trump has always depended on exploding a new mountain of his bullshit to disguise the current crisis. By the time this paperback is published, the election will have roughly seventy-five days to run, and those seventy-five days will sear themselves in your memory for their depravity, their cruelty, and their inhumanity. You will be beset with lies, deceptions, and temptations designed by the very worst of the very worst to crush your spirit and keep you home.

Unlike the Trump campaign's flirtation with the alt-right in 2016, this time they'll just hold hands in broad daylight. Trump knows that the racist elements of his base need red meat, preferably in the form of immigrant children. Expect more horror stories of caravans, this time with even more lurid tales of plagues, murderers, and human trafficking. Campaign ads will screech about sealing the border. It won't be long before kids in cages make the news again, with a government response of "So what?" rather than, "Dear God, what have we done?"

I wish I had better news for you, or some sunnier vision of the future where Donald Trump and Joe Biden will stand on a stage together and rationally debate policy, but it's not to be. Preparing yourself for the horrors Trump has in store will help you face the ratchet of suffering between now and Election Day.

RUSSIA, 2020

They're back. Of course they're back. Russians never walk away from equity, and their 2016 investment in Trump—let's be honest, Russians have been investing in Trump since the 1980s, just at the scuzzy Russian-mob level, not at Putin's rarefied heights—paid off spectacularly. It wasn't merely that watching Donald bow and scrape like some medieval peasant before his lord gave the Russians a constant thrill. They got the outcome they truly desired—a divided America, weaker in the world than ever before. They got the chaos they love and the deformation of America's political life into warring factions with nothing in common but their rage.

By late spring of 2020 the bot wars were on again, with Facebook and other platforms doing almost nothing about them. According to one estimate, 50 percent of Twitter accounts pushing to reopen the economy—even as COVID-19 roared on—were bots.[2] And the Trump campaign was laughing all the way to the bank. Digital propaganda works best in a vacuum, and the Biden effort is still struggling to dominate this part of the campaign. Voters are influenced by the kind of propaganda they see, and what they're seeing right now, just as in 2016, is Russian and Trump (but I repeat myself) agitprop with little countervailing message. Until Biden's digital effort scales, being alert to unsourced stories and aware that there's a war on for your brain is a vital defensive strategy.

Russian hacking continues apace, and you can certainly expect a number of October surprise bombshells to leak out through whatever version of WikiLeaks the Russians create this time around. Trump made eager use of leaks generated by Russian intelligence agencies in 2016, and most of America still doesn't understand the scope and power of their operations. We do now, though our government will do nothing to prevent it because Donald Trump thinks it helps his cause. The media needs to check itself before racing to print the fruit of Vladimir Putin's poisonous tree.

Fox and the Weapons of Mass Distraction

Donald Trump's love affair with Fox has soured a bit, but the biggest network in America is still overwhelmingly his most consequential support structure in the media. All the other Trumpian bullshit flows up to Fox, where it gets recast as "fair and balanced" and pushed back out to Trump's prole army.

You can expect Fox to continue to play its role as Donald Trump's lead enabler and the reinforcement mechanism that keeps him at the center of the hearts of millions of Fox viewers. Expect Sean and Tucker and Frau Ingram and Judge Jeanine Pirro, President of the Franzia Boxed Wine Case of the Day Club, to continue screaming every night about the imminent death of the republic at the hands of the Communists, the Chinese, the caravans, or lizard reptile space aliens.

Rupert Murdoch is obviously kept alive by harvesting the tears of orphans and those of Democrats who underestimate the reach and power of his media properties. Biden's smartest, toughest surrogates need to be trained to a hard edge and deployed on Fox to upset the comfy info-bubble that the network will produce. They are unaccustomed to pushback, and reaching the biggest audience in the political sphere is worthwhile even if you have to tolerate the clammy fish odor of Tucker's studio.

The DOJ as Trump's Law Firm

Bill Barr's role as Donald Trump's power lawyer will have an outsized effect on the 2020 campaign. As Barr swims like a great white shark through the waters of Washington, D.C., devouring the justice system in order to protect Trump and expand executive power, he'll happily weaponize the DOJ even further to ensure his patron's electoral success.

Barr is the sort of lawless, bloodless enforcer every strongman craves on their team. Respectable enough to give a thin, if barely passable veneer of legal probity to an administration known for its indifference to the law, Barr is Trump's DOJ Huckleberry. He's already shown his willingness to erase the morals, norms, traditions, and institutional imperatives that made the DOJ an independent office. Barr manipulated the Mueller Report and broke all the rules to attempt to get Trump crony Mike Flynn off the hook. Barr's ideological ferocity for preserving executive power goes beyond anything recognizable in a modern liberal democracy.

Barr's moves will be more aggressive and more dangerous as the campaign draws to a close. Expect a 2020 version of the Hillary emails, *shocking* revelations that just *happen* to hit at just the right moment as the election cycle ends. If Trump comes under the radar for (more) illegal actions, Barr will mumble about being nonpartisan— "*obviously* we'll get right on this after the election."

Think of Barr as a central member of Trump's campaign staff, empowered beyond your imagination, amoral beyond your wildest nightmares, and doing absolutely everything he can to reelect Donald Trump.

CHY-NA

Set aside that Chinese leader Xi Jinping has rolled Donald Trump like a cheap rug over and over again. Set aside Trump's infatuation with dictators, authoritarians, strongmen, and Central Command states of all flavors. The reason China is in the center of his campaign's attack messaging is because it popped up in a focus group and moves the kinds of male voters who flipped from Obama to Trump. Do I have to do all of this for you?

Welcome to the Sino-MAGA War 2020. This war will be as loud as it is stupid, given that both the United States and Chinese economies are now struggling in the aftermath of the COVID-19 crisis, and the status quo of interdependence between our two nations continues. Many elected Republicans are clinging to the anti-Chinese rhetoric because they understand that their association with Trump is killing them politically. They're looking for the Other, the scapegoat, and the Chinese pulled the short straw on this one. If blaming some vague Asian boogeyman for the Trump economic collapse means they might just escape the blast radius, expect more of the same.

My counsel for the Democrats is very simple: Don't get in a dumb fight about a dumb issue. Don't excuse China's authoritarianism, oppression, or shady practices. Dismiss it. China is a lot of things, but the shallow, transparent framing from Team Trump on this is boob bait.

Bring it back to the catalog of Trump statements about how much he loves Xi. Highlight how the "great trade deal" was always Trump bullshit vaporare. Point out how Trump was tricked and rolled by China's pet troublemaker, Kim Jong-un.

Remind voters consistently and loudly how the president has failed in handling China, and how Trump has done more damage to the American worker than China ever could have imagined.

A Base-Only Campaign

Donald Trump's election path has narrowed considerably in the past few months. Democrats need to be very clear that he's working to lock in and motivate his base, first, foremost, and only. And especially the base of the base: Trump needs to max out white working-class voters without a high-school education to levels never before seen, and it's going to be ugly. The campaign may talk a good game about African American and Hispanic voters, but it's the white, non-college voter, middle- to lower-middle-income, with a chip on his (and he's almost *always* a he) shoulder the size of a 747, and drugstore sunglasses in rural, exurban, and suburban swing states they're after. They've already given up on the college-educated GOP mom who walked away from the party in 2018.

The base-only strategy comes down to resentment, fury, and a barely hidden rabbit role of racial attacks, not so subtly coded dog whistles, and a continuation of their 2016 engagement with the darkest forces of America's racial fuckwits. Stephen Miller is of course still their inside man in the White House, so you can expect many, many speeches and policy decisions on the Wall and the importance of caging helpless children, and a general sort of make-America-white-again rhetorical platform when it comes to immigration. The anti-immigration crowd is easily activated, incredibly aggrieved, and, once engaged, hard to persuade otherwise.

The base-only strategy also means Trump may have to triage certain states he won in 2016 sooner rather than later. At the end of May

2020, Trump got into a war with the State of Michigan, which by all accounts was pivotal to his 2016 victory. He kept referring to Governor Gretchen Whitmer as "that lady" and threatening to cut off federal aid to the state if they didn't end an absentee-ballot program encouraging people to vote in the fall. Trump tweeted "Liberate Michigan!"—and he just may get his wish.

Trouble is rising among older voters, who once made up such a strong segment of Trump's base that his ticket could afford to be blown out by almost every other demographic and still hold on to a plurality in most states. Starting in April, however, Trump's campaign and Trump himself launched attacks on Joe Biden claiming he was senile. They produced the usual videos of stitched-together clips of Biden fumbling his words to push the narrative that he was suffering from dementia and/or mental illness. But by June the "Joe Is Senile, Old Folks Can't Lead" strategy was backfiring, as his once-rock-solid numbers in the senior demographic dropped sharply.

This is of course astoundingly ironic for Captain Covfefe. There are hours of tape with Trump mumbling, stumbling, speaking in tongues, and channeling the mystic voices from the great beyond as he mushmouths his way through press briefings, speeches, and visits with baffled VIPs. As they politely say, "Thank you for coming, Mr. President," they quietly wonder why someone in his family hasn't taken the time to talk to Trump about extended care in a skilled nursing facility.

Make the Fight with Obama One That Trump Will Regret

In the hardcover edition of this book, I encouraged the Democrats to get Barack Obama and Michelle Obama into this fight, not only as powerful advocates for African American voters but for the generation for whom they represented a vaunted ideal. The great tradition of former presidents' remaining largely out of the sharp-knives-and-pointed-elbows portion of their successors' elections has its merits, but since Donald Trump has chosen to engage in a war on Barack Obama, it's time for something new.

Trump's desire to seek revenge for the investigation into his ties with Russia by foisting the phony Obamagate conspiracy theory on the American people—for those of you living in caves, "Obamagate" is the ludicrous storyline that Trump's close ties to Russia and Putin's help in his 2016 race were all parts of a baroque effort by the Obama administration to persecute Trump and his campaign—is a gift. Trump's eager enablers in the Senate are falling over themselves to begin a 2020 version of "but her emails," and so Obama is liberated to get into this fight more directly.

On the weekend of May 20, with public graduation ceremonies canceled by COVID, Obama gave two virtual commencement addresses. Trump's reaction was, as you might imagine, not pretty. He demanded that his supporters in Congress and his media allies boost the message that Obama should be "held accountable" for the (imaginary) crimes of Obamagate.

Trump may be a reckless, relentless, day-trading political gambling addict, but I'm honestly surprised to see that he would try to take out Biden by using Obama, the most popular figure in American politics by far. No, it's not politically smart, but it is perfectly Trump. He felt himself slipping badly against Biden, so why not go after the black guy? At the very same moment that Trump brought up the Obamagate smear, Trump and the alt-right suddenly started to fall in love again. When Trump retweeted alt-right den-mother Michelle Malkin on May 16, 2020, it left the Gab crowd sitting in their mom's basement with unaccustomed erections because the great leader had once again acknowledged one of their own.

The secret is, it's no secret. Trump's racial motivations and attitudes are out there for anyone to see. The racial undertone isn't washed away when Trump declares "MAGA loves the blacks" or when he invites Diamond and Silk to the White House for a social-media summit. The overt and covert racial messages embedded in his "law and order" and "dominate them . . . take back your streets" demands during the unrest following the police murder of George Floyd appeal not just to the Trump base but to the ugliest edge of that base: the racial grievance mongers, the outliers, the dead-end anti-immigration and anti-civil-rights elements who felt validated and empowered by Donald Trump in 2016. I argued in my first book that these are the people who needed most to be purged not only from the Republican Party but from politics more broadly, but hey, what do I know?

RETURN OF THE RALLIES

Trump needs his sweaty Monster-Trump rallies like a junkie needs his stuff. His boundless black hole of need can never be sated—the love and adulation, the cheering, the smell of the Chinese-slave-factory MAGA merch. There is no substitute. There is no Suboxone or methadone to treat the addiction. Trump cannot survive long without the rallies. They are his safe space in a world turned against him.

No matter the risk, he'll hold those rallies. They work for him for three reasons. First, the rallies are a guaranteed way for Trump to commit news, to darken the press sky in the way for which he is notably famous. Trump doesn't go on the stage of these rallies and throw out racist tropes, wild lies, and metric kilotons of total bullshit for no reason. He does so because he knows that the national press corps is a machine built along certain design guidelines. Journalists feel duty-bound to report even his most outrageous utterances, his most vile racial claptrap, his insane lies, and his provocations. Sure, what he's saying flies in the face of truth, reason, consistency, and logic, but give me 750 words by 5:00.

In 2016, Trump's endless, repeated, Castroesque rallies were a primary factor in his ability to blot out coverage for every other campaign. He used them to brilliant effect, and will do so again. Should Joe Biden do giant rallies for the left? I would argue against it, because the MAGA rallies are going to be like a fucking petri dish of coronavirus, so let's avoid death-by-campaign-rally, shall we?

HERE WE GO

No plan of battle survives contact with the enemy. The idea that either Biden or Trump will be able to draw a straight line to Election Day will inevitably run into the brutal realities and terrible toll of COVID-19, a shattered economy, a world in disorder and chaos, and some other damn externality no one can plan to conquer in advance. The campaign has changed, the stakes are life and death, and for once in a very long time, we have a choice before us where the ideological differences between the two candidates are absolutely irrelevant. This is a battle for the soul and the survival of this country. This is a decision between competence and cruelty. This is an election that won't look like any other, and will be waged in a different and mostly digital fashion, but it will still come down to a choice between Joe Biden and Donald Trump.

I fought hard against Democrats for over thirty years of my long career. I'm still not in love with their various ideological predilections, but I wake up every morning knowing that being in this fight to defeat Donald Trump, striving to destroy the nascent nationalist-populist movement of which he is the figurehead, and putting country before party isn't just the right thing to do, it's the only thing to do.

Before COVID-19, one could be easily convinced that Donald Trump would go down in history as one of our very worst presidents. Now that we have faced untold misery and loss as a nation, and seen how a failed leader who thinks only of himself and who lacks even the most basic human empathy cannot rise to the occasion, this choice isn't really a choice at all. He was tested, and couldn't make even himself great, let alone this nation.

Trump's place in history is assured, and it is one of ignominy and shame. The only variable left in the eventual judgment of the Trump reign of error is whether the Democrats keep their heads in the game, run the race they must, and make Donald Trump a one-term president.

Joe Biden isn't a perfect man, but there's nothing in him of the darkness and need that drives Trump every day. Like all of us, he is flawed, he makes mistakes, and yet we can easily imagine this man forged by both experience and personal loss sitting down behind the Resolute Desk next January. That's an image that most Americans find deeply comforting.

By the time this paperback edition is in your hands, the campaign will have had a hundred twists and turns, a dozen make-or-break scandals, and God knows how many moments of tragicomedy as people stare at their tablets and ask themselves, "How can this be real?"

If you're reading this before Election Day, I hope you remembered to register, and to vote early. If you haven't yet registered, fuck you. Get it done. If you can vote early, and haven't yet? Fuck you. Get it done.

That damn cliché of "every vote counts" haunts me from overuse in every election from president to dogcatcher, but I want you to remember that this *is* a game of small numbers. Every damn vote really *does* count.

I know the pandemic and the shattered economy have changed our lives, and that the space we're in feels sad and alien. But our choice this year will mean more than any election we've ever faced in this nation.

Stay in the fight.

RUNNING AGAINST THE DEVIL

ELECTION NIGHT, NOVEMBER 3, 2020

Imagine you're a Democratic strategist, one of the top figures in the 2020 nominee's campaign. It's Election Night, and you feel something familiar in the air. It's a feeling of confidence, of rising joy and anticipation. It's been a long, tough campaign, but victory is in sight.

You're going to win, and you know it. It's a certainty. After four years of Trump, the Democrats are poised to claim a sweeping Electoral College and popular-vote victory.

Finally.

The last few weeks of October were a blissful whirl, with polling numbers looking strong across the board and your candidate joyfully working the crowds in swing states. She's a happy warrior, praised for her political skills and the subject of endless glowing media profiles. Almost every newspaper in the country endorsed her in the final week. America, after so many centuries of right-wing injustice, finally appears to have achieved a state of beautiful progressive *wokeness* and is ready for its bold socialist future.

After the debates, it was clear your candidate, though occasionally rattled by Trump's in-your-grill debating presence, had triumphed. She was smart, articulate, and progressive. She's everything you've dreamed about since Obama. Trump has been flailing, angrily tweeting a dozen times a day, stoking the MAGA base at an endless series of campaign rallies, and sounding crazier by the minute. He's punchy and tired, and looks worn-out.

You and your campaign colleagues have even started those elliptical conversations about what role you might play in a Democratic White House, mostly couched in the faux-modest "Oh, I just want to help the future president in any way I can . . ." tones of people who are already plotting for office space and picking out curtains.

A few of your older, wiser hands don't seem to share the infectiously optimistic Election Night mood. They lack the same sunny optimism the candidate displayed as she sat in the holding suite after the last long day of campaigning ended. They keep staring nervously at the FiveThirtyEight map and running the same mental calculations over Electoral College numbers they've done a thousand times. But hey, you feel *really* great about this.

The campaign's social-media metrics were weird the last few days, though, and your data and analytics people were sending increasingly worrying messages about the massive inflows of ads from brand-new super PACs and 501(c)(4) dark-money groups. You convinced yourself these were just the final gasps of the Trumpian grifters making a last buck on the Donald, or perhaps his Russian friends trying an end run. The Trump campaign and the RNC (but I repeat myself) ad buys were scattershot, and on issues that seemed off-kilter.

As the night starts, the ballroom is packed to the gills with eager, happy people ready to put Trump and Trumpism in the rearview mirror of history. The media risers, crowded with the A-talent from every network, are jammed. The results are about to come in, and the army of reporters in the back of the ballroom is in a near frenzy.

You didn't repeat the Hillary mistake of not visiting the states Trump and his Russian allies scored in 2016. Your candidate made the stops, though the crowds were never quite as large or raucous as you wanted. Your state organizers tell you they've got armies of volunteers knocking on doors, making calls, and driving turnout.

Hell, none of the final tracking polls showed Trump even close except in Michigan, home of Kid Rock and one of the most stark political divides between the city and suburbs anywhere in the nation. In Michigan, his numbers weren't just surprising; they were downright terrifying, but your pollster assured you it was an outlier and that you'd still take Ohio, Pennsylvania, Florida, and Wisconsin.

The exit polls were closer than you wanted but still looked good. As the first results were about to roll in, the AP, *Washington Post, New York Times,* Decision Desk, and *Politico* analysts started pinging you and the rest of the campaign's senior staff.

"What's going on in Michigan? Do you hear this stuff out of Florida?" Something is off the rails, and you don't quite know what it is yet.

By 9:30, it's not looking like you expected. Ohio is showing a razor-thin Trump lead. He's winning Michigan handily. Florida is Florida, and although you had projected a four-point lead, by 10:00 P.M. the vote total shows Trump up by 65,000 . . . and the Panhandle hasn't even fully reported yet.

Florida's enormous influx of Puerto Rican voters meant the Democrats were on track for a stunning victory there, right? Wait. Didn't someone mention in a meeting that the Hispanic turnout operation in Florida was a bit smoke and mirrors?

You post high numbers in South Florida, but everywhere else in the Sunshine State, Trump is tearing you apart. When the Panhandle does report, everything outside of the blue enclave of Tallahassee is posting numbers in the low 60 percent range for Donald Fucking Trump. Your mind flickers to an angry set of emails and Slack messages a few weeks before about avoiding the issue of gun control in North Florida, but your candidate insisted not only on an assault weapons ban but a ban on semiautomatics as well. Metrics show that north of the I-4 corridor you're losing everywhere except liberal Alachua and Leon counties by double digits.

"What the hell is happening in Wisconsin?" is your next question. With the Democratic gains in 2018, it seemed like a lock that Trump would go down in flames, especially after the disastrous scam of Foxconn left Wisconsin workers holding the bag for a failed deal with China. Wisconsin farmers had suffered terribly from Trump's trade war. When you see that the race is essentially tied, you think, "What in the actual fuck is going on here?"

A few thousand votes turn the easy layup of Pennsylvania into a disastrous loss. Hell, even Minnesota is closer than you thought. You get destroyed in Ohio, with record rural turnout offsetting the cities.

In nearly every swing state, you're losing everywhere outside the metros and the most affluent suburbs. Turnout is sky-high, which your models predicted would be great for your candidate, but even then you're just missing the margins.

That's why, come midnight, your candidate is in the suite, calling Donald Trump to concede the election. There are tears all around. You can hear Trump on the speakerphone, curt and smug. You dread seeing that first triumphant tweet from the once and future president.

The next morning, you begin to put together the mosaic of data points in your head from the last few weeks. You start to see the messages and strategies Trump and his campaign used that seemed lurid and absurd at the time but now begin to make perfect sense.

They weren't trying to win big, or swing the nation toward a new ideological polarity, or find the next savior. They were animals, trapped in a win-or-die moment, and they resorted to tooth and claw. You realize as the Electoral College numbers rise for the Republican that your campaign mistook Trump's sloppy, shambolic, hateful, stream-of-excrescence campaign for what was happening behind the scenes. There, for an army of professional Republican campaigners wedded to Trump out of desperate necessity, it was ride or die.

Suddenly, your candidate's detailed policy proposals, white papers, and granular knowledge of climate change, reparations for slavery, gun control, Electoral College reform, the Green New Deal, and healthcare reform weren't assets. Your pride in having the most progressive candidate and campaign since FDR turns to ashes in your mouth. Maybe giving Alexandria Ocasio-Cortez and Bernie Sanders keynote addresses at the convention, where they could declare fraternal communist solidarity with the workers of the world, was a mistake.

You understand too late that your race to the left to win the primary and secure the progressive ideological edge blinded you to the reality of largely center-right states on the Electoral College scoreboard. You handed Trump the weapon he used to cut off your head. Sure, Trump's lowest-common-denominator message was cultish, racist, and blisteringly stupid, but it was simple, constant, and repeated . . . and you kept feeding him issues to use against you.

Wall. MAGA. Judges. Socialism. Revenge.

You thought your progressive message was universal and that the swing states have the same political polarity as California, New York, or Massachusetts. You believed you could shame Trump and Trump voters into listening to the better angels of their nature by talking about diversity, inclusion, and liberal values. In reality, you were giving the Trump campaign fodder for the weaponized grievance machine that put him in office in the first place.

Boy (or your preferred gendered interjection), were you ever wrong.

The Republicans built a nearly invisible high-precision machine that hit the phones, emails, social-media feeds, and televisions of targeted cohorts of voters in swing states. They used issues and messages that seemed alien, discordant, or even silly. They distorted, twisted, and slandered your message, policies, and values, turning out the GOP's base vote by using your own candidate's progressive overreach and winning back just enough of that seemingly lost cohort of GOP women. Remarkably, they even kept the damage among Hispanics below the fatal level.

You lost to the worst president in history.

He didn't beat you; his record, his hideous personal behavior, the reeking cloud of corruption, and his broken economic promises made him unelectable. His divisive, shitty, be-worst reign was a stain and an embarrassment. You lost because you made the election into a referendum on policy, not a referendum on Trump. You went into a reality-television contest not understanding the rules, and the master of the genre kicked your ass.

In the words of the poet, sage, and philosopher DJ Khaled, "You played yourself."

Now that you've seen one future timeline for the 2020 election, let's try one that doesn't end with four more years of this umber clown wrecking everything we as Americans hold dear.

WHY THIS BOOK?

To paraphrase the political scientist Liam Neeson: "I have a very particular set of skills. Skills I have acquired over a very long career. Skills that make me a nightmare for people like you." For thirty years, I took those skills and put them to work electing Republicans. My clients didn't always *like* the advice I gave them, but when they took it, we won races, managed hideous political and personal crises, and reshaped the political battlefield in states across the country.

I no longer use those skills to serve the party I once loved. That party is gone.

I'm not telling you this as part of a job application. I'm telling you this because Democrats are going to lose to Donald Trump in 2020 unless they understand what my former team is about to do.

In this book I'm going to treat Democrats like a client. The Democrats are terrible at the work of electoral politics and they need to hear this. After thirty years, I've learned that in politics and crisis management, there are two kinds of terrible clients.

The first kind of terrible client knows they have a problem but becomes enraged and defensive when you analyze it for them, break it down, and prescribe a cure. Their anger over being told what's wrong and how to fix it is a natural but irritating bug of human nature. As a crisis manager, I'm almost always the bearer of bad news, tough love, and rigorous correctives.

These clients *know* they've screwed the political pooch. They *know* you're right. They *know* that no matter how many times they roll the problem over and tickle its belly, the situation isn't amenable to being ignored. But they *hate* you for the work of extracting them from the situation they created. The resentment they feel—even when you're successful—is because you made them stare into their own moral voids, personal and professional failures, and most of all, cowardice.

"No, ███████████ U.S. OFFICEHOLDER. I know you *like* to fuck highly specialized prostitutes who charge more per hour than my mortgage, but you *may not* and *here's* what we're going to do to rehab your shitty reputation" is not a recipe for making them love you, but it is a recipe for saving their political career.

Some of the Democrats reading this will be in that first category. You'll admit the problems in your policies and party, particularly in re Donald Trump. You won't like much of this book, or me, but you'll understand I'm not here to mock or judge your politics. Rather, like a political oncologist, I'm going to give you a way to treat the cancerous orange tumor consuming our nation.

The other kind of terrible client denies there's a problem. They pretend the brutal articles about their financial sleaze or their taste for strip bars or doll porn (honestly, I'll take this one to my grave) don't exist. I once had a client look at me in complete sincerity and say, "No one is going to see a mug shot from a town that small."

Sure, pal. No one is going to find the dick pics you sent to some rando on Chaturbate or see your Bumble profile? No one is going to find the recordings of your phone-sex sessions? (True story: In one of my most evil campaigns, I *didn't* use six hours of phone-sex recordings by a U.S. Senate candidate we were up against. I did make a traumatized intern listen, and when I asked for a summary of the opponent's phone-sex interests, he replied: "Anal. So much anal." I didn't use them, because I had something that polled better.)

Many of our Democratic friends exist in a beautiful fantasy bubble, as though the GOP's twenty-year march through their electoral numbers across the nation had never happened. For them, history began in 2018.

They ascribe all their losses to imagined bogeymen like gerry-mandering or the Koch brothers or *Citizens United,* because the deeper causes are too painful to examine honestly: policy and cultural disconnects, reliance on generational superstar candidates, and crappy campaigns run for the base alone while scorning and insulting the middle. "But we won X!" is a sad cover for the systematic, slow trend line of their loss of power in both Congress and state governments, particularly in the South and Midwest. We Republicans weren't geniuses. You made it easy for us.

Some of the Democrats reading this will be in that second category. This book will piss you off, and you'll rationalize hating it because you think it's just some asshole Republican telling you to be more like Republicans. Honestly, I'm not.

This book is not a value judgment on any particular political philosophy. I'm not telling Democrats that they're wrong on any single economic, social, environmental, or foreign policy question. I mean, they *are* but that's not the point.

I'm going to tell the truth about how Democrats' feel-good intentions end up as political branding disasters. My job is to show you the *real* rules of the 2020 election game, and to explain how Democrats' policies are frequently box-office poison in red and purple states.

I'm telling you this because Democrats are very prone to shooting themselves in the foot, snatching defeat from the jaws of victory, and blowing the simplest political tasks out their rectums.

Hillary didn't win, and she had a *billion* fucking dollars of advertising and organizing behind her. *Hillary* didn't win because the Democratic Party is systemically bad at elections, misread the populist appeal of Trump, underestimated how well his racial appeal worked, and didn't drive to the damn net every minute of every day (oh hai, Wisconsin). They stubbornly refused to understand that many of their boutique policies repel the Walmart voters they must *absolutely* win in states that aren't deep blue. In 2016, they came across as entitled to the office, instead of wanting to earn votes with hustle and humility. They can't make that mistake twice.

Donald Trump is a terrible, horrible, no-good president. He'll go down in history with asterisks next to his name for endemic corrup-

tion, outrageous stupidity, egregious cruelty, and inhumanity, for diminishing the presidency and the nation, and for being a lout with a
terrible wig. But he's trapped, desperate, and will do anything—and I
mean *anything*—to win.

So, yeah. I'm going to treat Democrats like a client, with tough
love, real talk, and a commitment to a shared victory. You won't always like it, but for the good of the republic, and for your own good,
I hope you'll listen. *I* won't like a lot of the outcomes, but Donald
Trump is a bigger threat to America and its future than a Democratic
president.

No policy victory is worth the damage he has wrought. No slate of
judges can offset the destruction he has done to our institutions and
our values. There is no moral accommodation with Trump, no safe
path away from his authoritarian statism. As with nuclear weapons,
only deterrence works. Only strong institutions and strong leaders
can offset the chaos and dissension that follows Trump.

He can scream "no collusion, no obstruction" from the grave, and
it won't change the fact that he owes his election to the Russians and
obstructed justice in trying to cover it up. He'll be remembered for a
spectacularly failed record in foreign policy. Despite his tough talk
about being the world's toughest negotiator, he has been routinely
rolled by foreign adversaries, leaving America less safe and less respected in the world. His deficit spending puts drunken sailors to
shame and makes the eyes of the few remaining fiscal conservatives
pop out.

His overtly racial appeal is beyond shame. His ongoing flirtation
with xenophobic arsonists over immigration and his long game of
footsie with the racist virgins of the alt-right (but I repeat myself)
have left the country more divided than anyone could have imagined
in the post-Obama era.

He has done more damage to the institution of the presidency
than Nixon and given the country a White House clown show with a
cast of the least competent, least ethical, least sympathetic, and least
appealing supporting players in any administration in memory.

There's only one thing that can save him, and that's a Democratic

Party too stubborn, undisciplined, and foolish to get out of its own way.

The Democratic Party is on the verge of doing the impossible—handing Donald Trump the 2020 election. Even with the table set to eat the Republicans' lunch in 2020, the Fyre Festival of political parties is on the verge of fucking it up once again, and it's time someone gave them the tough love they so obviously need.

My Democratic friends will have one of two reactions to this book. Some will stomp off, huffing, "Thanks, but we don't need you to pick our nominee. SANDERS FOREVER, BRAH!" Some will distrust any Republican, even one who sacrificed his career, lifelong friendships, and arguably his sanity to do the right thing. (Fuck me, right?)

The smart ones will realize that, though my tough-love approach isn't what they want, it's what they desperately need.

Think of it this way: When a senior KGB officer who decided he'd had enough of throwing people into the gulag or supporting a corrupt kleptocracy walked into an American embassy during the Cold War, the right response wasn't "Fuck you." The correct response was "Hey, we'd LOVE to check out this boatload of intel, plans, strategies, and data you've collected while you've been kicking our asses." It was "Oh, so *that's* how you did it."

I'm coming in from the cold, whether you like it or not. I have a low tolerance for stupidity, and by God, I *will* overcome your stubborn resistance to the truth. This will not be over soon. You will not always enjoy this.

———

First, a confession. Yes, I would prefer that a conservative hold the presidency. Not a Trumpian, new-era conservative of this currently hot flavor of nationalist authoritarian dickishness, but one of the old, vanished era when we governed like adults, behaved like civilized people, and held on to both our principles and our humanity. I also want my own fighter aircraft and a volcano lair, but that's not happening, at least this election cycle.

The Republican challengers (as of this writing, at least) look like a field of also-rans, and the independents look like spoilers, so I'm stuck telling the Democrats how to avoid their usual mistakes, run the right campaign, and defeat Donald Trump.

Why the hell would I do this? Am I a suddenly far-left, woke social justice warrior who's gone all pro-abortion, pro–gun control, big-tax socialist? Am I a RINO sellout? Am I trying to please my masters in big media? Is this a guidebook from the vengeful deep state? My Trump Republican critics will call this making common cause with the enemy. I know it sounds pious, but I really do put country over party, particularly when the party I served for a generation is on a headlong path toward becoming a collection of mere votaries to a maniacal cult leader.

It's a common trope that every election is the most crucial election in history. This time, that cliché has both the danger and the benefit of being true. Unless there is a viable challenge to Trump and—just as important—to Trumpism in 2020, America is poised to transform into a different, darker, and more dangerous country. His embrace of nationalist populism may be accidental or incidental, but it's spreading fast and it's dangerous as hell.

I'm going to tell you these things not merely because I loathe the damage Trump is doing to our nation, or because I think your policies are good for America. If Democrats win, I'm going to hate it rather a lot.

But there's more at stake than political and ideological preference now.

I'm doing this because the party I worked for, fought for, and sweated over for thirty years didn't just abandon people like me who couldn't stomach Trump; they're putting the entire American experiment at risk. I'm telling you this because Trump and his enablers shredded every ideological predicate that drew me to conservatism and the Republican Party—the old-fashioned stuff like following the Constitution and the rule of law, limits on state power, tradition, honesty, decency, and sanity.

I'm doing it because I'm sick of the moral and political contagion he's spread across the country, and sick over the collapse of a once-great party. I'm doing it because I'm repulsed by how Republicans have abandoned even the paper-thin excuses that let them make the switch to Trump in the first place.

I'm on this journey as a man without a party, a rebel in the Trump era, because the man covering the Oval Office with his ichor is an existential threat to American values, institutions, the Constitution, our system of government, our security in the world, the rule of law, and, you know, the little stuff like the future of humanity.

I'm willing to burn down the village to save it.

Here's my promise to Democrats: I'm going to walk you through this as someone who has run the exact same playbook against your candidates that you're about to face. I'm going to show you the flaws in your operating system that Republican consultants and candidates have hacked time and time again. This book is a road map for defeating Trump in 2020 for the Democrats, written by a Republican who knows how and why the Democrats often lose big elections they should win.

Why listen to me?

Why listen to a man who believes in a set of principles and philosophies many of you find anathema? I hope you'll read and implement the ideas in this book with the understanding that there really are things more important than a transient political outcome. I hope that, like me, you'll put country before ideology and the survival of the idea and ideals of America before the resentments over how many times I kicked your ass down the block.

We're on the same side now, and that side is America.

THE CASE AGAINST TRUMP, OR FOUR MORE YEARS IN HELL

Tweets from Donald Trump's Second Term

@realDonaldTrump: The TRADE WAR has made AMERICA SO GREAT. Don't believe the lying FAKE NEWS about record farm and manufacturing bankruptcies. This tiny, 50% correction in the market is a FAKE NEWS LIE. This trade war was so easy to win! I sent Chinaman Xi a MESSAGE.

@WSJ: As Depression Looms, Trump's Trade War Rages

@Bloombergbusiness: Markets down 50% after Trump sends "dick pic" to Chinese premier Xi in latest trade war skirmish.

@BreitbartNews: Trump's manhood wows globe. Women beg for his seed.

FOUR MORE YEARS IN HELL

Words fail to describe how bad four more years of Donald Trump would be for America and the world, to say nothing of the Democratic Party. In the beginning, I joked about the Mad Max hellscape that awaits us in the Trump era, but it's gotten much less funny over time.

Why am I telling you this? You know this, right?

I'm telling you this because at some level Democrats still seem to believe that this is a mere political contest, with traditional limits and boundaries. They still think this is an election like any other, where they will turn out the base and scrap over the remaining voters in the center, trying to get back to the Oval Office along the paths laid out through the long, sprawling history of American politics.

But this isn't just any election; it is an existential moment for America. This is either the last election of the nation we understood and loved, or the first of a long reset where we restore our honor and image after Trump's term.

Campaigns often claim that the present election will decide what the America we leave our children and grandchildren will look like. This is rarely true; most elections aren't epochal choices between light and darkness, liberty and servitude, good and evil.

This election? Yeah. It's the real, apocalyptic deal.

Pick one: our messy, flawed, wonderfully sloppy democratic re-public stumbling toward the shining city on the hill, or a kingdom of cruelty and utter corruption led by a family of authoritarian klepto-crats in thrall to foreign powers.

In those terms, you'd do anything to win, right?

Right?

Watching the 2020 Democrats, that answer isn't clear. Some seem willing to chase their ideological fantasies instead of a decisive victory; others are unable to focus on a single, strategic truth—that this election will be fought in fifteen or so swing states and will be entirely a referendum on Donald Trump.

So what's it going to be? A real campaign, or a purity contest for the edges of the Democratic Party?

Choose now and choose fast, because the clock on the 2020 election is running. The only thing you can never get back in an election is time. You can raise more money. You can do more ads. You can change your speeches and messages. You can do more calls, interviews, and town meetings until you collapse from campaign exhaustion. But you can't get back a single week, day, or hour. Time, tide, and the battle of 2020 wait for no one.

All reelection campaigns are a referendum on the incumbent. All of them.

This presidential race is the ultimate referendum on the politics, character, persona, and actions of a man who has proven himself to us in a thousand awful ways. His enablers and ball-washers spend their lives in a state of constant revisionist panic, lunging from "He didn't say that" to "He didn't mean that" to googling "How can I enter the witness protection program?"

Trump cannot be shamed. He cannot be embarrassed. He cannot be controlled, and he cannot resist his impulses. Turning this election into a referendum on Trump is a gift for Democrats, not a burden.

Democrats don't need to sell the progressive base on opposition to Trump. They don't need to sell the rank and file. They don't need to sell African Americans. They don't need to sell most Hispanics. They do need to make the case that Trump is a mentally and morally unwell man, and that he sold a pack of lies to the voters in the fifteen or so swing states that matter in 2020. Democratic base voters gave us a preview in 2018, and they're ready to rock again in 2020.

The following chapters outline the case to be made against Trump in this referendum. They look at how deeply Trump's next four years will damage the American system, and the American people. If the stakes are outlined more starkly and more directly, Democrats might—in spite of themselves—understand how vital it is they fight this fight as it is, not as they wish it to be.

Tweets from Donald Trump's Second Term

@realDonaldTrump: As you know, Israel considers me King of the Jews. You might not know due to the lying media that I am also considered by many to be the next incarnation of the Dali Lama! THANK YOU FOR THIS HONER! Do you think I should also be POPE?

@YaleDivSchool: Wait, what?

@TheHolySee: (⊙_⊙)

@DalaiLama: New phone. Who dis?

AMERICAN SWAMP

The Trump White House is lavishly and obviously corrupt to a degree unprecedented in modern American political history. Yes, we can drag back to Warren Harding and Teapot Dome, or Ulysses Grant's multifarious scandals, or Andrew Johnson and the spoils system's corrupt and corrupting influence, and yes, all presidential administrations are touched by corruption, though generally in trivial, marginal ways. In the modern era, we've had only one real standout: Richard Nixon.

Until now.

Trump makes Nixon look like a rookie, a small-ball piker. He makes the nontroversies of Obama, the Bushes, Clinton, and Reagan feel utterly trivial by comparison. Carter, the most reviled Democratic president of my youth, was practically a Sunday school teacher. Oh, wait. He was a Sunday school teacher.

Richard Nixon's corruption sprang from a raw desire to protect his political power and position. He wasn't in it for money or even adulation. Can you imagine Nixon with Trump's neediness for love? Yuck. Lyndon Baines Johnson really just cared about the game; everything else was gravy. Clinton enjoyed the game, and certainly cashed in after office, but he was much more about chasing interns than dollars while in the White House.

No, Trump, a man who is sui generis in so many shitty ways, has taken the White House and the nation to new lows when it comes to corruption. Far from draining the hated swamp, the Trump administration careens from one scandal to the next. America watches transfixed as one after another personage is fired or quits, investigations are launched into all kinds of possible wrongdoing, and lobbyists carry on in a rumspringa that a Hollywood screenwriter would find absurdly overdrawn.

Democrats, who too often focus on policy, not the players, are finally catching on. With the 2018 Democratic takeover of the House, the oversight function of the legislative branch is getting a long-needed workout. Instead of chasing deep-state demons as Fredo Nunes did during the first two years of the Trump administration, the Democrats are finally investigating the extraordinary degree and depth of corruption that orbits Trump. They're moving too damn slow, but they are moving nevertheless.

The grifter demimonde cashing in on Trump should come as no surprise. His lawlessness and contempt for ethics is a feature, not a bug. He ran as "too rich to be bought" but governs as "hey, sailor, wanna date?" While the scammers have always been a part of political fundraising, this Trump generation is exceptionally shameless. Trump's venality and willingness to fleece the GOP rubes doesn't repel them—it's what attracts them.

Democrats must understand that corruption is always a killer app in politics, parting even hard partisans from candidates. The referendum against Trump is in part an anti-corruption message, highlighting through clear narratives and illustrations that Trump is a tool of K Street and that the D.C. corruption that swing state voters associate with their own misfortunes is more extreme and corrosive than ever. If Democrats can't tell Americans a tale of how greed, corruption, and self-dealing define Trump's Washington, they need better writers.

FOUR MORE YEARS: A DEEPER AND MORE FETID SWAMP

Trump's followers, sycophants, clingers, and the joyous corps of lobbyists have an obvious plan for 2020 and beyond. It's a plan that works on one assumption: Get while the getting is good. Eat, drink, and snatch all the federal largesse we can, for tomorrow we may die, or be indicted.

Whether it's lobbyists for Wall Street banks, big coal, the payday-loan industry, private prisons, or any other number of economic vampires, the Trump kakistocracy really does have something for everyone: nepotism, cronyism, pay-for-play, backroom deals for donors, abuse of power, lying to Congress, threats and intimidation, and, as a bonus, monetizing cruelty to children. And the first term was just a preview.

The next four years will make the Trump administration's first four pale in comparison. The kleptocratic festival of crony capitalism, lobbyist giveaways, consumer-screwing protections for predatory lenders, environmental rapine, immigration cruelty, and fiscal insanity in his first term was a warmup act. In the second, all the political restraints are off.

Trump, who ran for president to reboot his failing brand and faltering image, has monetized every moment of his occupancy of the Oval Office to sell hotel rooms and golf course memberships. He'll be looking for the big cash-out in ways no prior president ever could. Trump Tower Pyongyang, here we come.

Trump and his scavenger spawn Don Jr. and Eric will spend the next four years working every angle they can to springboard his postelection empire of middle-tier resorts into every third-world satrapy with a decent beach and lax extradition standards.

Corruption is a disease. In healthy societies, it's a chronic but mild ailment. With a moderately balanced diet and exercise plan, and occasional treatments, it's bothersome but rarely fatal. It's why governments (hey, even ours) have laws against self-dealing and nepotism, government ethics watchdogs, mandatory conflict-of-interest reporting requirements, and bright lines on using government office for personal enrichment. Those things function as an ethics immune system that sends T-cells racing to the source of infections and diseases and fighting back.

We no longer live in a healthy political society.

Trump's fluke win put him in the most powerful office in the land,

and alongside his Large Adult Sons and his older daughter, the Trump enterprise has cashed in, bigly. Trump himself is, of course, still intimately involved with the family business.

The endless revisions of his con-in-law Jared Kushner's financial and personnel security reports point to how that side of the Trump family business is monetizing government. Did Kushner's backing of a Saudi/UAE blockade of Qatar pressure Brookfield Asset Management—which just happens to be largely owned by Qatar's sovereign wealth fund—into making a deal to save the Kushner family's fortunes? Given Jared's repeated evasions and revisions to his financial disclosures, we will likely never know. I, for one, would be shocked to find gambling going on here in Casablanca.

As for Trump's financial disclosures, to say nothing of his elusive tax returns, the degree to which any sane person puts the slightest credibility in them is a key marker on the sucker scale. You'd have to be as dumb as Deutsche Bank to believe them, but there have been no punishments, no sanctions, no consequences. Given the House Democrats' unwillingness to hammer Treasury secretary Steve Mnuchin for ordering the cover-up of Trump's tax returns and for refusing to comply with black-letter law on this matter, Trump knows the second term is his time to pillage. What's Congress going to do? Send a strongly worded letter?

Trump will lie, punt, sue, and evade on every financial disclosure; he'll spend a second term more comfortable than ever with monetizing his position. He'll allow his sons to continue their domestic development games with a nod and a wink to various foreign powers. Jared will be Jared, and Ivanka will reboot her international branding operation. Every major meeting and summit will be held at a Trump hotel or resort, and feature, as did both the 2019 state visit to Britain and the G20 summit in Japan, the Imperial Trump Family on full display.

For the Trump crime family, the next four years will be a lavish opportunity to extort every last thing they can get out of everyone who comes on their political radar. The "fuck you, pay me" mentality of the Trump enterprise will become even more vivid, and the menu of prices for government services will become more apparent. "You want to invade Kraplakistan? Sure, buy two dozen F-35s, and be sure to throw in Eric's commission, and we won't say a word."

Trump is a demonstrably cheap date on the corruption front, apparently hoping to make it up on volume. You don't think that foreign governments, international criminals, and expat oligarchs from around the globe buy blocks of Trump condos and fill wildly overpriced D.C. hotel rooms and event spaces every night just because they read a Yelp review praising the linens and spa services, do you? You don't think that people like Cindy "Happy Ending" Yang are buying memberships to Mar-a-Lago because the omelet station is to die for, right?

Donald Trump is sending a signal, loud and clear, that he's for sale, satisfaction guaranteed. Far from the Greatest Negotiator Ever, he's the easiest lay in White House history. In the second term, foreign and domestic powers will start cashing in their chits, and the losers will be the American people.

As a demonstrably weak and not very bright man, Donald Trump has proven throughout his personal and business history to be an easy mark for those types of approaches. His second term will be an era when his raw, unending greed further compromises the presidency and the nation. Far from the incorruptible, swamp-draining billionaire his yahoos imagined, Trump is a pay-to-play, small-ball narcissist who is vulnerable to emotional and financial bribery.

The consequence-free corruption of the first term will slide into a second, where it will become normalized and mainstream. It's another short slide from there to an American political system in which corruption, self-dealing, and criminality become the central tendency of government.

If the president is for sale, so is everyone else, and—spoiler alert—nations where endemic corruption takes hold aren't stable, prosperous, or small-d democratic for long.

Trumpism corrupts, and absolute Trumpism corrupts absolutely, so expect more unsubtle stories of political payoffs by powerful interests. In 2019, sanctioned Russian oligarch and Putin bestie Oleg Deripaska *mysteriously* announced that his firm, Rusal, would build a new aluminum plant in the United States, in Mitch McConnell's home oblast of Kentuckistan.[1] It struck one columnist and some Senate Democrats as a *remarkable* coincidence that McConnell blocked bipartisan efforts to stymie Russian election interference in the 2020 election shortly thereafter.[2]

Expect many, many more examples of Trump donors being handed the keys to the kingdom and free rein over the various satrapies in which they take a monetary interest. As a note, a coal lobbyist now runs the Environmental Protection Agency, a pharma lobbyist runs the Department of Health and Human Services, and, for a time, a defense lobbyist ran the Department of Defense. All this happened when Team Trump still had to think about reelection.

Expect more cabinet and subcabinet members to dwell in limbo as "acting" this-or-that. By naming "acting" secretaries of departments and having those departments staffed by armies of "acting" minions, Trump can avoid ever having his hires truly vetted and examined for conflicts of interest.

As for the Trump 2020 campaign, its leadership will be a ripe target for both foreign and domestic interests. Paul Manafort, Mike Flynn, Carter Page, George Papadopoulos, Michael Caputo, Roger Stone, and the rest of the 2016 dog's breakfast of scumbags were all eagerly hustling for cash from anyone and everyone who would stroke a check.

Why should the 2020 team be left out? Anyone who can influence Trump by saying "X loves you and they're donating to the Trump slush fund—I mean campaign fund, sorry" will suddenly find themselves with many new best friends. The majority of the Trump folks today look at the few who got prison time as outliers. They've seen the money made by Trump 2016 veterans, and nothing drives their behavior like the lure of the long green.

"It won't happen to me," they think. "I'm dealing with a reputable Russian oligarch."

Tweets from Donald Trump's Second Term

@realDonaldTrump: Because the Wall has been so powerful, so big, so effective at STOPING Terrorist MS-13 child solders, I have Ordered the creation of the TRUMP DOME over all of America. The TRUMP DOME will truly make America RESPECTED.

@MIT: Delete your account.

@BreitbartNews: SPACE DOME ALMOST COMPLETED. Trump Dome will stop all aliens!

@Drudge: MS-13 SPACE CARAVAN APPROACHES!

THE CRAZY RACIST
UNCLE ACT . . . ISN'T AN ACT

As much fun as it is to mock Donald Trump's daily rage-tweeting, self-fellating, and bald-faced pathological lying, it's increasingly clear Trump is not a well man. This is not simply President Munchausen. The Republican excuses of "It's just an act" are going to wear thin when Trump wakes up one morning and demands to see the pretty nuclear fireworks because Ecuador or Monaco or Brigadoon offended him in a dream. In the summer of 2019, Denmark barely ducked a rain of radioactive fire after refusing to sell Greenland to Trump.

Of course, the idea that Trump was a wild card, an unpredictable bullshit machine, was held dear to the hearts of many Washington Republicans hoping to deflect attention from his spectrum of pathologies by pretending to possess some secret decoder ring. They hoped they could wink-and-nod it away as an artifact of his mystic deal-making prowess or his keen insights into human behavior. For their own survival and sanity, they hoped and prayed the ignorant, crazy racist uncle act was just that—an act.

Spoiler alert: It's not.

They—like much of America—discovered you can't trust a word he says. It took a while for them to realize he wasn't playing a dumb and dangerous liar; he is one, and always was.

It's also time that we talk about Grandpa's racism, because I'm pretty sure at this point it isn't some clever strategy to lure in the white male non-college demo with a nationalist-populist message, and is actually just, well, straight-up racism.

The long arc of Trump's racial rhetoric goes from Mexican "rapists" at the beginning of his campaign to "shithole countries" to "both sides" in Charlottesville to "invasions" at the southern border to calling a majority-black district of Baltimore "rat and rodent infested." This president isn't a subtle racist. He's not the kind who wants to white-glove it with pretty rhetorical dressing about culture and heritage.

His endless attacks on immigrants, his quest for his illusory border wall, his lies about caravans and criminals surging over the borders are all of a piece; it's part of repeatedly stoking his base with his racist air-raid siren. Trump-allied "conservatives" have tried to put a pretty face on white nationalism with policy conferences, gussied-up versions of *The Daily Stormer,* and an alt-lite media complex, but racial animus is still at the wretched heart of his filthy movement.

A lot of Trump's arena events are a couple pointy white hats short of a Klan rally, and even when a chain of white nationalist gunmen slaughtered Americans in Gilroy, California, and El Paso, Texas, and at the Tree of Life Synagogue in Pittsburgh, the beat went on. His overtly racist attacks on the "squad" of four Democratic congresswomen who all—*quelle surprise!*—happen to be women of color was swiftly followed by a blistering series of attacks on the late Representative Elijah Cummings of Maryland, who—stop me if you've heard this—was African American.

I've written at length about Trump's racial history, and the picture is hideously below the mark of what America deserves in a president; he's an awful, dark stain on our history. What the first term makes abundantly clear is that it's not an act, it's not a strategy, and it's not something the American people can bear. It is exactly who he is: a fucking racist. The referendum on Trump's racism will play out in 2020, and well beyond, costing the GOP seats, status, and support for generations.

They have no one to blame but themselves.

IT'S ALL DOWNHILL FROM HERE

Which leads us to what he looks like in a second term.

Cognitive decline is an ugly, hard reality for millions of Americans. As the Silent Generation slips into their final years, and the oldest Boomers join them, families all over America confront Alzheimer's and many other tolls of aging. For many afflicted with a loss of memory and ability, this decline is a sad, steady reduction in the joys of life.

For Trump, it's part of the reality show, though not one he wants to focus on. Comparing Trump now with video clips from a decade ago is chilling. The slippage in his verbal acuity is marked. His rages and explosions of temper aren't part of an act; they're no longer controlled or controllable. The nearest contemporary parallel was the second-term decline of Ronald Reagan. Americans sensed the terrible gravity of Alzheimer's pulling at him, but he was still surrounded by largely competent people and was, on the whole, a healthy man. For all the disagreements Democrats had with him, Reagan could never be considered an impulsive narcissist with a hair-trigger temper and no concern for others. Reagan actually bothered to understand nuclear weapons and the risks they posed, unlike President Missile Parade. Trump's lack of knowledge should terrify you as much as it does me, especially as his cognitive decline continues apace.

Given his hold over the cabinet, there's no workable solution for this president's combination of apparent mental infirmities and uncontrolled urges and racist fuckery, suggesting a second term will be more dangerous than the first.

The madness, the narcissism, the eccentricities, the pathological lying, the delusions of both persecution and grandeur are rationalized and normalized now. The remaining cabinet members are men and women who have capitulated, morally and mentally, to the realities of this president. It's not leadership and policy that keeps them in line; it's terror. They wake up every day knowing that the moment they move or speak against him, they'll be fired, Twitter-shamed, dismissed as mere coffee boys, and victims of brutal news coverage from Ibn Fred's Trumphadi media outlets.

Pulling off a Twenty-Fifth Amendment play against Trump based on his mental state is utterly justified, and utterly impossible, given the composition of bootlicks, yes-men, edge-case weirdos, and corrupt satraps in the clown-car Trump cabinet. Trained professionals have assessed and written about the increasing signs of dementia and instability in Trump; I'm just an amateur cognition specialist, but I keep expecting him to go full Cypress Hill on the White House lawn one day and ask the press, "Who you trying to get crazy with, ése? Don't you know I'm loco?"

Today, he's still bounded by a burning desire for reelection, and he knows at some level he has to pretend to observe the forms from time to time to throw America off the scent of his problems. That's why after moments of national tragedy he gives hammy speeches where he seems like a glitchy Trump droid reading words off the screen.

Mumbling through teleprompter speeches one moment and veering off the next moment into wild ad-libs of stream-of-consciousness blurting, Trump is a shadow of even his 2016 self. We all know that cognitive decline is, tragically, a one-way street.

Don't forget, kids: The crazy racist uncle act isn't an act . . . and he still controls America's nuclear arsenal.

Sleep tight!

Tweets from Donald Trump's Second Term

@realDonaldTrump: Some lying liberal media who are FAILING BADLY and will soon be bankrupt like the Bezos Washington Post are reporting that Stephen Miller was arrested for making a suit from a woman's skin and eating her. FAKE NEWS. He did NOT EAT HER! Stephen is doing a GRATE job!

@PressSec: Correction: Mr. Miller did not eat the woman in question raw. Unlike degenerate migrants, Mr. Miller cooks his food.

CRUELTY AS STATECRAFT

All bullies display two distinct characteristics: cruelty and weakness.

As for Trump's cruelty, nothing represents it better than the way our government has treated immigrant children under his watch. The catalog of abuses belongs in the International Criminal Court in The Hague. The administration's immigration policy is deliberate, planned, and engineered to shock the conscience. Trump is often conflicted on whether he wants to own this policy; some days he denies it's happening at all, other days he blames Obama, and still others he capers and giggles about it.

On the days he doesn't want the full heat of President Stephen Miller's circus of child incarceration, mistreatment, and infant deaths to fall on him, he denies it with vigor. The pictures tell a damning story, and the statistics are worse. The man who never hesitates to never hesitate when it comes to tweeting is strangely inert on actually fixing the program.

The first "kids in cages" moment was a turning point for Trump and the nation. In 2016, the insults he hurled at his fellow candidates, the disabled, John McCain, and others all had a towel-snapping edge to them, as if he was just a boobish bastard who didn't know where the line was. Now, his impulses toward cruelty are backed by government policy, and the results are a human rights disaster.

Trump lost control of the narrative the moment the story broke.

The president's political arsonists, desperate to stop the "brown-ing of America," believed they had a surefire winner for the core of the Trump base. I'm sure that during the planning meetings they felt secure in the knowledge that Fox, talk radio, and the Trump media would cheer his aggressive steps against the horde of toddler MS-13 trainees. Engineered as a political spectacle of cruelty, the plan failed in its efforts to stem the tide of refugees and asylum seekers from Central America, so of course the Trump team doubled down, over and over.

Americans have powerfully rejected this policy, embraced the plight of these kids, and showed an outpouring of support that re-flects the very best of America's values. The reaction of the vast ma-jority of Americans to Trump's policy was and is horror.

This cruelty is still playing out in squalid detention centers and ICE roundups along the U.S. border. As immigrant children are forc-ibly separated from their parents and placed in cages inside ware-houses where they are maltreated and malnourished, America looks on in horror.

If you're looking for a referendum point on Trump with the subur-ban demo of former Republicans, this is it. If Democrats are looking for a referendum point with anyone with a basic scrap of humanity, this is it.

The cliché "This is not who we are" has suddenly taken on more weight, and it's important to outline for voters how Trump's cruelty and bigotry damage our national soul. This is a message Democrats can and must use to complete the divorce of women voters from the GOP. If Democrats can't build an entire suite of messages and ads around this story, I don't know if anyone can help them.

IT STARTS WITH KIDS IN CAGES. IMAGINE FOUR MORE YEARS.

What do you think happens when this program gains additional bu-reaucratic momentum? What happens is a series of perverse incen-tives where instead of standing up to this deeply un-American, entirely outrageous, and inhumane cruelty the government normal-

izes it. It becomes the same old Nuremberg just-following-orders defense in which the outrageous becomes the expected and the cost in
lives is offset by bonuses, performance awards, and promotions.
Deep inside the bureaucracy, government is always unaccountable,
and this is even more true of Trump's government.

The abuse of immigrants will accelerate for a host of reasons in
the second term, the most consequential of which will be that the
Republicans around Trump will understand that he's saddled them
with a generational problem with Hispanics. Even red states like
Texas will experience profound erosions of Republican political
strength, almost entirely because of the damage their cooperation
with Trump has done to them with Hispanic voters. Set aside Texas
for a moment and consider that Florida, Arizona, Georgia, and North
Carolina are experiencing rapid growth in the legal immigrant population of Hispanics, and those folks are going to be voting soon—and
their American-born children will follow them. For them, Trump is
a racist who hates them with a fiery passion, and in politics, people
always return hate for hate.

That's why the efforts to close the border, to stop asylum seekers
and refugees, and to largely end even legal immigration will be front
and center in Trump's second term. The abuses will ratchet up in
order to frighten desperate immigrants—at least according to the designs of the architects of this monstrosity—into staying in their as-
signed shitholes. This is a last-ditch shot at the big prize of Making
America White Again.

Like junkies, the base of Trump's anti-immigrant cult will need
more. It's not enough to just see children in cages. It's not enough to
see mothers having their kids torn out of their arms. Oh, no, they'll
need more to feed the monster, and Trump will provide it. Stephen
Miller now largely runs the Department of Homeland Security and
Immigration and Customs Enforcement, so expect that the leaders of
those agencies will be held to his standards.

He wants a theater of abuse and cruelty, and he'll get it.

Tweets from Donald Trump's Second Term

@realDonaldTrump: No one has worked harder than my beautiful wife Melania to #BeBest even though no one on social media has been nicer than Your Favorite President. No wonder she is so attracted to me!

@JustinTrudeau: Cool story, bro.

@FLOTUS: Justin. DM me. XXX

TRUMP'S ECONOMIC
BULLSHIT MACHINE

A central presumption of Trumpism was that he would ensure a unique and persistent form of economic prosperity. The sugar rush of the tax cut is waning and the end of the Fed's easy money policy is coming. Trump is about to own a stock market correction, an overextended economy, massive new debt and deficits, and the inevitable train wreck of a trade war run by morons.

All of his economic mistakes are accreting into a mass of errors and evils that will hit Trump voters, and hard.

Democrats can and must use working- and middle-class examples of the foolishness of the Trump economic model to actually communicate that they give a damn instead of proposing some ephemeral and unsaleable "Yay, free college!" and "We'll all build solar panels" nonsense that voters no longer buy. Trump is vulnerable in the area he perceives as his greatest strength.

The trade war is a perfect example of Trumpism and its combination of blistering ignorance and robust cronyism. Part of a backward economic theory from the 1600s, it hurts the very people it was ostensibly launched to help. It has harmed farmers, ranchers, timber, manufacturing, tech companies, and small businesses all while driving up costs to American consumers. Far from being "easy to win," this trade war is already lost, and Americans are paying the price.

To reach the target set of voters Democrats absolutely must win in

2020, the most important countervailing message against Trump is simple: He lied to you. Political lies are perfect weapons for dividing previously loyal voters from the pack, and history is replete with examples. George H. W. Bush went to his grave knowing that, while he'd done the right thing for the government in 1991, the tax increase he supported broke a promise to the GOP base. "Read my lips" was the political lie that the GOP's rank and file would never forgive. Barack Obama promised "You can keep your doctor" and lost the House of Representatives a year later.

A fundamental predicate of Trump and Trumpism is that economic nationalism is the secret sauce both politically and as a national economic policy. After feeling screwed, pressured, abused, and left holding the economic bag in bad times and good for generations, American working people viewed the reality-TV character Trump played on *The Apprentice* as a man who would restore good-paying jobs and increase their paychecks.

But Trump has bent the economy to the point of subatomic collapse and continues to do so every day.

The working class of America hasn't seen wages rise, nor the prosperity of Silicon Valley and Wall Street trickle down to their neighborhoods. Trump promised a fundamental change from the way Americans outside the coastal prosperity zones lived, but every promise is a lie, every commitment nothing but a con, and every policy a Potemkin village. Polling shows that top-level happy talk about the economy is working; Americans are generally optimistic about their situation, as they were throughout the Obama era. But storm clouds loom, and as always, the bailouts won't go to them but to Wall Street and the banks. They're worried already.

Below that is a deeper concern. The cost of housing, college, and healthcare haunts Americans. They can't pay for retirement. They can't afford to truly save money. The stock market bubble is a beautiful boat on a toxic ocean.

From promising "great healthcare" to destroying the now-popular Affordable Care Act (can I get a sarcastic "Thanks, Obama" from the Trump-right media?), Trump's broken promises now have a cost.

The promised auto, coal, steel, and manufacturing jobs aren't just fiction; they're a cruel lie to people who spent the last three decades in a slow, painful decline.

Trump's lies convinced many working-class Americans for a reason. They're rightly pissed off, stressed out, and lost. They're looking for a return to a time when a guy or a girl with a high school education could hold a steady job, afford a home, raise a couple of kids—in short, lead a middle-class life. They aren't trying to be the next tech billionaire. They simply want to live that American dream they grew up believing in.

Both parties stood by as the world changed. From laissez-faire "let the markets decide" dickishness on the right to the vaporware promises on the left, neither party understood that these voters are pissed. Like all predators, Trump can sense the weakness in his marks, every time.

Coal jobs ought to go the way of, well, coal jobs. We're better than coal at this point for so many reasons, but Trump's wily populist bullshit broke off parts of the Democratic vote in southwestern Virginia, Ohio, and Pennsylvania. Trump's pressure on companies to bow to his 1950s (or is it 1850s?) vision of industrial policy produced chaos, not opportunity. Coal, despite his promises, isn't coming back.

Democratic candidates can't come in blind to their own failures. We saw both Clinton and Obama promise to restore jobs, manufacturing, unions, and the rest of the old signifiers of Rust Belt America with a gauzy, hazy "Well, we'll retrain you to become an organic solar panel installer and holistic home healthcare aide." This crap rings hollow for many of the people in Wisconsin, Ohio, Pennsylvania, Michigan, and the rest of the former industrial heartland.

Trump's lies had a different edge and character. His deceptions were more pointed, more racial, and xenophobic. In Trump's portrayal, the evil MS-13 gangs weren't here just to murder your entire family but also to take your job. Their insidious taco trucks would replace the local Culver's just as their insidious DNA would brown your neighborhood beyond recognition.

Democrats need to start hitting this message early and often, because many voters are already primed to listen. The slow growth of awareness about Trump's inability to tell the truth on the economy even when he doesn't need to lie has an arc something like this:

"Well, Trump's a salesman. He's selling."

"Well, I still trust him. He may be a liar, but he's our liar."

"Well, the media lies, too, so fuck off, libtard."

"Trump's playing eighty-seven-dimensional chess and he's lying to own the libs."

"I guess there aren't going to be fifty new steel mills and coal mines here in Ohio."

"The bank just repossessed my John Deere combine harvester."

Here's the painful irony: The big-picture economy, which is largely out of any president's control, is the real source of this president's political strength with voters who like him. The SSRN poll for CNN in June 2019 had a striking finding. Of those who approve of Trump, a plurality of 26 percent said they do so because of the economy, more than twice the next most-frequent answer. In the same economic issue basket, 8 percent cited jobs as a reason for liking him. On immigration, 4 percent said that's the reason they like him.

When it comes to other aspects of Trump's persona, support falls to the single digits. Just 1 percent said they approve of him because he's draining the proverbial D.C. swamp. A whopping 1 percent said they like him because he's honest, which proves you can fool 1 percent of the people all the time.

All of this is a sign of trouble ahead for Donald Trump, because his economic record is a rickety construction prone to collapse from external forces at any moment.

A BUBBLE, READY TO POP

The long, sweet climb in economic prosperity we've enjoyed for a decade comes down to the decisions of two men and one institution: George W. Bush in taking the vastly unpopular step of bailing out Wall Street in the 2009 economic crisis, and Barack Obama for flooding the economy with economic stimulus in his first term. The Federal Reserve enabled both of these decisions by issuing an ocean of low- or zero-interest credit for ten years. Sure, the bill will come due someday, but the party is still going. While Trump took short-term political advantage of it, every bubble gets pricked by the old invisible hand. In the current economic case, the blizzard of Trumpian bullshit will inevitably hit the fan.

We're awash in trillion-dollar deficits, the national debt is asymptotically approaching infinity, and we have a president who's never hesitated to borrow and spend well beyond his means, or to simply throw up his hands and declare bankruptcy when it suits him. We never did—and most likely never will—tackle entitlement reform. Nations don't get to go bankrupt; they collapse.

The GOP passed a tax bill that is performing exactly as expected and predicted: A handful of hedge funds, America's top corporations, and a few dozen billionaires were given a trillion-dollar-plus tax benefit. Even the tax cut's most fervent proponents know that its effects were short-lived, the bill is coming due, and in 2022 or thereabouts it's going to lead to annual deficits of close to $2 trillion.

When the bubble pops, the correction hits, and Wall Street investment firms and banks go tango uniform, Trump will bail them out before you can say "golden parachute." The "average guy with a 401k" who is going to get crushed in the next drop? Not so much.

The lobbying class will make a final thrust for the remaining sectors of the economy not dependent on crony capitalism as facilitated by K Street. The president continues to pick winners and losers in the economy, selecting companies who are "nice to me" for favorable regulatory treatment.

The current wave of consolidations, bigger-is-better, and monopoly-adjacent corporate mergers in tech, defense, agriculture, telecoms, and retail will be greased along by a Trump White House that does everything but post a price list outside the Oval Office. Canny CEOs will maximize shareholder value by sucking up to Trump in the usual ways: lavish campaign donations and even more lavish praise of the wonders of his fabulous leadership, incandescent intellect, and totally realistic-looking hair hat.

The next four years of Trump will also bring an unprecedented amount of direct, personal, and, of course, economically disastrous interference from Trump in the business of the Federal Reserve.

America's central bank is, in the mind of the Donald, merely one more adjunct of the White House, another cabinet department to browbeat into submission.

Trump's public whining over the Fed's slow grapple with interest rates at the end of a decade of easy lending and quantitative easing is understandable; the same Fed policies that fueled eight years of economic uplift under Obama have fueled the first part of Trump's administration.

Trump wants the Fed not only to continue the current spending spree but to expand it. His slow escalation of pressure on the Fed finally got the attention of economists when he ripped out this doozy of a tweet on April 14, 2019: "If the Fed had done its job properly, which it has not, the Stock Market would have been up 5,000 to 10,000 additional points, and GDP would have been well over 4% instead of 3% . . . with almost no inflation. Quantitative tightening was a killer, should have done the exact opposite!"[3]

Now, I know you're thinking what I'm thinking: "Quantitative tightening" isn't a phrase in the Trump lexicon, unless it has to do with plastic surgery for his spouse du jour. Not to mention that the guy who literally went bankrupt multiple times while running casinos is trying to tell the cautious, smart minds at the Federal Reserve how to manage the U.S. economy. This, as in all things Trump touches, will not end well.

In the words of Noël Coward, "There are bad times just around the corner." The gulf between prosperity at the highest reaches of the economy and stark terror at the lowest is growing wider. I'm not saying this as some kind of Bernie-bro socialist. I'm saying it as a conservative who sees that federal government protections have allowed the investment sector, and the folks who can afford to game the tax and regulatory systems, to enjoy a boom like no other.

In a second term, President Trade-Wars-Are-Easy-to-Win will doubtless reap some of what his policies on trade have sown in the last few years. The global order of (largely) free and (mostly) fair trade is shifting quickly to our economic, political, and military rivals in the world, opening new markets where we have now boxed ourselves out. As sweeping change continues to move the global economy toward technology, services, and nano- and biotech, Trump's retro trade policy will continue to bankrupt American farmers and manufacturers, strengthen our adversaries, and cost American consumers billions in new taxes.

All of this is building toward an economic disaster out of proportion to the mere correction we would experience after a long period of growth, all else being equal. No, the collapse next time won't just be awful; it'll be made more dangerous and destructive by an economic ignoramus trying to rage-tweet the country away from the economic cliff.

My suggested portfolio in the coming Trump depression is gold, ammunition, and canned goods.

Tweets from Donald Trump's Second Term

@realDonaldTrump: Because You are so Proud of the Greet Job I do as your FAVORITE PRECEDENT, I have issued an executive order which is totally legal and cool to do called Prima Noctis. Lay back and think of Trump, American lady women.

@BigBillBarr: Totally legal, sir! If the President says it, it's law. That's in the REAL Constitution.

@realDonaldTrump: THANK YOU Bill Barr for stoping the Witch Haunt!

@HillaryClinton: Da fuq?

GENERALISSIMO TRUMP AND PILLOW FORTRESS AMERICA

Democrats lost a meaningful fraction of their male base after 1980 because they were perceived to be weak on national security. They reinforced this impression over and over, squandering the Democratic foreign and military policy legacies of FDR, Truman, and JFK. They now have an enormous opportunity, as both a moral and a political force, to take back the high ground on defense, security, and terrorism—to mount a ringing, Kennedy- and Reaganesque defense of America's role as a force for good in the world. Part of the referendum on Donald Trump is to show where the grubby rhetoric of the United States as a transactional, mercenary force leads, and how a man fueled by profound ignorance, low biases, irresistible impulses, and obvious weaknesses for praise and money put America at risk in an unstable world.

Even in the first term, the indictment is powerful. Trump has given the Democratic nominee a perfect opportunity to reclaim the mantle of being the national security grown-up in the room. He's a foreign policy failure and a constant danger to national security. The case makes itself: From Putin to North Korea to Iran to ISIS to Saudi Arabia to NATO, Trump turned U.S. foreign policy into a pay-to-play humiliation, coupled with a juvenile, shit-talking style that sounds more like something from a third-world, beret-wearing caudillo from the 1970s.

We're suffering from diminished credibility, influence, and security in the world, and the knock-on effects of this era will ripple out for decades, building a series of problems that will haunt our diplomats and damage our interests. America's foreign and military policy inflection points are marked by big, transformative moments and small mistakes that mushroom into slow-burn conflicts we can't quite win but don't quite lose.

Trump's endless self-aggrandizement as the Greatest Negotiator in the History of Mankind™, a human quantum computer of dealmaking prowess that would break the wills, hearts, and backs of our trading competitors, military rivals, and players on the global stage turned out to be the largest nothingburger in the history of dealmaking. At this point, I wouldn't trust Donald Trump to negotiate for a 1999 Hyundai at a used-car lot, and no one else who's watched him over the last two and a half years would either.

On trade, every single deal that Trump promised would be quick, easy, and immediately profitable has been a flop. The rebranded NAFTA is still NAFTA. The trade war with China has left the Xi government in a stronger position than ever, while devastating Midwest farms and industries. Trump's trade record is one long on bluster and higher costs for Americans, followed by concessions to the ostensible targets of his policy.

On foreign relations, from NATO to the Baltics to South America to the Persian Gulf, Trump has left allies wondering at the source of his affection for their enemies and his animus toward their leaders. From the Helsinki debacle in which Trump sided with the Russian leader over his own intelligence services[4] to the weakening of NATO to Russia's conflict with Ukraine, Trump has been outstanding as Vladimir Putin's lapdog. He treats journalist-murdering Saudi Arabian rising-star Mohammed bin Salman with kid gloves, including providing U.S. intelligence and firepower for the Saudi war against Yemen.[5] Far from making America safer, the president has left even our most loyal friends in doubt about our intention to honor our commitments abroad. He's cast us as a pay-to-play mercenary force and has divorced us from the international priorities that once defined American power in the world.

We once were a beacon of freedom and liberation for the oppressed and those held in tyranny. A long line of presidents from both parties held that America plays a unique role in the world as a trusted defender of freedom, a model for other nations. But Trump's America is transactional. With Trump, it's "Fuck you, pay me."

In July 2019, diplomatic cables sent by the British ambassador to the United States, Kim Darroch, were leaked, resulting in his resignation. In the leaked emails, Darroch stated the unvarnished truth about Donald Trump: "We don't really believe this administration is going to become substantially more normal; less dysfunctional; less unpredictable; less faction-riven; less diplomatically clumsy and inept." The ambassador described Trump and his team as "uniquely dysfunctional" and noted the deep divisions and internecine warfare inside the White House. He predicted the Trump presidency could "crash and burn" and "end in disgrace." Remember, these are the observations of an *ally*.[6]

GATHERING STORMS

What does four more years of the Trump Doctrine look like on the world stage?

Best case? A diminished America. Worst case? Cleansing sea of radioactive fire.

Global economic downturns often lead nations to do stupid shit on the world stage and at home. The Great Depression is only the best-known example of this, but the pattern repeats, and with the global economy riding the brakes since the fall of 2019, our chances of economic conflicts erupting into international conflicts are rising fast. Add in the disruptive nature of Trump's trade war with China and the deliberate destruction of generational alliances, and Trump will be uniquely remembered as a president whose policies weakened the nation at every turn. His fool's luck has been that—so far—we have avoided the horror of a terrorist attack, a hot military confrontation, or some other foreign policy externality. Luck, however, is not a national security strategy, and luck famously and consistently runs out.

Our overseas partners' confidence in America's national security and intelligence community is severely damaged; they know Donald Trump's hatred for the IC, and they know he is filling its leadership ranks with his toadies. An unsung story of American foreign policy success that was built on a foundation of quiet work by intelligence professionals working with our allies has fallen apart and will degrade further under Donald Trump in his second term.

Our close alliances are strained as never before. A frazzled NATO feels the eager heat of Russia's breath in the east, with the Baltic states, Poland, and Germany wondering if we're about to see a new Cold War, only this time with the United States more friendly to Russia than to the West. America's role as a NATO ally will continue to degrade as Trump's bromance with Putin, his extortion of the allies, and his utter ignorance of the traditions and meaning of the Western Alliance is demonstrated time and again. But hey, Trump Tower Moscow will make it worthwhile, right?

South Korea and Japan, our closest Asian allies, will face a China unconstrained by the leverage of U.S. trade to normalize its behavior and a North Korea emboldened by Trump's elevation of Kim Jong-un to the status of an equal partner. Kim has been able to survive sanctions and threatens the stability of the region only by Trump's goodwill. The DPRK will have enjoyed a long head start on developing effective intermediate-range nuclear weapons because Donald Trump gave it to them on a platter.

At least Jared Kushner will broker Middle East peace in the second term.

Oh. Wait.

The State Department will become an even more demoralized mess. Secretary of State Mike Pompeo has gone down a path toward being the ultimate Trump sycophant. His leadership in U.S. diplomacy and protection of our allies is constantly compromised by attempts to apply the proper suction to Trump's ass.

Trump's eagerness for "wins" will continue to collide with the realities of a hard world of hard leaders. The Chinese will never give him a victory. The Taliban are salivating for the departure of U.S. forces from Afghanistan so they can return to their accustomed medieval savagery toward women and apostates. Russia will continue to behave as if they have—to paraphrase LBJ—Trump's pecker in their pocket. And by "pecker" I mean "mushroom-shaped object."

Trump's short temper, lack of knowledge or experience in national security matters, and inability to see beyond the time horizon of his next tweet will, in the event of a more kinetic crisis, leave American forces and interests at risk. God forbid an American warship fails in battle, or a Special Forces unit can't complete a mission. He'll likely declare them enemies of the people and issue a tweet to mock their shortcomings.

The bad guys know the same things our allies know: This is a weak man in a weak White House. He is unreliable, untruthful, and unmanageable. No matter how many flyovers and tank displays are arranged to keep him clapping like a toddler, and no matter how tough he talks on Twitter, they've got his number . . . and America in their sights.

Tweets from Donald Trump's Second Term

@realDonaldTrump: Fake news media and Democrat haters and losers won't admit my new Cabinet Member are the greatest Cabinet in history! No one can disagree that I am the best Cabinet secretary and I'm doing a GREAT job for America!

@nytimes: In a controversial move, President Trump replaces Cabinet with 16 mirrors.

ALL RISE: PRESIDENT McCONNELL'S COURTS

If you want to know the most potent excuse any Republican has for defending Trump, it's the courts. Give Trump four more years in office and President Mitch McConnell and Vice President Leonard Leo of the Federalist Society will have fundamentally reshaped the federal bench.

The next person elected president, even if we only play out the usual actuarial results, will name at least two new justices to the U.S. Supreme Court. Trump's approval of the McConnell-selected Neil Gorsuch and Brett Kavanaugh is already a powerful judicial legacy.

McConnell, a canny player at this game, has been given carte blanche by this White House to pick young, smart, Federalist Society–approved judges for these seats, and he has moved with lightning speed. The courts will be a long echo of McConnell's and Leo's ideological preferences, and Democrats underestimate this at their enormous peril.

Now, Trump wouldn't know any of his nominees beyond Gorsuch and Kavanaugh if they came up and bit him on the ass, but he is crafty enough to know that his people love them some judges. He has learned the language of conservative judicial fetishism—the mirror image of the old language of liberal judicial fetishism. "We can't win the policy outcomes we want in Congress or in the states, so we'll name our ideological fellow-travelers to the bench to get what we want." It's the ultimate spoils system; your besties get jobs on the bench for life, and you get to rack up policy wins that have the force of law. When liberals did this for a generation, I was told it was Very Very Bad and Must Be Stopped. Now? Not so much.

Democrats do need to saddle a bit of the blame here. In November 2013, Harry Reid undid the judicial filibuster rule for lower-court nominees. Everyone warned Reid at the time that someday Democrats would reap a terrible whirlwind for blowing up one of the Senate's long-standing norms. Reid was hailed as a masterful legislative player, a genius, a man who would finally help Obama get his people on the federal bench.

What could go wrong?

Mitch Fucking McConnell could go wrong, you dolts.

If you know Mitch, you knew the moment Reid nuked the judicial filibuster that McConnell was making book on the day he'd be able to return the favor. He looks harmless, but Cocaine Mitch is a specialist in the political art of "Fuck me? No, fuck you," and when McConnell fucks you, you stay fucked.

Democrats have almost no tools in the toolbox, even with the Senate currently split with fifty-three Republicans, forty-five Democrats, and two Democratic-leaning independents, to stop McConnell from filling up spots on the federal bench with conservative judges. In the old days, it took forty-one votes to pop the brakes on any nominee. Now the GOP has enough wiggle room to lose three squishes in any tough vote and still have Mike Pence as a hole card. Pence, as you might imagine, relishes the prospect, and said as much during the confirmation battle over Brett Kavanaugh.[7]

The scorecard as of the summer of 2019 is grim for the Democrats. President McConnell's two Supreme Court picks were confirmed, with Democrats impotent to stop either. The lesson that the contentious, ugly Kavanaugh fight taught Republicans was that the base loves one thing more than Donald Trump: conservative justices on the Supreme Court. Even Trump-skeptical Republicans were drawn into the fight on the side of Kavanaugh; it was a rare moment of almost complete unity on the right.

In the U.S. courts of appeals, the legacy is even more powerful. The Senate has confirmed forty-one nominees to that bench, including a number of fresh, young conservative faces to the notoriously left-leaning Court of Appeals for the Ninth Circuit. For those of you not inside the conservative judicial movement (try it, the parties are lit), the Ninth is an article of particular obsession with conservatives.[8]

At the district court level, there are almost a hundred new judges seated as of today. My liberal friends may think, "Oh, these are dumbfuck Trump cronies. Most of them didn't even go to Harvard Law." This is a mistake.

These conservatives are young, sharp, and aggressive players of legal and judicial hardball. They'll have a profound effect on the legal landscape of this country. You don't have to *like* the Federalist Society, but you have to respect the farm-team system and the Long March strategy they adopted. What they've executed in two short years is a remarkable feat of judicial engineering.

More are coming. Many, many more.

If Trump wins four more years, McConnell and the Senate Republicans (in the likely case they maintain their majority) will move to fill more judicial vacancies at every level; they'll work with partners outside government to push cases through the increasingly conservative judiciary to engineer results that future Democratic presidents and Congresses will have enormous difficulty overturning.

As a conservative, I don't hate every one of President McConnell's choices, but also as a conservative, I dislike judicial activism on either side of the political equation and abhor judicial fetishism. A few conservatives are quietly wondering if some of the nominees moving through the system and onto the bench aren't a wee bit *too* committed to a view of the law that may not, you know, fully embrace the rights of individuals over corporate interests.

Liberal folk heroine Ruth Bader Ginsburg (b. 1933) is impressively spry, but the clock of mortality is running in us all, and her chances of surviving Trump 2.0 are, again according to the actuarial tables, not high. Sonya Sotomayor (b. 1954) and Elena Kagan (b. 1960) are hale, but Stephen Breyer (b. 1938) is getting up there. Among the conservatives, Clarence Thomas (b. 1948) isn't exactly a spring chicken, but liberals will be less exercised if it's a conservative replacing a conservative. Trump's chances of naming another justice if he's reelected aren't just good, they're almost inevitable.

If that's not a motivation for my Democratic friends to do whatever it takes to mount a winning 2020 campaign, imagine a Supreme Court with four McConnell-picked justices. It's hardly an impossible scenario.

Hell, if they really need a kick in the pants, try this on for size: Associate Justice of the Supreme Court Lindsey Graham.

Tweets from Donald Trump's Second Term

@realDonaldTrump: Mike Pence was a man I barely knew. A part-time volunetter covfeve boy who no one really saw. Everyone knows Ivanka will be the best VP in History.

@VP: I'm honored to have served the tallest, most handsome, most brilliant President in the history of all mankind, in this or any other universe.

@FoxNews: Tune in this Saturday at 3:30am Eastern for the premiere of the Mike and Mike Gospel Comedy Hour as Mike Pence and Mike Huckabee present their wholesomely heterosexual comedy stylings.

THE ENVIRONMENT

If you wanted to build a caricature of a movie-villain environmental monster, Donald Trump fits the bill. His love of coal is as irrational as his fear of cancer-causing windmills.[9] (Honestly, I don't know either, folks. Some of his cray is just utterly inexplicable.) Trump knows he's on the wrong side of this, but that sweet, sweet lobbying money and those working-class voters who buy into the cruel nostalgia of hard-workin' coal miners in Ohio, Pennsylvania, West Virginia, and elsewhere are a powerful draw.

Part of his contempt for the environment and the natural world comes from his upbringing in New York City. Trump is a germophobic weirdo who spent the majority of his life in a glass tower. His rare moments in the natural world are on groomed, highly fertilized golf courses. Teddy Roosevelt was a famous outdoorsman and adventurer. Ronald Reagan was most at home under the clear skies of his beloved California ranch, on horseback or cutting brush. George H. W. Bush loved the waters off Maine. His son embraced the wide, sere spaces of Texas and his ranch. Barack Obama, raised in Kenya's . . . sorry, *Hawaii*'s pristine environment, loved biking and swimming.[10] He took his family to national parks, and while perhaps you couldn't call him a rugged outdoorsman, he was at least happy to be out in the sun.

Trump? Not so much.

Trump may believe moving his quivering ass from a golf cart to the green counts as cardio, the same as hiking the backcountry in Yellowstone, catching the waves off Laguna, or kayaking through the mangroves in Florida Bay, but no. The weird golden-throne-loving Manhattanite in him doesn't get the value of America's natural wonders and rich biodiversity or how a clean environment is a core element of quality of life in the modern world. He's lived inside an air-conditioned tower all his life.

Kellyanne Conway, desperate to bring suburban women back into the GOP, has forced Trump to give a few deeply awkward speeches about the environment where he grimly plods through the teleprompter and looks about as comfortable as he would hip-deep in raw sewage.

Maybe I'm spoiled and biased—I live in North Florida, one of the most beautiful places on earth, where I enjoy fishing and boating, hunting and camping, and seeing it from above as a private pilot. The sense that it's all at risk now in a flurry not of mere deregulation but of aggressive, dickish destruction for the sake of lobbyists and corporate sponsors of Trump makes me sick to my stomach. Look, not every regulation from the EPA is sensible, balanced, cost-effective, or environmentally useful; but the Trump approach, to shred them all in a rush to please donors and troll environmentalists, is beyond reason.

In the next term, expect the very worst for America's environment.

Trump's 2019 promise to gut the Endangered Species Act is a hideous measure of how low his regard for posterity has sunk. The insistence that the protections in the act are somehow stopping the American economy from growing will have ramifications that stretch far beyond his lifetime—extinction is forever. Gutting protections for wildlife, and removing wilderness and parks designations that comprise vital ecosystems for these species, is a deliberate, ugly element of the Trump state. Protecting these species is a matter of work that has been undertaken now for a generation, and once they're gone, they're gone. This isn't simply a matter of conservation versus industry. It's a matter of responsibility to our children and grandchildren, our legacy for the future. I'd get the kids out to the national parks as soon as you can, folks. At this rate, they'll be paved over for Ivankalands and Don Jr.'s House of Endangered Meats before the end of the second term. Why bother with pristine National Wildernesses when they could be so much better repurposed as either oil fields or Trump Wilderness Adventure Golf Resorts™?

Clean water? Endangered-species protections? What's a little extinction and permanent habitat loss when we need to MAGA? Isn't some lead and E. coli poisoning worth it when we've got so much winning going on?

Coal will continue to gather the lavish government protections and benefits it received in the first four years of Trump. Agribusinesses will continue to live with market protections that screw consumers, destroy farmland, and encourage the widespread use of pesticides. Big Corn will continue to make billions on subsidized ethanol.

He's gotten away with most of it in the first term under a frenzy of executive orders and the fog of war generated by other scandals, the Mueller investigation, and his usual cloud of bullshit that darkens the sun with its density. Washington has essentially been too busy to focus on the damage his EPA and White House are doing to America's environment.

When the second-term political pressure is off, the oil and natural gas folks are already expecting a bonanza in that he'll radically expand offshore oil and gas drilling leases and permissions, including off the coast of Florida. There's a burning irony here, because Florida is, in large measure, Trump country. It was the jewel in the crown of his swing-state pickups in 2016.

As your ambassador from the most purple (and weirdest) state in America, I can tell you exactly why Donald Trump took Florida off the list in 2017 when he announced he would allow expanded oil and gas drilling off the coasts of the United States. He did it because then-governor and now–U.S. senator Rick Scott called and tore him a new one over the issue. It would have cost Scott and now-governor Ron DeSantis their 2018 elections.

Florida may be deep red on some issues—income taxes, guns, and school choice, to name a few—but it is powerfully pro-environment when it comes to preserving the unique quality of life we all enjoy.

No, I'm not talking about our abundant Native American casinos (try the fried alligator; it's transcendent) or our high strip-clubs-per-square-mile ratio. No, I'm talking about offshore drilling.

I've worked in Florida politics for thirty years. I've studied what makes voters tick from Key West to Pensacola and every weird Florida Cracker-ass -burg and -ville in between. If there's a unifying issue in my home state, it's that everyone—white, black, Hispanic, rich, poor, coastal, and inland—hates offshore drilling. As in all things political, it didn't matter whether the fear of the damage drilling might cause was rational or irrational; it was there. But in April 2010, with the BP Deepwater Horizon disaster, it was game over. The massive oil spew cost the Panhandle billions and caused environmental damage from which the region is still recovering. Now the fear is very rational. Our lives and economy depend on a clean environment. Florida gave Trump its vote in 2016. He's almost certain to give it the finger after 2020 and allow drilling off our shores.

As for climate accords of any sort, forget it. We'll fall behind the rest of the world not only in the emerging clean energy sector but in any meaningful reductions in carbon emissions. Republicans (me included) were furious when Barack Obama "picked winners and losers" in the energy sector. Trump's team is doing the exact opposite kind of winners and losers game; regulations are a cost seeking to induce behavior, and they're going to flood the zone in favor of the carbon economy for the next four years to monetize their elimination of regulatory checks on bad behavior.

Even in an administration known for an almost comical level of conflicts of interest, grand and petty corruptions, and the appointment of a constellation of clowns, government rejects, and Trump University grads without the slightest area knowledge of the world, Trump's appointment of a coal lobbyist to head the EPA stands out. Team Trump's EPA and Department of the Interior are catchments for people who are poorly qualified and deeply unethical, even for Trump world. The second term will draw even more of the dregs into Trump's administration, so expect more lobbyists to collect government paychecks while deregulating the industries they'll return to the moment they leave. Bonus time!

As a conservationist Republican, I realize my concerns are out of step with the new "deregulate your donors" strategy of the Trump era. This is one of the legacies of Trump and Trumpism that we will not easily live down. In a second term, Trump won't worry about the politics of drilling off the coasts, of coal mines dumping waste into creeks and rivers, and Lord knows what supervillain-level industrial and agricultural products that will get to either enter or stay on the market because the right lobbyists stroked the right check.

In a second term, Trump's expansive use of executive orders to accomplish things Congress wouldn't touch with a long, sterilized pole will continue, and likely with a sense of greater abandon. The crony capitalism of the coal and fossil fuel sector, the promotion of coal ("Papa . . . I have the black lung"), and the lowering of water-quality standards leave this Teddy Roosevelt–style Republican and so many other folks cold.

By the end, don't be shocked if Trump removes the United States from the International Whaling Treaty because Eric Trump found a fisherman's sweater at Barney's and a harpoon on eBay.

Tweets from Donald Trump's Second Term

@realDonaldTrump: Because of the small disturbance outside my Rally in Dogsbreath, Alabama last night, I am declaring Antifa to be a Terrorist Organization. They attacked the peaceful marchers. There were good people on both sides!

@CNN: Revitalized Klan holds torchlit parade outside Trump rally, attacking counterprotesters.

IMPERIAL TRUMPS

Eight years of Trump sucks, right? It's terrible, isn't it? I mean, it *can't* get worse, right?

Right?

Oh, you cockeyed optimists.

As in all things Trump, it can get much, much worse. If he wins in 2020, we're never getting rid of these dolts. Even if shit goes really, really off the rails, Immortan Don and the rest of his Mad Max crew will still be racing around the desert far into the future.

A second term guarantees the rise of the Imperial Trumps, a family cult built on the remains of the moldering corpse of the GOP, featuring all the warmth of North Korea's Kim dynasty and a kind of Hapsburg-jawed je ne sais dumbfuck rien.

The fantasy self-image of Donald Trump has always been that of royalty, and as I wrote in *Everything Trump Touches Dies*, it's just that pesky Article I, Section 9, Clause 8 of the Constitution that forbids titles of nobility. Since he's not, you know, famously dedicated to the Constitution in most areas, why this one?

Get ready for Donald Trump Jr., a man who speaks the fluent asshole dialogue of the own-the-libs Trump Party, to rise to the top of the 2024 GOP primary ranks. The dynastic talk that was once treated as a joke (even by me) is already growing around both Don Jr. and Ivanka. Poor Eric is left out, but then again, he always has been.

The Trump family—including the creepy automaton Jared

Kushner—will continue to view the American government not as a sacred trust but as an ATM for their crapulous enterprises and nation-state-level grifting. While Kushner's ambitions don't appear to be especially political, his exploitation of his high office as Grand Vizier to Emir Donald has been spectacularly profitable for his companies. As for Trump personally, his hotels, golf courses, and clubs were *miraculously* both popular and profitable for *unknown reasons*.[11] (Pardon me while I recover from that epic eye-roll.)

By the fall of 2019, it was clear that Trump had even managed to suborn the military into spending money that benefited his resorts and golf clubs when stories broke of Air Force cargo flights to the Middle East making unusual stops at his golf resort in Scotland for hotel accommodations and fuel.[12]

The ambition that drives the Trump spawn these days is powerful, and the corruption and collapse of the GOP as a party will enable their dynastic fantasies to play out with real consequences for the country. The Orange Kardashians will have the brand power of Trump, as well as the shameless hucksterism of Fox and the degraded conservative media, behind them. Mark my words, even the "respectable" elements of the conservative media will soon be producing think pieces on why Don Jr. is the bridge from raw Trumpism to a smoother, smarter populist nationalism.

As for Mike Pence, who briefly held out a secret hope that he would be the heir to the Trump movement by combining his adoring gaze, talent for bootlicking, and slavish Donald über Alles suck-uppery, well, Trump treated Pence like any other wife or business partner and has already signaled he's going to fuck him, and not in his usual two-pump-chump way. When asked if Pence would follow him as president, it would have cost Trump nothing politically to shout out his VP, but he punted. Loyalty is an alien concept to Trump, except to his own progeny.

Ivanka, though never accepted in Washington, still hopes to shape an image of the smart, Aspen- and TED-Talk-friendly modern technocrat who just happens to be the daughter of the warlord. I once had a "serious journalist" with robust access to the Trumps tell me, "She stops so many bad things. She's a net positive." Bro. Just because

Ivanka calls you and says "I'm stopping bad things" doesn't make it so, but like her father, she knows how easily duped the media can be.

Installing Ivanka and her android husband, Jared, in the White House was already the greatest display of nepotism in presidential history, but by the summer of 2019 Jared and Ivanka had become the awkward party guests at events like the Tokyo G20 meeting. Trump's work to frame Ivanka as the First Princess led him to include her in event after event with world leaders, to incredibly awkward effect. It wasn't the first time he'd thrust his groomed but talentless daughter into the spotlight, but it was one of the most embarrassing.

Her presence was deeply unwelcome at a number of events where she tried to run with the big dogs of world affairs, sparking an #UnwantedIvanka hashtag that ran wild on social media. She drew grumbles and cold shoulders from other world leaders offended that the adult child of a reality-star president was treating them as props in the drama of her personal ambitions.[13]

Trump made sure that his then national security advisor, John Bolton, was exiled to Mongolia during Kim Jong Don's surprise visit to see his bestie Kim Jong-un.[14] Apparently, though, it was Take Your Daughter to See a Nuke-Curious Genocidal Madman Who Starves His People and Tricks the President of the United States Over and Over Again Day. Trump brought Ivanka to Korea with him because of course he did.

Don Jr. might as well have a Pepe back tattoo, given how beloved he is by the alt-right and how frequently he boosts the social-media posts of the assorted race-war flotsam that follows his father. He's already teased about running for governor of New York or mayor of New York City, but a better bet will be a quickie relocation to Montana or some other state, at least nominally, before he launches his political career. Junior has spent a lot of time on the campaign trail and has learned the ropes. Expect to see him at the center of the Trump efforts in 2020 and as a constant presence on social media.

Lucky us.

Even Eric the Wide-Gummed and Tiffany have been dragged along for some of the high-profile state visits and glam events. Trump wants to maximize the reach of the brand, even for the children he loves the least. This is how real dynastic politics come to America, not with a bang but a reality show. For the Trumps, it'll be easy—with the rigid control of the GOP this president exercises, there will be none of those pesky primary elections the Bushes and even the Kennedys had to endure.

Yes, the Imperial Trumps are here to stay. Get ready for four years of the right-wing press writing strained profiles of the Strange New Respect that Ivanka is generating among conservatives, and how the first woman Republican president might not be Nikki Haley but rather the deceptively smart and successful fashion icon supermom Ivanka Trump, who is surprisingly down-to-earth. They'll "discover" she has an easy, self-deprecating sense of humor.

She'll even appear on Colbert or (again) SNL, poking fun at her image, and even—just a bit—at her famous father. Even skeptical conservative media will find themselves drawn to how the Princess Royal now represents the Trump nationalism without the rough edges and ugly tweets.

One other factor about the soon-to-be endless presence of Trumps in our lives: They're breeding like rabbits, so if we don't play our cards right now, they'll have enough offspring to get a majority in the U.S. Senate before long.

Tweets from Donald Trump's Second Term

@WSJ: With the passing today of Rupert Murdoch, sons Lachlan and James announced that the Fox News organization had been nationalized by President Trump. "We're thrilled to cut out the middleman," said a statement from the brothers.

@realDonaldTrump: The merger of Fox and the Greatest Presidential Administration Ever (ME!!) is GOOD for America and BAD for the Fake News haters and losers. CNN and MSNBC are Next!

@MSNBC: Nah, bro.

@CNN: What they said.

OUR NATIONAL SOUL

I f Trump wins reelection, freedom, opportunity, and equality will no longer be the normative social forces shaping the next generation of American children. They won't be taught that this is a country of marvelous provenance and a glorious future. Instead, they will be steeped in the essence of Trumpism: nativist, negative, and fundamentally pessimistic. The Other is the enemy. They'll learn the long-discredited notion that ethnicity defines character. The sort of stereotyping that met the nineteenth- and twentieth-century immigration waves— drunken Irishmen, dour Germans, lazy Spaniards, fiery Italians, and inscrutable Chinese—are back with a vengeance under Trump. It's one step short of the Department of Homeland Security having a Phrenology Division to screen migrants.

A generation will learn its behavior from the worst role model since Saddam Hussein.

Instead of learning that complex and persistent national challenges need solutions based on innovation, leadership, teamwork, and accountability, they'll learn to hail the warlord with the biggest social-media following and the most wild-eyed support. Tweet-shouting "Only I can solve!" and engaging in endless bluff, bluster, and bullshit with no follow-up will be good enough.

They'll learn that lying about everything, all the time, is the way great leaders operate, and that truth is a fleeting, conditional construct based on the president's whims, moods, and blood-sugar level.

They'll learn what Garry Kasparov said so presciently in 2016: "The point of modern propaganda isn't only to misinform or push an agenda. It is to exhaust your critical thinking, to annihilate truth."[15]

They'll be taught that it's OK to keep people fleeing from shithole countries and desperate for refuge in cages like animals. They'll learn to shrug at the sight of a father and his daughter drowned in the Rio Grande as they try to cross into America to seek a better life. They'll learn that the way to stop illegal immigration is to tear children from their parents and incarcerate them in for-profit detention centers where they're held under bright lights twenty-four hours a day—blankets, soap, and toothbrushes optional.

They'll be taught that mocking the disabled and the disadvantaged isn't to be greeted with disdain and anger, but rather a hearty "Womp womp!" They'll be taught that egregious racism is bad only when you get caught, because, you know, "both sides."

They'll learn that the president can sexually assault women for decades and get away with it as long as he claims they are "not his type." "Grab 'em by the pussy" is the new "Shall we dance?" and paying women for sex is OK, as long as it's on the back end of a deal with an airtight NDA.

What they will learn, every day, is that threats, intimidation, serial deceptions, bullying, bluster, and bullshit are a full substitute for character. They will learn from the master of cons that after he took the highest office in the land with a series of brazen deceptions and help from hostile foreign governments,[16] he faced absolutely no consequences.

They'll learn that this man's history of business failures and his sordid personal life, including paying hush money to a bevy (I love the chance to use "bevy"—sadly underplayed word) of porn stars, actresses, models, pageant contestants, and God knows what other random victims of his lusts, is perfectly acceptable for the president.

What a *spectacular* role model for the youth of America.

Four more years of a president normalizing the worst behaviors, enabled by his political party, will result in a generational change. JFK's lofty postwar New Frontier resonated for a generation of leaders. Ronald Reagan shaped my cohort of young conservatives on matters of economic freedom and national security. Barack Obama shaped millennial attitudes and values on issues of inclusion and diversity.

Donald Trump's legacy will be a generation of young people comfortable with casual cruelty, rampant dishonesty, and revenge as pillars of our politics. They'll combine the dissonant images of a "Fuck Your Feelings" T-shirt and a string of pearls to clutch when anyone questions their behaviors.

As I've said before, Trump isn't Hitler. Hitler had normal-sized hands and the ability to concentrate for more than thirty seconds.

Trump is, however, cut from the same modern authoritarian cloth as the leaders he publicly and slavishly worships: Vladimir Putin, Viktor Orbán, Kim Jong-un, Rodrigo Duterte, and others.

Trump and his acolytes display a fundamental contempt for the American experiment and an obvious, persistent attachment to the trappings, affect, and untrammeled power of strongmen. A decent president would view these men with contempt and disgust; Trump views them with envy.

The Founders—whom Republicans once revered but whom they now conveniently forget—knew it. Madison wrote in *Federalist* 10, "Men of factious tempers, of local prejudices, or of sinister designs, may, by intrigue, by corruption, or by other means, first obtain the suffrages, and then betray the interests, of the people."[17]

Trump is a complete package of the Founders' greatest fears—delusions of royalty, appeals to the basest appetites of the polity, populism over small-r republicanism, and vulnerability to the blandishments of foreign powers who so obviously are welcome to corrupt him with gifts or flattery of his ravenous ego.

To date, his actions have had the possible check of the 2020 election hanging over him, which has influenced him whether or not he admits it. Trump needs to win reelection to continue his nation-state level, god-tier grifting and to avoid prosecution.

He thrives not on a competition of ideas but on the division of the country. Our parties and politics will follow him down, fighting a dirtier, more savage battle until we've forgotten what it means to share even the most common baseline with our fellow Americans.

The cold civil war is warming by the day. He's not the only centrifugal political force, but he's the most powerful.

This will only accelerate if he is reelected. There will be no end to his ambition and no check on his actions. He will conclude that he's the winner who wins, and for him that will justify everything in his catalog of errors and terrors. We've learned there is no bottom with Trump, no level to which he won't sink, no excess he won't embrace.

The future I've described in the preceding chapters isn't inevitable, but if Trump wins a second term as president, it is all too likely. I never want to leave you with anything but a sense of existential dread, so let's do something about it, shall we?

Tweets from Donald Trump's Second Term

@realDonaldTrump: Forget What the Fake News says. Our GREAT AG Bill Barr says a 3rd term is totally legal if I issue an executive Order! Me and Vice President Ivanka are going to Keep America GREAT . . . FOREVER.

@BigBillBarr: Yes, sir. Totally legal. Super legit. Very cool.

@nytimes: Trump Plunges Nation into Constitutional Crisis

@WashingtonPost: End of the Republic; Trump's Dynasty Begins

@FDRLST: Trump's Bold Plan to End Gridlock

@NRO: At least we got some judges.

@BreitbartNews: LONG LIVE THE KING!

THE MISSION

Your mission is tough but simple.

Defeat Donald Trump.

The preceding chapters offer just a glimpse of another four long years of Donald Trump in office. I didn't even touch on the corruption of the Justice Department, the long-term impact of the ludicrous debt and deficits, the attacks on the free press, and other further corrosions of American values and virtues that are assured if he is reelected.

The 2020 election is the one last chance the American people have to slam on the brakes and turn this country off a path to authoritarian statism, racially motivated nationalism, and ingrained corruption that sullies our history and image forever.

You probably liked this part of the book. It's all the robust and richly deserved Trump-bashing you've come to love, and I love delivering. The next part? Not so much.

You know you've got a problem in 2020. It's not just Trump.

It's you.

So ask yourselves: Even if this gets uncomfortable, are you in for the win?

Are you willing to do the things you need to do?

Are you (in the words of Van Jones) willing to drop the radical pose to achieve the radical ends?

Are you willing to compromise, to show strategic patience and personal discipline?

Are you willing to listen to a person you view as an enemy on every axis but our shared loathing of a man who is poised to destroy this nation?

Are you willing to practice raw, pure, amoral politics before ideology?

Honestly, I have my doubts.

Trump is a flawed, awful shitbird of the worst order, a historical accident mutating into a political and moral monster who, as much as he deserves to lose, might not. Democrats looking at national polls are deluding themselves that this race will be easy, or that Trump will go down—or leave the White House—without a battle from hell.

I can promise you one thing: I will never give up this fight.

Every day, from now until the time I can salt the earth over his grave, I will do everything in my power to stop Donald Trump and his enablers. I hope that by now, if nothing else, you know that about me.

We may hate him for different reasons, but I hope we're united in the understanding that his defeat is an existential challenge for this republic, and that odd alliances, political compromises, and joint operations are worth the discomfort we may feel as we step back from our ideological priors.

Donald Trump is the devil in human form, and the battle against him requires all men and women who believe in the dream of America and the continuation of this republic to stand together to destroy him and all his works.

You know I'm in this fight until the last dog dies.

So my question for you is simple.

What the fuck are you gonna do?

PART 2

THE MYTHS OF 2020

Every campaign, particularly a presidential campaign, operates inside a bubble of its own deeply held beliefs. Inevitably, campaigns create strategies that seem brilliant inside the bubble but cannot survive the hard collision with political reality.

They view the country as one homogenous entity, not as it is, a patchwork of regions, cultures, and ethnic groups. They think every idea that comes from their pet think tanks is precisely what a restive electorate is seeking. They chase political fashions and trends, extrapolating too much policy from too little data. The GOP and the Democrats alike fall victim to this cognitive mistake. Both sides try to resist them, and fail.

I made a career in the GOP helping to take Democratic seats by exploiting the mismatch of policy to politics. Republicans became masters at leveraging Democrats' insistence on picking candidates based on what policies they *like* versus what *wins*. Many Democrats campaigned in an alternate reality, believing the myths of the campaign as they desired it to be, not the one they truly faced. We, by contrast, were cold-eyed, clearheaded operators.

Democrats are already doing every goddamned thing they can think of to lose to this moron, making the same mistakes they made against Nixon, Reagan, George H. W. Bush, George W. Bush, and Trump. I feel dirty putting them all on the same list, but as a professional campaign guy and trench-historian of American presiden-tial politics, I know how those men beat the Democrats, and how those wins have iterated down the political chain in the last fifty years.

It's evident from a mile off that Democrats are setting themselves up to reelect Trump by making 2020 into the anointing of someone who strokes their ideological happy place rather than someone who could, you know, win.

The previous election provides a vital lesson for Democrats in 2020. Forget about Russia, economic anxiety, or Trump's celebrity. The lesson is that you ran a candidate who existed in your *heads*. In your heads, Hillary Clinton was the most accomplished woman in American public life: a warm, lovable, approachable leader ready to shatter the glass ceiling and govern as a wise and merciful Athena.

The real Hillary Clinton was a greatest-hits album of Democratic Party mistakes wrapped up in a candidate: unlikable, cagey to a fault, cautious, a terrible combination of turgid and defensive on the stump, and cursed with a campaign that promised the moon and delivered little outside the deep-blue states. They left easy votes on the table and phoned in the last weeks of the campaign. When they should have been rolling up votes in Milwaukee, Detroit, Pittsburgh, Cin-cinnati, and Broward County, Florida, they were picking out curtains in the White House and scheming over jobs in the administration. Hillary was a perfect proof case that Democrats are holistically bad at politics.

The run-up to 2020 seems little different.

Sure, sometimes Democrats pull a generational candidate like Bill Clinton or Barack Obama, or find a theme that resonates, or build a smart campaign infrastructure, but for the most part, they can't do all three at once. Like juggling, it's hard. Like juggling chain saws with a live ferret in your pants, it's also dangerous. (You practice first with a dead ferret in your pants. Don't ask.)

In 2020—for the sake of the nation—they can't afford to put ideo-logical indulgences over strategy, or reliance on the witchcraft, folk-lore, and anecdotal evidence of campaigns over the mathematics,

demographics, and operations of a sure-footed, focused election effort. They can't afford to make this election anything other than a
brutal referendum on Donald Trump.

This part of the book will outline the campaign-killing myths of
2020. Pay attention. The final exam is in November 2020.

Scenes from a Trump Focus Group

The following is a transcript of a focus group of Republican voters outside of ▓▓▓▓▓ [rhymes with Smaukesha], a major suburb in the key swing state of ▓▓▓▓▓ [rhymes with Smisconsin].

MODERATOR: Hi, everyone. Thank you so much for coming. I hope everyone got something to eat and drink. Please let me know if anyone needs a bathroom break before we start. I'm ▓▓▓▓▓▓▓▓ from the ▓▓▓▓▓▓ ▓▓▓▓ Polling Company and I want to thank you all for taking the time to come out tonight to talk to us.

BRIAN *(male, white, 56, some college)*: The fifty bucks didn't hurt.

(Sound of laughter in room.)

MODERATOR: OK. Let's get started. We're here tonight to talk about Donald Trump and your vote in 2020.

MARCY *(female, white, non-college, 49)*: That's *President* Trump, Praise Be upon Him.

MODERATOR: Uh, OK, Marcy.

MARCY *(hisses)*: Infidel.

IT'S A NATIONAL ELECTION

No. It isn't. It's not even close to a national election. It's an election in about fifteen Electoral College battleground states, and don't you forget it. I'm going to keep reminding you of this, because if you take away no other lesson from this book, let it be that.

Every time I hear "Hillary won the popular vote," I cringe.

The correct answer to this is "And?"

Winning the popular vote and $5.45 gets you a venti mocha latte at Starbucks.

It. Means. Nothing.

Every person on the Democratic side who brings up this tired, dumb, irrelevant point again is really in contention for the political Darwin Award.

Here's a phrase Democrats need to take out of their game plan for 2020: popular vote. Pretend it doesn't exist. You need to understand the rules of the game, once and for all.

You're not playing a game of winning the popular vote, and whether you like it or not the game is exclusively about victory in the Electoral College.

Them's the rules.

Say it with me: "The only game in town is the Electoral College."

Now say it again, with feeling: "The only game in town is the Electoral College."

Now say it with your raging, Samuel-L.-Jackson-in-a-Tarantinomovie face: "*The only motherfucking game in town is the motherfucking Electoral Fucking College.*"

Fight where the fight is. Ignore where it's not. It's not in California. It's not in New York. It's not in Massachusetts. If the Democratic campaign or a single political committee on the left spends a goddamn dollar in those states or visits them for any reason other than fundraising, they're helping Donald Trump. The only states in your campaign are the target states on the Electoral College map.

I feel like a Bubba Sun Tzu trying to instruct my Democratic friends who think this is a fifty-state campaign effort. Bless your hearts. The campaign is already over in thirty-five states. Done. Cooked. Kaput. Finito.

You're fighting an election in ten to fifteen states. Most of them aren't blue. Some are pretty red and getting redder. (In a later chapter, I'll outline how to fight and win in them.)

"But muh popular vote" has become such a tiresome refrain that it betrays something more fundamentally broken about the Democratic Party approach to elections. It's a stark disconnect from reality as it stands today, and the reality you will most certainly face in November 2020. No, you're not getting rid of the Electoral College in 2020.

Which is of course why the Democrats can't stop talking about it. (Did I mention they're bad at politics?)

The major players in the Democratic primary field—and nearly all of the fringe cases, some of whom are now out of the race—bought into the idea that we should abolish the Electoral College and spent valuable time on the stump in the spring and summer of 2019 talking about it.[1]

And talking about it. And talking about it.

Elizabeth Warren, Comrade Bernie, Beto O'Rourke, Julian Castro, and Cory Booker all made dumping the Electoral College a tentpole of their early campaigning (as did, among the early dropouts, Jay Inslee and Kirsten Gillibrand). Warren attacked the Electoral College with both passion and commitment: "I believe we need a constitutional amendment that protects the right to vote for every American citizen and makes sure that vote gets counted. . . . And the way we can make that happen is that we can have national voting and that means get rid of the Electoral College."[2]

Even Pete Buttigieg, a man who is demonstrably smarter than most of the field, got on board with this absurdity. In a profile by *The Washington Post*'s Greg Sargent, the South Bend, Indiana, mayor and Flavor of the Month in the pre-Biden spring of 2019, said: "We need a national popular vote. It would be reassuring from the perspective of believing that we're a democracy."[3]

Leaving aside the constitutional concerns and political impracticality, this is one of those hothouse flowers of an issue that take on a life of its own in a party seemingly dedicated to stoking its base with promises they can't keep on issues that won't move votes. Every iota of energy and focus on an issue so esoteric and specialized is wasted. Not only is the Electoral College not going away in 2020, it likely never will.

When it fails to come to pass, it will demoralize and anger Democratic primary voters. They will feel cheated by the system, when in fact it was never going to happen. It's one thing to promise your daughter a pony. It's another to promise her a unicorn.

This is the kind of messaging failure that tells working-class Democrats, centrists, and soft-Republican voters in the key states that the Democrats will chase any dumb rabbit rather than talk about things that might, you know, matter to them on Election Day. All the talk of things that can't happen in 2020 makes me fear for a Democratic base who believe some deus ex machina maneuver will save them. It won't. In politics, God helps those who help themselves, and devil take the hindmost.

Some Democrats are rubbing their little paws together, imagining some pre-2020 miracle . . . like the National Popular Vote Compact passes and the GOP forgets to litigate it into oblivion, or that other political unicorn gallops onto the scene and we become a direct democracy. This is worse than fantasy. This is political malpractice.

Donald Trump knows—and so do his little Russian friends—that the Electoral College is the ballgame.

You want to change the Electoral College? Go for it some other time. I think it's spectacularly dumb, both un- and anti-constitutional, and would have a boatload of unintended consequences. By all means, give it a shot, but rest assured: It's not going to win the 2020 election as an issue, and the rules of the game are not going to change before November 3, 2020.

This is the kind of thinking that gets you four more years of Trump.

Scenes from a Trump Focus Group

MODERATOR: So, you're all here tonight because you're committed Trump supporters, but tonight we're going to ask you about some of your reservations in supporting Trump in the 2020 election.

TODD *(male, white, some college, 64)*: You might as well just stop right there. We're not changing our minds. It's Trump, or we're gonna have sharia law. And welfare for MS-13.

MODERATOR: I think MS-13 isn't Islamic.

TODD: Nope. Islamic. Rush said so.

MODERATOR: I believe they're from . . .

TODD: They're from one of the Mexicos. It was on Fox. Or Facebook. I saw it.

MODERATOR: Well, moving on to . . .

TODD *(angry)*: Maybe you're an Islamer.

MODERATOR: I'm Lutheran . . .

TODD: Maybe you want that Mexican sharia up here. But not me, and not Mr. Trump. No, sir.

THE POLICY DELUSION

One thing about Democratic campaigns that is entirely predictable and relentlessly exploited by the GOP is their addiction to policy. They talk about what they *want*, rather than doing what they *should*. Without a superstar candidate—and let's be honest, no one in the 2020 field possesses the natural political gifts of a JFK, Bill Clinton, or Barack Obama—they need to focus on a winning strategy that avoids telling Americans what they really want to do.

"But policy!" you cry, right until the tidal wave of ads distorting your policy hits.

We've seen it over and over again—a top-down, rigid ideological checklist of programmatic messages that sound like a focus group at a Democratic Socialist Alliance meeting in Burlington, Vermont, shocks Democratic candidates by exploding in their faces, because the ideas are at odds with the way Americans speak, think, and live.

Many 2020 Democrats, notably Elizabeth Warren, have produced a corpus of policy papers and plans both voluminous and deeply granular. Some of it is serious, smart, and robust work. It's also worth precisely the paper it's printed on. A few press nerds read the papers, and then they disappear into the campaign memory hole, except when they're being weaponized against the candidate.

Do you know how many Americans are going to pull the lever for the Democratic nominee because of this or that policy paper on court-packing, reparations, gerrymandering, or late-term abortion?

I don't care how much intern blood, sweat, and tears went into those papers, the answer is: not enough. Even seriously worked-out policies on big issues largely fail to hold public attention. This is, after all, America.

The issues that excite Democratic voters when they watch the debates aren't top of mind for the average voter, particularly those in the target states. Over and over throughout campaigns, Gallup, Pew, other public pollsters, and every private political pollster run Most Important Problem panels. Hardly any of the boutique issues ever rise above 5 percent. The big-picture stuff—the economy, healthcare, national security—does, but even then, policy as a winning campaign strategy is an illusion.

It's a hard 2020 truth, but none of it matters. Not one bit. No matter what consultants, pollsters, and policy geeks tell you, this race is about Trump. Policy distracts, and the Fox-Trump distortions of your policy distract absolutely.

Now, I like policy people. I like their big, sweaty brains, their good hearts, and their ability to concentrate on questions that make my eyes glaze over and to reduce those questions to cogent answers. Liberal, conservative, libertarian, they're all such cute nerds you just want to squeeze them. In campaigns, though, they show up with the veggie platter, and I show up with oysters and a case of Champagne.

Say it with me, so we get off on the right foot: This race has absolutely nothing to do with policy. This race is about Trump and a competing candidate's personality and presentation, not about soon-forgotten policy papers and the administrivia of running a government.

Policy is a luxury good in this election because this race is against a man, not a party, a platform, or an ideology. Democrats are fighting a cult and a cult leader, and until they realize that the referendum against Trump is about *Trump,* he has the winning hand.

Some Democrats think this is about picking someone who motivates their base into towering heights of political passion. They think they need the hottest, purest, wokest strain of AOCisma policies to get their voters fired up. The truth is, the Democratic base will be there with heat like a nuclear fire, no matter what. They're passionate, motivated, and hungry for a win. To use a technical political term, they fucking hate Donald Trump.

What about healthcare? Gun control? The Electoral College? Climate change? Medicare for All? The Green New Deal? Reparations? Nope. Sorry. It's all noise at best. Every media consultant working for Trump will merrily take those policies and twist, turn, and recast them as fodder for attack ads. You'll never understand that once those messages are on the air, post hoc arguments are worse than useless.

There are some policy attacks that work, but they're about Trump's actions, and thus part of the referendum on *him*. Which ones? Here are a few: Show voters how Trump tried to eliminate healthcare coverage for preexisting conditions, highlighting how his corrupt government screws over working families. Educate voters on how the trade war is wrecking their economic future, and how farmers and manufacturing are both being crushed. Call out Trump's cruelty and brutality toward immigrant children. Call him out as the unrepentant racist he has proven himself to be.

Trump has handed Democrats all the weapons they need to defeat him; they just need to use the right ones for the job. This race must be a referendum on Trump, or the Democrats will lose. You are already tired of hearing me say that, but it's the truth and you need to internalize it.

Why give the GOP weapons in the messaging war to isolate, intimidate, manipulate, and terrify your target voters and motivate Trump's base? Why allow them to scare the hell out of people with messages like "Democrats will take away your private health insurance," or "They're coming to seize all your guns," or "They want to give free healthcare to criminal illegal aliens"?

Don't think for a moment that Republicans won't turn your well-meaning policy papers into operatic terror messages to be bellowed out by the Mighty Wurlitzer of the Trump Right media apparatus. They have your number on this, and they're very, very good at ringing it. I did this to your candidates, over and over, and Trump has a dozen Rick Wilson types with an unlimited budget and zero shame.

They understand the Electoral College play, and that the fifteen or so target states are to the right of the coastal blue enclaves on issues like climate change, abortion, guns, taxes, and almost everything else. Why would Democrats give Trump and his allies the sword with which to cut off their heads?

Some Democrats will object that I'm recommending shallow, content-free campaigning.

You got me. You're right.

So what?

It's smart and cynical, and if you need to beat a man who practices pure, unadulterated opportunistic politics, you'd better be ready to practice pure, unadulterated opportunistic politics.

Don't believe me? Have you been living in a cave? Have you taken a Marie Kondoesque vow of digital celibacy because too much news fails to spark joy?

May I remind you of death panels, migrant caravans, the war on Christmas, creeping sharia, Hillary's emails, Seth Rich, the Clinton Body Count, babies being killed after birth, Antifa, and a thousand other weaponized issues and stories Democrats laughed at, saying "How absurd, darling. Is this organic kale slushie gluten-free?" while Republicans ate their political lunch?

There's an organized system for creating these weaponized outrages. I know; I helped build it. Republican candidates and consultants exploited it in races across the country. No policy from the Democrats will ever be seen with even an iota of good faith, and everything they commit to a policy paper is like show notes for the latest Muslim Illegal Immigrant Soros Deep State Antifa Hour on Fox.

Democrats don't have to play by the GOP and Fox (but I repeat myself) rules.

Democratic voters have already demonstrated the aforementioned sweeping, powerful, almost unprecedented hatred of Donald Trump. It drove a host of new candidates into office in 2018, not only in Congress but in hundreds of down-ballot races. Democrats don't need policy to make their voters turn out against Trump. Those people will crawl over broken glass to vote against him, as they did against his minions in 2018.

Until Democrats grapple with the fact that they must make the case against Trump to the few voters who can still be swayed—in other words, not his base or theirs—they're playing on Trump's battlefield, and by his rules.

More bad news: There's an equal, if thankfully smaller, fire on the other side of the political divide. The Trump base may be smaller, but as two and a half years of painful experience demonstrates, Republican unity behind Trump is virtually unshakable. He is the parasite that ate the GOP from the inside out as an ideological force. In 2020, they'll be utterly united, motivated, and angrier than ever; we're moving away from red-hat, spittle-flecked, rally crazy and approaching bomb-vest crazy. I wish I was kidding. They are dead-enders, the last guys in the bunker.

Fox News, talk radio, the debased clickwhores of the Trumpist conservative commentariat, social media, and those ever-helpful Russians will continue to be all-in with Trump, pouring a constant drip of fear poison into the minds of his base. You're not going to change many of their minds.

For Democrats, the voters they need are right in front of their eyes: the large and growing cohort of Republican women who broke away from the GOP, and the white, Democratic men who broke for Trump in Ohio, Pennsylvania, Wisconsin, Michigan, and Florida. Democrats who recoil at actually messaging to these old white dudes, writing them off as a lost cause or viewing them as an intractable enemy, are miscategorizing these voters.

For many, their choice to go with Trump was diffuse; they voted out of anger and bitterness at a system that shanked them. It was the end-product of a successful thirty-year War on Hillary.

After a string of broken promises—Thousands of coal mines! New car plants! So much winning on trade!—many of these voters are in the wind. Democrats need a candidate who makes a moral and personal case against Trump using language and messages that don't sound like something spewed up by a mushy focus group or overheard in the living rooms of Cambridge, Potrero Hill, or the Upper West Side. As Bill Clinton speechwriter David Kusnet once said, "Speak American."

Donald Trump's 2016 "policy" fit on a trucker hat. As expressed at a hundred rube rallies, it was raging xenophobia, revenge against brown people, a Wall, and what was essentially a long, cheap riff on his wealth, power, intellect, and sexual prowess. Smart people in the GOP laughed it off.

The Democrats howled. How could this simpleton hope to win the election? We have so many people from the Center for American Progress and Brookings on our staff! We have a Lake Michigan Grass Carp Mitigation plan on our website! We published a slide deck on our campaign's gender-pronoun policy!

Over and over again in elections up and down the political scale, simple, robust messages on heavy rotation triumph over complex policy. Some voters pretend to be interested in policy and to base their decisions on it, but in the end, they're mostly faking it.

Once in a while, pollsters will sneak a policy test question into surveys to subtly call out the bullshit of people who say policy matters in elections. The questions go something like this: "Have you heard of the Wilson-Santiago Bill?" Of course, there's never a Wilson-Santiago bill, but guess what? Somewhere around two-thirds of voters will tell you they have.

The next question sets the trap: "Do you favor or oppose the Wilson-Santiago Bill?" Sure enough, they'll answer, generally along the usual statistical distribution curve.

Given that the issues you discuss on the 2020 campaign trail need to be laser-focused on Trump and a contrast to his actions and policies, I want to close with a simple principle I've applied for a couple of decades in professional politics: In a Walmart Nation, don't run on boutique issues.

Or, as a campaign mentor once said to me, "Never underestimate the power of dumb."

Language matters. Presentation matters. Charisma matters.

Policy? Not so much.

Scenes from a Trump Focus Group

MODERATOR *(eyeing Todd, warily)*: So, moving on to our next issue, I'd like to talk to you about the president's verbal attacks on members of Congress who happen to be people of color. Does this make you more or less likely to support him in 2020?

KAREN *(white, 40, college)*: Well, Mr. Trump has to defend himself.

KYLE *(white, 42, college)*: I just wish he'd been able to stop all those planes on 9/11. He was only able to take out twenty of the twenty-four planes al-Qaeda sent. *(Tears up.)* Mr. Trump was down at Ground Zero when it happened. Just like when he saved his whole unit in Nam.

MODERATOR: I think that was Robert Mueller in Vietnam.

KYLE: He was saving those boys from the rubble when Obama was laughing it up at the White House. He had a secret mosque built there, you know.

MODERATOR: I'm pretty sure he wasn't there, but . . .

KYLE *(growing venomous)*: He was there. I saw the meme about it on the Patriotic Patriots MegaMAGA Facebook group. Obummer was laughing about it.

MODERATOR: George W. Bush was president at the time . . .

KYLE: Liar.

AMERICA IS SO WOKE

Contrary to social-media Democrats, most *actual* Democrats who live out in the real world aren't screaming for the blood of the aristos and ordering bespoke pitchforks, torches, and solar-powered electric tumbrels made by wymyn-run collectives.

The January 2019 Pew survey asked Democrats if they'd rather their party become more moderate or more liberal. The answer was clear: 53 percent said they wanted a more moderate approach, and 40 percent wanted a more liberal approach.[4]

This is a lesson that is apparently nearly impossible for Democratic activists to learn, even with the results of 2018 staring them in the face. The midterms did not see a wave of far-left, ultraprogressive neosocialists swept into office, all having satisfied an ideological litmus test set by the likes of Alexandria Ocasio-Cortez. In fact, the great victories of the Class of 2018 came from more moderate Democrats.

Democrats won by running candidates who—and listen closely because there will be a quiz later—matched the politics and attitudes of the districts. How did Ben McAdams of Utah win a seat with a Republican advantage of twenty points? By not being a Bernie-bro hard progressive, that's how.

Political analyst Charlie Cook, using his Partisan Voting Index,[5] scores congressional districts by voter performance and party preference. The 2018 election showed that the Democrats could compete in red and purple areas, particularly suburbs, when they ran more moderate candidates. In New York, Max Rose won the R+8 seat on Staten Island. Abigail Spanberger captured the Northern Virginia seat held by Republicans for a generation. Katie Porter famously captured California's 45th district in the heart of Republican Orange County.

None of them ran as hard progressives either. They're not the candidates of Woke Twitter and the furthest reaches of the left. AOC has the hot Twitter feed; they had real races in tough seats. They're Blue Dog Democrats, New Democrats, and just, well, Democrats. Pelosi's DCCC—for once—didn't insist on an ideological litmus test.

There are only two groups who believe the country is filled to the brim with eager Marxist social justice warriors determined to smash the capitalist patriarchy, seize the guns, burn down the churches, and ship the Murdochs off to a reeducation camp. The first group is the clichéd cadre of Marxist social justice warriors, who are few in number but loud in volume. The second group is Republicans, because Fox has become very, very skilled at—to use a technical term of the political arts—scaring the shit out of people.

For the GOP, the culture clash between hard progressives and most of America is a prime opportunity. They listen closely to it. They stoke it. They exploit it. It doesn't matter if this is right or wrong, or if progressives huff off and say, "Well, Middle America is too stupid to understand modern monetary theory or that there are 740 genders anyway." The scaring-the-shit-out-of-Middle-America system exists to trap progs like hogs in a baited field.

Here's a pointer: Think "Sheboygan, Wisconsin," not "Cambridge, Massachusetts." Think "guy who works with his hands," not "graduate student working on her master's in intersectional feminist interpretative dance with a subspecialty in mime and puppetry." Think "United Auto Workers," not "Democratic Socialists of America."

But don't take it from me. Take it from Barack Obama (who, despite what I heard on Fox, is not actually a Kenyan Muslim commie sleeper agent sent here to deliver on the Bill Ayers/George Soros plan to bring a Pol Pot–style far-left government to the US of A; if Obama was the peak of the progressive secret plot for world communism, he was *really* bad at his job). In the spring of 2019, Obama understood that the huge Democratic field would inevitably become a proxy for the long-running battle between party pragmatists and party purists. "One of the things I do worry about sometimes among progressives in the United States . . . is a certain kind of rigidity where we say, 'Ah, I'm sorry, this is how it's gonna be.' And then we start sometimes creating what's called a circular firing squad where you start shooting at your allies because one of them is straying from purity on the issues. And when that happens, typically the overall effort and movement weakens."[6]

Whether you're a Republican or a Democrat, showing a little ideological daylight between yourself and the edge cases in your own party during the general election is helpful and smart politics. As a rule, your base is with you by that point, *but you need more than the base to win.* Winning politics is about addition, not subtraction. The shrinking, but still sizable, pool of independent and undecided voters is a nontrivial target in the key Electoral College states, and a winning Democratic candidate who understands them will rather quickly realize that these folks aren't exactly *Chapo Trap House* listeners.

In 1968, Roger Ailes helped shape Richard Nixon's campaign as the candidate with a secret plan to end the Vietnam War and restore peace. He ran as a technocratic centrist with a culture-war underpinning. The eggheads and libs were out protesting the war and dropping acid; Nixon was the candidate of the silent majority. There's a lot of Ailes/Nixon DNA in the 2020 race for Trump.

In 1980, Reagan walked back from the Goldwater edge with a tonal shift in how Republicans ran. The optimistic, big-picture, economic-uplift message wasn't tailored to the "drown government in the bathtub" faction. It was the cultural comfort the avuncular Reagan brought—and the unapologetic pride in America—that helped move the famous Reagan Democrats into pulling the R lever.

George H. W. Bush ran largely on his own biography (and rightly so), but his 1988 campaign promised to soften the harder edges of the Reagan Revolution. He talked about volunteerism, dignity, and compassion. It didn't please the Pat Buchanan wing, but it helped win a contentious, hard-edged election in 1988 against a perfect exemplar of the East Coast liberal elite in the form of Michael Dukakis.

In 1992, Bill Clinton understood that the broad "Reagan Democrat" coalition was up for grabs because of economic changes and a changing global landscape. His push on topics like enhanced penalties for drug crimes, government reform, changes to welfare-to-work rules, and the revival of manufacturing hit a moment in the culture when a centrist good ole boy from Arkansas didn't—and this is important—scare the shit out of people. He made it nearly impossible for my side to turn him into a Dukakis or, worse, a Ted Kennedy.

I know it gets lost in the events of 2001 and the wars in Iraq and Afghanistan, but George W. Bush's 2000 campaign talked a lot more about education and "compassionate conservatism" than people recall today. It was enormously appealing in suburban districts and regions for a reason: It was built in a lab to be just that. The message was "better schools," not "bomb Iraq back to the Stone Age."

Barack Obama ran and won in 2008 as a technocratic centrist, essentially scanning as a liberal Republican. Trust me, we tried to scare the shit out of people on him, and it frankly just didn't work because he knew the value of his cool, charismatic, pleasant, "welcome to my TED Talk" demeanor. That part about scaring the shit out of people? Not so much.

Don't get me started on Trump—I know, it's too late not to get me started—who detonated every GOP orthodoxy under the sun. You can disagree all you like on the details of the policies his Republican predecessors used to get there, or whether those policy choices are resonant in the 2020 moment. The point is clear: As candidates, they all understood how to expand their voter pool. Math is your friend, and so is some even token independence from the hard edges.

One trick I and many others have used to win races against the left is simply to treat the Democratic base as it is, not as the Democrats think it is. DSA members won't believe this, but not every Democrat is a screaming progressive with a knife in their teeth ready to board the USS *Plutocrat* and start slitting the throats of the idle rich.

Not every Democrat thinks abortion is without a single moral question. A hell of a lot of Democrats own and carry guns. Some Democrats aren't sold on government as the solution to every problem or tax increases as a universal good. Many of the 110 million holders of private insurance are Democrats and want to keep it, thank you very much.

Some of my liberal friends are hissing through their teeth right now, "Well fuck them. Traitors. Filthy counterrevolutionary kulaks. Wreckers! Saboteurs!" They look at centrist and moderate Democrats as worse than Republicans. They're worse because they're unwoke. Woke liberals believe that if only Democrats feed the progressive edge of the party they'll magically discover a turnout model that sweeps the electoral board. This is a delusion that won't die. (And yes, Republicans who believe that just winning enough white non-college evangelicals will ensure a majority play the same dumb game.)

By all means, if you want to reelect Trump, treat the very real cohort of moderate, centrist, and even—I know, you're shocked that these words exist together—conservative Democrats like outcasts. If you want to know why the GOP beat your asses sideways across the South and West, it's not racism; it's that you piss off 25 percent of your own base, over and over, and the GOP scoops them up.

Let's look at the numbers, shall we?

First, the big picture from reputable public polling. Knowing the composition of your own base is the most fundamental skill in data-driven politics. If you understand your base, you know how much you need to do to push the needle to 50 percent plus 1.

The conventional wisdom on the Democratic Party is that it's gone so far left that JFK would be a conservative Republican and Bill Clinton a RINO squish, and even Barack Obama would have his political priors questioned at the monthly All-Party Congress of Ideological Purity and Swift Justice to Unbelievers.

The Hidden Tribes of America project dove into the American electorate in a seminal 2018 study that examined the deep political divisions in the country today, in both major parties. It's worth a look when it comes to the Democrats' choices and campaign in 2020. This will involve numbers, not just pissy righteousness, so bear with me for a moment.

The analysis of the Hidden Tribes project built a typology of Democratic voters with five broad categories and three divisions. The categories, in decreasing order of liberalism, are Progressive Activists, Traditional Liberals, Passive Liberals, Moderates, and the Politically Disengaged. The three divisions into which each fall are their percentages in the total population, in the Democratic electorate, and on social media.

The powerful distortion field of Twitter (and trust me, I live there far too much of the time, so I fully confess to its shitty power) and other social-media platforms is driving candidates to positions that have political costs down the line. Again, I'm not judging your positions, progressives. I'm telling you the numbers aren't what you think they are. Math is a cruel mistress.

Let's break it down:

Progressive Activists are the center of the woke universe. They're the ones who think, "Has Media Matters sold out? Is there someone like Bernie, only really committed to the struggle?" They're young, educated, and super-white. Here's how Hidden Tribes describes them:

Progressive Activists have strong ideological views, high levels of engagement with political issues, and the highest levels of education and socioeconomic status. Their own circumstances are secure. They feel safer than any group, which perhaps frees them to devote more attention to larger issues of social justice in their society. They have an outsized role in public debates, even though they comprise a small portion of the total population, about one in 12 Americans. They are highly sensitive to issues of fairness and equity in society, particularly regarding race, gender, and other minority group identities. Their emphasis on unjust power structures leads them to be very pessimistic about fairness in America. They are uncomfortable with nationalism and ambivalent about America's role in the world.[7]

They represent just 8 percent of the American electorate, 22 percent of the Democratic voter base, but 39 percent of the social-media cohort. This is the most vocal, activist part of the base, and they scream loudest for the issues on the edge. If you're worried they'll stay home if Dems don't check every one of their ideological wish lists, you should be. For this group, the more you make this a pure referendum on Trump, the better.

Just a pointer from a guy who has used the words, positions, and policies of the farthest left to divide Democrats in the past—they're a gold mine for the Trump campaign and its allies. They're the comical villains of the conservative cartoon hour; they're free-access conservative agitporn. We highlight the policies the right and center find unacceptable and claim they're what otherwise centrist and electable Democrats believe.

Traditional Liberals are Democrats of a certain age, which means they're more likely to vote, and more likely to have a long record of loyalty to the older iteration of the Democratic Party. They're gonna pull the D lever, trust me, but they'll do it with a smile for a Joe Biden, less so for a Democrat from the far edge of the progressive side. Here's the rundown from Hidden Tribes:

> Traditional Liberals reflect the liberal ideals of the Baby Boomer generation. They maintain idealistic attitudes about the potential for social justice in America, yet they are less ideological than Progressive Activists. They also are not as intolerant of conservatives. They have strong humanitarian values, and around half say that religion is important to them. Traditional Liberals are significantly more likely to say that people "need to be willing to listen to others and compromise." . . . Overall, Traditional Liberals respond best to rational arguments and are inclined to place more faith in the viability of American institutions, even if they are disillusioned with the country's current direction.[8]

Traditional Liberals represent 11 percent of the country overall, 25 percent of the Democratic electorate, and 22 percent of the social-media cohort. In the age of Trump, they're the real heart of the Democratic Party. For them, it's not just our politics he's damaging, it's the country and its meaning.

The Hidden Tribes project's Passive Liberals are less politically engaged, and more driven by the feel of the political climate than by deep policy or political questions:

> Passive Liberals are weakly engaged in social and political issues, but when pushed they have a modern outlook and tend to have liberal views on social issues such as immigration, DACA, sexism, and LGBTQI+ issues. They are younger, with a higher proportion of females (59 percent) than any other segment. . . . Passive Liberals are also the least satisfied of all the segments. They are among the most fatalistic, believing circumstances are largely outside their control. They are quite uninformed, consume little news media, and generally avoid political debates, partly from a general aversion to argumentation and partly because they feel they know little about social and political issues.[9]

Passive Liberals are 15 percent of the population, just 2 percent of the Democratic voter pool, and 1 percent of the social-media cohort. They're a slightly harder target to turn out, and there is a small danger of their just staying home to tune out the noise, but a close focus on them in the target states could pay enormous political dividends.

The Politically Disengaged are the toughest nut to crack in the Democratic base, and were a rich hunting ground for Donald Trump in 2016. These are the Obama-Trump Democrats, and ignoring their anger or trying to sell them airy bullshit policies is a dead loser:

> The Politically Disengaged group most resembles Passive Liberals in having lower levels of income and education and being less engaged in following current affairs. Fully 41 percent are making less than $30,000 per year, and approximately one in four have gone without food or medical treatment at least

somewhat often in the past year. They diverge from Passive Liberals in being more anxious about external threats and less open in their attitudes towards differences. For instance, they are the most likely to say that being white is necessary to be American and that people who hold other religious views are morally inferior. They are more concerned about the threat of terrorism and are quite closed to the view that Islamic and American values are compatible. They are practically invisible in local politics and community life, being one of the least likely groups to participate in political rallies or vote in local elections. They are the least well-informed group on all measures of political knowledge. They are also the most pessimistic about the possibility of reconciling differences between the factions. Overall, this makes the Politically Disengaged a challenging segment to persuade.[10]

They make up 26 percent of the population, 14 percent of the Democratic vote, and just 3 percent of the social-media cohort.

These people are largely deaf to the hot arguments of social media's political domain. You can bet your last bitcoin the Trump team has people looking at this group to find ways to split them from the Democrats again. You won't win them with government-subsidized transgender abortion; you might win them by calling out Trump's bullshit and making them understand he won their 2016 vote with the same kinds of lies that have left them cynical about work, education, and America itself.

Ah, Moderates, last on the list but first in my heart. Moderate Democrats in particular are reviled in the climate of today, but only because the progressive wing keeps believing this country is one single region, entity, value set, and belief structure. Here's what Moderates look like in the Hidden Tribes study:

Moderates reflect the middle of the road of public opinion in America. They tend to be engaged in their communities, often volunteer, and are interested in current affairs, but uncomfortable with the tribalism of politics. They tend to be socially conservative and religion plays an important role in their lives. They feel conflicted on certain social justice issues, including same-sex marriage, and they are slower to embrace change. They mostly disapprove of Donald Trump as president and overwhelmingly believe that the country is headed in the wrong direction. . . . They also think that political correctness has gone too far. They dislike the activism and what they see as extremism of both progressives and conservatives. While they think feminism has gone too far, they also recognize sexual harassment as an important issue. They support the notion of sanctuary cities and want undocumented immigrants to have better treatment. They tend to seek less radical solutions than Devoted or Traditional Conservatives, such as building a border wall. They are worried about the state of America and feel that American identity is slipping away.[11]

Moderates are 15 percent of the American electorate, 24 percent of the Democratic base, and 13 percent of the Twitterati. You read that right. There are more Moderate Democrats out there than hard progressives. This is especially true in—wait for it—the targeted Electoral College states. The pernicious idea that the Democratic Party's voters respond only to messages on the purest left edge of the spectrum is as politically destructive as it is common.

These moderate voters may not be with the party line on every issue. In the targeted Electoral College swing states, they may roll their eyes at the far-left language and policy assertions so popular on the primary-debate stages, but they're unified on one matter: Trump. This is why the battle is about America versus Trump, not progressive versus moderate or progressive versus conservative.

If you're a pollster, strategist, or data scientist, the moderate cohort of voters is the most intriguing play in the game. Democrats could take them a message of restoring normalcy, tradition, and comity in our politics, but their reflex action is the opposite. The treatment of immigrants is a clear vector into the hearts, minds, and votes of this group. I call this group Biden Democrats, and they're out there for a smart candidate unwilling to mouth every far-left shibboleth to snatch up.

SOCIALISM, NOW MORE THAN EVER

Some folks wondered why during his 2019 State of the Union speech Trump said, "Here in the United States, we are alarmed by new calls to adopt socialism in our country. Tonight, we resolve that America will never be a socialist country."

This wasn't a mistake, or Trump being Trump. It was a deliberate decision based on polling, demographics, and an understanding of at least the Plato's Cave version of the contrast between capitalism and socialism. Trump's pollsters—even the ones he fired for telling him the truth about how bad his overall numbers are—are not idiots. They know socialism qua socialism is a hard, hard sell in America.

Now, the dirty but open secret of socialism in America, one conservatives tend to underestimate and liberals overestimate, is this: Americans are OK with a splash of socialism, but they don't want to call it that.

In 2019, the same farmers in deep-red areas of deep-red states who would fetch a shotgun before letting their daughter date a socialist are lapping up the benefits of a benevolent state. Medicare, Medicaid, Social Security, and now Obamacare are rickety, marginal, and on a path of catastrophic overspending and demographic disaster, but they're exemplars of the eternal political-economy problem of Free Shit. Once voters are given a benefit—even a terribly managed, inefficient, unsustainable benefit—they will fight like hell to keep it.

People don't think of government benefits as socialism, even if they are.

As a result of Trump's train-wreck trade war with China and the rest of the world, Midwest farmers have lost many of their international markets; to mitigate the political damage, the Trump administration has showered them with "relief payments" to the tune of over

$28 billion. It's red-hat instead of red-banner socialism. But don't dare call it that—it's just the government redistributing wealth because of its failed attempt to manipulate markets and dictate production. Song as old as time.

The fact that the Democrats running for president are all aflutter about socialism in 2020 is a sign they've bought into the myth that America is finally ready to tear down the edifice of market capitalism and create a country where the workers control the means of production and the beet harvest always exceeds the goals of the Five-Year Plan. I know, I'm a smartass, but the conceit that democratic socialism will be front and center in the 2020 campaign is delightful if you're Donald Trump's campaign team. They're thrilled.

Watch how the word "socialism" will rise from Trump's blubbery lips again and again over the coming year. It will be for one reason: Socialism per se has a horrible branding problem.

The socialist brand comes with a lot of political overhead that isn't going away, given that history presents us with far too many cases where socialism went hand in hand with bodies stacked like cordwood. No, not always, but often enough to blot its copybook permanently. "But Sweden" doesn't make up for "But Stalin." Democrats (and I'm looking right at you, Comrade Sanders) who just ignore Stalin, Mao, Castro, Maduro, and others ought to know better.

Even the Holy Grail of American socialism—universal, single-payer government healthcare—has slipped badly in public polling. In 2003, 62 percent of Americans favored a single-payer system with no private insurance. That number was down to 41 percent in a July 2019 *Washington Post* poll, so of course the majority of the 2020 Democratic field stick their hands up when asked if they'd trash the private health-insurance market that covers 180 million Americans. Because of course they do.[12]

No matter how many times you try to change it, the cultural and economic operating system of America is market capitalism with some socialist accessories. Yet the lonely voices in the Democratic primary field who understand that market capitalism—as flawed, inequitable, manipulated, cronied-up, and corporate as it's become—

is still much closer to the aspirational vision Americans embrace were greeted with derision and were mostly marginalized in the 2020 field.

For being a clunky and terrible candidate in a number of areas, Elizabeth Warren has gotten closer to a winning message, broaching the idea that a government doing socialist-adjacent things doesn't have to be socialist itself. It's smart politics. My conservative eyebrows are raised. As an ad guy and message strategist, I think she's closing in on something that resonated with the Trump base the first time around—that the little guy without an army of lobbyists in Washington, D.C., gets fucked and everyone else gets rich. I hate to admit it, but she's not even wrong.

This is a message window for Democrats if they can just skip playing "The Internationale" at the convention.

Trump can and will try to box Democrats in on support for communists like Venezuelan strongman Nicolás Maduro. It would help—and I know this is difficult with red-diaper Bernie in the party—for the Democratic nominee to end the reflexive defense of socialism when it's in the authoritarian frame of a Cuba, Venezuela, or China.

If you think 2020 is the time and place to litigate socialism, democratic or otherwise, just resign yourself to a generation of Trumps in the White House. It may be popular with voters born after the end of the Cold War, but may I remind you who votes? Old people vote. Old people who remember we fought a twilight struggle against fucking communism and who still view socialism as communism's slightly cleaned-up cousin.

A major poll from Public Opinion Strategies—some of the very best in the business, on either side of the partisan divide—in February 2019 started probing the socialism question ahead of the 2020 election, testing the following proposition with likely 2020 voters: "The country would be better off if our political and economic systems were more socialist, including taxing the wealthy to pay for social programs, nationalizing health care so that it's government-run and redistributing wealth."[13] Democrats love them some socialism. By a margin of 77 to 19 percent, they agreed—they are ready to embrace the glories of our postcapitalist future despite it all! All hail the record tractor production at People's Heavy Industrial Plant 16!

Republicans? Well, duh—83 percent disagreed with the proposition, compared to 14 percent who were OK with it. Independents are also opposed to socialism in America, 37-to-56 percent. You know who else missed sending in their dues to the People's Revolutionary Collective Fan Club? Suburban women, 57 percent of whom are opposed, and voters in eleven of the swing Electoral College states for 2020 report opposition at 54 percent.

There's more cold water in this bucket. While younger voters are dreamy-eyed about socialism by a 53-to-40 percent margin, older voters—again, you know, the voters who vote—oppose it, 60-to-38 percent.

Luckily for the Democrats, a glorious revolution is upon us and they won't need independent voters, suburban women, or old folks! And who needs those swing states, anyway? You can just run up the numbers in California . . .

Oh. Wait.

Scenes from a Trump Focus Group

MODERATOR: Now, I want to talk a little bit about the president and truthfulness.

BUD *(50ish, CPA)*: Well, we like a little sales talk. It's good. He's a salesman.

MODERATOR: Can you say he's always trustworthy, mostly trustworthy, or something else?

KATHERINE *(40ish, suburban)*: Well, I voted for him because Hillary was the real liar. After she murdered all those children, I could never trust her again.

BUD: After he went over and fought those ISIS boys hand to hand and then bought Greenland, I was sold.

MODERATOR *(voice tightens)*: I don't believe he bought Greenland.

KATHERINE *(interrupts)*: Greenland is a state now. I'm just worried they're going to have sharia law there. And Mexicans. Are Greenlandians whites?

MODERATOR: But the market is down—down by a lot.

BUD: Fake news, my friend. Fake news. The market is doing great, it's just the media lying about it to hurt Mr. Trump.

KATHERINE: I don't know if Greenlandishmen are socialist. Lordy, I hope not.

(At this point, the camera behind the mirrored glass of the focus-group facility picks up a noticeable tremor in the moderator's hands.)

KUMBAYA

All this Democratic intramural spritzing and primary scrapping is just good clean fun, isn't it? It's just the feisty process of electing a unifying candidate who will bring even the most disparate elements of this most disparate party together as one, all hands on deck, all backs to the capstan, right? They'll all come together in the end, right?

Sadly, history doesn't suggest this will be the case. If Democrats don't enforce some hard, punitive party discipline on anyone who wants to play games with the nominee or the fall campaign, they're going to give Trump a wonderful opportunity to churn their divisions into a full-scale meltdown.

Ambition is a heady drug. As of this writing, the Democratic field has somewhere around ten candidates of varying degrees of seriousness, and a few persistent hangers-on without the political wherewithal to win a race for middle-school class president. As of October 2019, you still have a goddamn New Age fortune-teller in the race, for fuck's sake. Those in the serious tier are followed by a group of could-be candidates and a horde of people there because the barriers to entry are lower now than at any time in the past.

Some are running on the notion that if a no-account prank candidate like Donald Trump ran for and won the GOP nomination for president, why not spin the wheel? "It could happen to me," they whisper to themselves. "I could catch fire," they tell donors, "I only need to have my moment on the debate stage and for Trump to tweet about me." A field this large—as this book goes to press, there are enough Democrats in the race to fill a platoon—the elbows are flying, the purity shit-checking is rampant, and the hostility is getting pretty marked.

It's a bitter, tough race. These folks obviously aren't going to walk out of this political Thunderdome without some bruises and scrapes, but for the love of God, Democrats, keep your eyes on the prize. You need to herd all the cats of your normally unmanageable party behind the nominee, and focus on making 2020 a referendum on Donald Trump, not a scrap inside your own team.

Granted, calls for Democratic unity from an apostate Republican are a bit unusual. But I want to talk about what became a famous analogy from the 2016 election. In an essay published under the nom de douche Publius Decius Mus, later revealed to be Michael Anton, the writer compared the 2016 election to the doomed Flight 93 of September 11, 2001. He argued that unless Hillary was defeated, death was certain for all that Republicans held dear. Storm the cockpit and die? Possibly. Sit quietly and let the terrorists fly the plane into the White House or the Capitol? You're dead either way.

Anton's argument to his fellow conservatives concerning the highly unorthodox, and to many distasteful, candidate Trump was this: We need to put aside our long-held conservative ideas and ideals to get to the goalposts. Storming the cockpit with Trump is better than sitting quietly while the Democrats steer America toward a progressive apocalypse from which it would never recover. It was a painfully facile argument on one level, since Hillary was hardly going to seize the means of production for the workers or impose sharia, but it persuaded many on the right. And Hillary wasn't—what's the word?—insane. Can serious people argue that Donald Trump, who is in control of our nuclear arsenal, isn't at least *potentially* batshit crazy?

For Democrats, this really *is* a Flight 93 election—except the emergency isn't to elect Trump, but to beat him. Unless Democrats put aside their internal grievances, beefs, ideological wish lists, and purity-posse threats to stay home in November, they might as well expect Trump for another four years, and his spawn in the White House for decades after.

In 2008, once Barack Obama won the Democratic nomination, and then the White House—and against the advice of some of his most passionate supporters—he drew Bill and Hillary Clinton closer to him. First, he had Bill and Hillary as part of his campaign surrogate operation, and later named Hillary as his Secretary of State. This was good, unifying politics. He didn't want a flank exposed, and understood the Lyndon Johnson truism about having people inside the tent pissing out rather than outside the tent pissing in. Obama was smart and lucky. The Clintons accepted the embrace, cautiously at first, but both sides benefited from the alliance.

In 2012, perhaps Hillary Clinton believed that in setting aside her anger and hurt over losing to Obama in 2008 she had set a precedent for putting party first. After all, when the insurgent Obama had taken down the Democratic Establishment Death Star that was her campaign, she was graceful to a fault:

> The way to continue our fight now—to accomplish the goals for which we stand—is to take our energy, our passion, our strength and do all we can to help elect Barack Obama the next President of the United States. Today, as I suspend my campaign, I congratulate him on the victory he has won and the extraordinary race he has run. I endorse him, and throw my full support behind him. And I ask all of you to join me in working as hard for Barack Obama as you have for me.[14]

She went to work, first on the campaign, and later as one of Obama's most loyal and effective cabinet members. It was a win for her, and for Obama.

Perhaps when she won the nomination in 2016, Hillary expected Bernie Sanders, her most persistent rival for the nomination, to do the same. Yeah, not so much. Sanders, that bitter old fart, may have capitulated, but he never truly stepped up with the support she needed from his faction of the progressive base. Many Bernie bros in 2016 sat on their hands, stayed home, and in some cases voted for

Trump. When will Democrats learn that Bernie is in a party of one: the Bernie Party? The nominee in this cycle will need to watch for Angry Old Commie Throws Hissy Fit, 2020 edition.

The Democratic Party isn't without its own "Fuck it, burn it all down" elements, and in the 2016 election, and the opening acts of the 2020 election, many of those people seem to flock to the banner of Bernie Sanders.

Now, I know what you're thinking: "Isn't it time for a president who can praise Soviet Communism in Russian and mean it?"

Democrats cannot afford to let Bernie drag the race into the late summer of 2020. They can't afford a messy floor fight or months of the media narrative of "Can X unify the party with Bernie still sniping?" It's going to take some time to convince his "my way or the highway" supporters that knocking Trump out of office is more important than ushering in the Workers' Paradise with Comrade Bernie at the helm. It sucks for the eventual nominee, but Bernie's pattern of behavior, if repeated, is a significant problem.

Anyone who has spent even a moment on social media knows who the Bernie elements are: the blue-state version of Trump's online army, with some live humans, some bots, some foreign-propaganda agents. They respond with livid, spittle-flecked outrage at any word about Bernie that doesn't declare him the ideological second coming of Lenin, the vanguard warrior for whom the American proletariat has been waiting, and the man who will burn Wall Street to the ground and build a socialist paradise from its ashes.

The reality isn't as lofty. He's a grumpy, mean old bastard who stomped off in 2016 after doing the absolute minimum for Hillary Clinton's presidential campaign. He's become a marketing and branding candidate, milking his email lists with Make America Collectivist rhetoric and policies just a notch short of the *Bernie Sanders Eat the Rich Cookbook*. (Though I'm told his recipe for Oligarch à l'Orange is magnificent.) Bernie's retirement fund—pardon me, ongoing political advocacy—depends on maintaining that edge-case rhetoric. He's the Commie Ron Paul.

In a year when Democrats had a stark, bright-line ideological contrast before them—sane, stable-to-a-fault HRC versus Donald

Fucking Trump—one group stood out in switching their party preferences radically: the Bernie bros. Somewhere between 10 and 15
percent of Sanders voters switched their preference on Election Day
to Trump. These aren't principled progs; they're arsonists.

Bernie is Trump reelection insurance.

If he's the nominee, I say to my Democrat friends, get ready to
lose forty-five states. If he's not, prepare for Bernie to mutter a few
words of mealy-mouthed support for the Democratic nominee and
then keep on being Bernie. I don't think Bernie will do anything for
the 2020 Democratic nominee, and I'm not sure the Democrats have
the capacity to alter his behavior in the slightest. The dream of progressive perfection dies hard. The Democrats need to get the Bernie
progs in line, and fast. They can't afford 15 percent of Bernie's voters
to either vote for Trump or stay home; this would mean having to
overshoot even more in the purple and red swing states on the Electoral College map.

Democrats should also keep an eye on Putin shill Tulsi Gabbard,
because I'd put money down she'll be announcing a third-party run
once she gets trounced in the Democratic primary. As Jill Stein demonstrated, even a small bleed of voters on the left side of the Democratic equation can be catastrophic in the general.

Every serious candidate, and the eventual nominee most particularly, needs to keep the house in order, and that starts with reminding
every Democratic also-ran that defeating Trump isn't just the top job,
it's the only job. The Democratic donor class is split at the moment
among the top-tier candidates, but they have a vital role to play in
patching the party together after a winner emerges. These moneyed
powerhouses need to tell the wannabe candidates that they're going
to have another chance to run someday, but unless they get out of the
race quietly, play nice, and work hard for the ticket, all hell will befall
them.

Scenes from a Trump Focus Group

MODERATOR: Finally, I'd like to ask the group why it is you stick with Donald Trump. We've talked about the damage he's done to the economy here in █████████ with the trade war. We've talked about how he isn't truthful. We've talked about the broken promises. We've talked about his . . .

CARL *(white, 60)*: He's just like us.

MODERATOR *(a note of sarcasm)*: You mean you're a lunatic with four bankruptcies, three wives, and an itchy Twitter finger?

(Silence.)

MODERATOR: I apologize. I wasn't referring to you, sir. I was speaking of—

CARL *(angry)*: You blasphemed the God-Emperor.

MARCY *(whispers)*: Heretic.

KAREN: Heretic.

ALL: Heretic! MAGA!

MODERATOR: If we could just . . .

(At this point, the lights flicker briefly and one of the focus-group participants locks the door.)

YOU'LL GET OBAMA'S
MINORITY TURNOUT

In the 2016 presidential election, there was a 1.1 percent decrease in the total number of votes cast by African Americans and a 4.5 percent decrease in black turnout as compared to 2012. Seems trivial, doesn't it? Just 1.1? 4.5? Hardly.

Those numbers were a cataclysmic drop-off in African American voters and cost Hillary Clinton the election. Hillary won 88 percent of the African American vote compared to Barack Obama's 93 percent. In a counterfactual alternate history of our times, if major African American population centers in Milwaukee, Detroit, and Philadelphia had turned out for Hillary even at 90 percent, she may well have offset Trump's Electoral College edge.

It didn't help that Hillary Clinton is the whitest, most school-marmish person in America, and that African Americans were never going to peg the needle for her as they did for two terms of Obama. Her campaign still, fatally, assumed both in their top-level political calculus and their voter models that Clinton would enjoy the same support.

As with many things in the Clinton 2016 campaign, the only response is "What the fuck?"

At this writing, it's unlikely that the nominee will be an African American, though Senator Kamala Harris ran a campaign that's kept her in the top tier of Democratic candidates, but she couldn't quite close the deal in a field with Biden, Warren, and Sanders. She may well be on the ticket in the second spot. Having her as president or VP would—probably—have an effect on black turnout similar to Obama's in 2008.

The raw, real politics of 2020 demand that the Democrats get their shit together when it comes to their most loyal and vital constituency. African Americans have given the Democrats their votes with stunning regularity and consistency for decades. The only differences come with turnout rate. They may not be voting for Trump, but the key question is whether Democrats are turning them out to vote at all.

One African American operative who worked for Obama shook his head when I asked if the Clinton campaign's African American outreach was effective. "Well, some people got paid," he said, "if that's what you're asking."

You may have noticed by now that Donald Trump's support with African Americans is . . . what's the word? Oh, yes: abysmal. Racism will do that.

The struggle of the GOP to play the "Look at my black friend" game in the era of Trump is a monumental lift, and largely results in merely nervous laughter. Those great voices of the civil rights struggle like Diamond and Silk, Candace Owens, and Sheriff David Clarke haven't exactly altered the political chemistry for a presidency that reeks of racism from stem to stern.

The profound and fundamental question is how Democrats move African American voter performance into the region they need to secure victory in the Electoral College target states.

For black voters, the referendum on Trump is in one dimension: racism, not race. With the rising tide of racial violence inspired by Donald Trump's rhetoric, and the large presence of covert and overt racists in his base of support, I'd argue that the path to activating African American voters leads through Charlottesville.

While some Democrats have adopted the idea that reparations is an issue sufficient to drive African American turnout, I'd argue as a guy sensitive to the politics of race (after an upbringing in both the Deep and New South—the Venn diagram is complicated) that the idea that Trump is bending the arc of history in the wrong direction is more compelling than a reparations plan. It was a momentarily hot issue in the Democratic debates, but in a Democratic primary Fox News will turn it into THE BLACK LIVES MATTER–ISIS CONNECTION! CAN PRESIDENT TRUMP SAVE US? It's an issue with little growth potential in the general voting pool; just 26 percent overall favor reparations.[15] Perhaps surprisingly, only 58 percent of African Americans favor them.

Winning the African American vote likely comes down to the two people who stand as political superheroes in the black community: Barack and Michelle Obama. Both of them have sky-high popularity across the board, and the Obamas' unique ability to move, motivate, and turn out African Americans cannot be underestimated. The nominee needs to put any ego aside, make the ask, and do whatever it takes for the Obamas to come out and hit the road for the last six months of the 2020 campaign.

The only reasonable answer from the first African American First Couple is "Yes, we can."

Scenes from a Trump Focus Group

At this point, the video and audio recording of the focus group become difficult to interpret. The nude figure of the moderator is seen tied to a primitive altar constructed by the participants out of office chairs and focus-group dial-testing equipment.

FOCUS-GROUP PARTICIPANT (unknown): BLOOD. BLOOD FOR THE BLOOD GOD.

(The one-way mirror becomes obscured by the smoke in the room from the fire set near the base of the altar. As the smoke thickens, the only words that can be made out over the guttural incantations and screams of "MAGA!" "KAG!" are those of the moderator as he descends into the final moments of madness before his death.)

MODERATOR *(screaming):* You people can't really fucking believe this garbage. You *can't*. Can't you see he's *completely full of shit? What the fuck is wrong with you?*

ALL: MAGA! MAGA! Cthulu fhtagn!

MUH YOUTH VOTE

You chase it every damn time.

Democrats are all aflutter, every damn election cycle with the idea that the youths are coming out in droves, this time. *This* time there's a massive tidal wave of kids ready to rock the vote. Hold on a moment while I recover from that eye roll. Memorize this rule: Old people vote. Repeat it until it sinks in.

The youth vote is a moving target, a political unicorn running through a field of poppies, shooting rainbows from its ass. Democrats in particular seem to spend an enormous amount of time trying to activate 15 percent or so of the voting pool in general elections (lower in the off-cycle races). Yes, youth participation was up in 2018, and meaningfully so. The percentage of millennials who voted in 2014 was nearly doubled in 2018.

Want to know why?

Because the oldest millennials (for our purposes, people born between 1980 and 2000) are closing in on forty, the age when voter participation tends to kick up. Even the youngest millennials are now leaving college and dealing with the cruel fate of their college loans and all that the departure from Mom and Dad's nest entails. In big, broad strokes, millennials are voting because they're aging up.

Millennials are aging out of the youth vote, but the Democrats still overplay the idea that the youths can be turned out if only they strike some alchemical formula combining college loan relief, Taylor Swift, Obama, and Rock the Vote.

Wow, you're thinking, this sumbitch is cynical. The children are the future . . .

As is often the case, Democrats reading this will glare balefully at me, puff out their cheeks, and intone, "Ackshually . . . Barack Obama proved . . ."

Obama proved nothing.

He goosed the youth vote with eighteen- to twenty-nine-year-olds by 2 percent to 17.1 percent, but here's the hard reality: If not a single young voter pulled the lever, he still would have won the 270 votes in the Electoral College he needed to beat John McCain. NBC polling analyst Ana Maria Arumi ran the numbers state by state, and when she pulled out the under-thirty demos, the map flipped in only two states: North Carolina and Indiana.[16]

Now I'm really gonna break your hearts about who and what moves the youth vote. The modern era's peak youth vote wasn't for Barack Obama in 2008 or 2012; youth turnout in those years was 17.1 percent and 15.4 percent, respectively. It wasn't for Bill Clinton in 1992 (17.7 percent) or 1996 (14.9 percent).

No, the peak youth turnout in the last thirty years was in 1988, when teen heartthrobs and sex symbols Mike Dukakis and George H. W. Bush were on the ballot. That year, turnout for eighteen- to thirty-year-olds was 18.1 percent. Nothing sends the kids today rushing the stage like a septuagenarian preppy and a fusty Cambridge nerd. In the words of political scientist Eddie Murphy, "Bitches throw they panties on the stage."

I know, I know. You don't believe me. "But muh youth vote."

I'm going to stop you there, because you know who does vote? (Stop me if you've heard this.)

Old people vote.

You know who votes in the swing states where this election will be fought? *Really* old people. Instead of high-profile videos with Cardi B (no disrespect to Cardi, who famously once threatened to dog-walk the egregious Tomi Lahren), maybe focus on registering and reaching more of those old-fart voters in counties in swing states.

If your celebrity and music-industry friends want to flood social media with GOTV messages, let them. It makes them feel important and it's the cheapest outsourcing you can get. Just don't build your models on the idea that you're going to spike young voter turnout beyond 20 percent.

The problem with chasing the youth vote is threefold: First, they're unlikely to be registered. You have to devote a lot of work to going out, grabbing them, registering them, educating them, and motivating them to go out and vote. If they were established but less active voters, you'd have voter history and other data to work with. There are lower-effort, lower-cost ways to make this work.

Second, they're not conditioned to vote; that November morning is much more likely to involve regret at not finishing a paper than missing a vote.

Third, and finally, a meaningful fraction of the national youth vote overall is located in California. Its gigantic population skews the number, and since the Golden State's Electoral College outcome is never in doubt, it doesn't matter. What's our motto, kids? "The Electoral College is the only game in town."

This year, the Democrats have been racing to win the Free Shit election with young voters by promising to make college "free" (a word that makes any economic conservative lower their glasses, put down the brandy snifter, and arch an eyebrow) and to forgive $1.53 trillion gazillion dollars of student loan debt. Set aside that the rising price of college is what happens to everything subsidized or guaranteed by the government.[17] Set aside that those subsidies cause college costs to wildly exceed the rate of inflation across the board, and that it sucks to have $200k in student loan debt for your degree in Intersectional Yodeling. Set aside that the college loan system is run by predatory asswipes. The big miss here is a massive policy disconnect—a student-loan jubilee would be a massive subsidy to white, upper-middle-class people in their mid-thirties to late forties.

I'm not saying Democrats shouldn't try to appeal to young voters on some level, but I want them to have a realistic expectation about just how hard it is to move those numbers in sufficient volume in the key Electoral College states. When I asked one of the smartest electoral modeling brains in the business about this issue, he flooded me with an inbox of spreadsheets and data points. But the key answer he gave me was this: "The EC states in play are mostly old as fuck. If your models assume young voter magic, you're gonna have a bad day."

PART 3

ARMY OF DARKNESS: TRUMP'S WAR MACHINE

Some days, you can almost convince yourself he's trying to lose this election. It feels like he's sabotaging himself with the tweets, the crazy talk, the scandals generated by his own slips of the tongue and thumbs.

Shake it the fuck off.

Of course he's trying to sabotage himself. His entire life is a pattern of self-sabotage and self-destructive lying, whore-humping wandering cock syndrome, boom-and-bust spending, and bumping business uglies with a constellation of sleazeballs.

It doesn't matter if he's trying to lose. The hard political reality is that the machine under him is doing everything they can to prevent it, and that the investment Fox has made in their pet president will serve as a powerful countervailing force against even his most damaging actions.

Trump, for all his fuckups and follies, still has a better-than-average chance of reelection. I'm going to outline the powerful assets and forces arrayed in Trump's favor. I do this not to scare you, but to give you a clear-eyed perspective on just how difficult beating any incumbent president can be, to say nothing of one with the skill set in entertainment, transgression, and social-media manipulation in this president's arsenal.

Do not mistake his clownishness and stupidity for a campaign that's incompetent. The consulting people around him are not dumb, and they're going to have unlimited resources. Underestimate my former colleagues and their appetite for survival at your peril.

White House Diaries: Melania Trump

I am hatings him, of course.

How couldn't I? Of course, I should not be writings this diary, but I am trapped here in this White House and honestly, without visitings to border camps, or Be Besting, I am so boreds.

Diary, I will tell you the things. All of the things.

First, let me say, because you are not being surprised, that Jared is creepy. How you say? As a mofo. Some day, he murders us all in our sleeps.

Seconding, you know Donald is badnesses, da?

Someone ask me at Be Best event, "Why is Donald so cranky in morning?" I say, "How I know? Prenup says no touching until after Melania has had chardonnay and sun is down."

You will ask questionings, I will answers.

THE TRUMP 2020
WAR MACHINE

Donald Trump may be a terrible president, a terrible candidate, and a terrible human being, but in 2020 the entire apparatus of the GOP will form a shield around him. The consultants, ad makers, pollsters, and operatives may have a rogue candidate, but they'll simply focus on burning the Democrats to the ground and then stirring the ashes. I know these guys. I was one of them until I grew a soul.

They'll have Fox News and its massive viewer reach, the corrupted and degraded "conservative" media, and Donald Trump's chekist friends from Russia weighing in. They'll work every minute of every day on ways to—and this is a technical term, so bear with me—fuck you over, regardless of what Trump tweets, what lunacy emerges at his rally-du-jour, or what idiot squawking comes out of the president's lie hole.

Guys and girls in my former business can and will transform any lack of Democratic discipline into attacks that cut you off at the knees. You might think it's absurd to transform the Green New Deal into "They want to take away your hamburgers and airplanes," but middle Americans famously don't read policy but do watch television ads. And guess what? It's now an article of faith in the Midwest and South that the Green New Deal is there to ban meat and motorcars.

EARNED MEDIA

Let's get one thing straight about earned media: It is the campaign, and the Democrats start with a massive disadvantage. Donald Trump is the most effective, powerful, and amoral user of earned media in the history of American campaigning. His massive Twitter and social-media footprint and his pet state-media organs amplify every signal, no matter how mendacious or misspelled. His 60 million followers—including a few million bots controlled by foreign intelligence services (ahem, @Jack!)—will echo, signal-boost, share, and spread every message. If Trump tweeted the word "fart," he'd get 100,000 likes and people would sing his praises for breaking down the old barriers of presidential stodginess.

Pitching long-lead, deep-think stories about your candidate is a fool's errand. Trump will literally tweet a dick joke to splash a new wave of controversy over whatever media fire you kindled so carefully. Pitching single-line themes of the week is similarly pointless. "Healthcare Week" will be rolled over by whatever toilet-tweet he rips out that morning along with his twice-weekly KFC dump.

Trump's power resides in earned media propelled by social media. Twitter is his singular megaphone, and he understands the way the mainstream media is drawn to it like moths to a flame. He knows that every tweet is breaking news and will create hours of work for reporters across the media. He relies on it. There is some evidence his tweets are diminishing in impact and reach,[1] but this is like saying a punch from Mike Tyson won't still knock you on your ass.

Trump's control over the media agenda is relentless, but it's neither perfect nor inevitable. The Democrats' earned-media teams need to work reporters, hard and constantly. They need to call bullshit on Trump's lies and crazy talk and then immediately reframe Trump's message as part of an indictment on him. Bridge back to your angle, no matter what bullshit Trump and his spokes-harpy Kellyanne Conway vomit out.

THE POWER OF GIVING NO FUCKS

Donald Trump's game is the base and the base only, which, though it limits his ability to seek and persuade new voters, also liberates him from much of the hard work of politics. He will never, ever look over his shoulder and think "Uh-oh. Have I crossed a line with the PC speech commissars? Have I offended the [select your disadvantaged group] community? Did I use the wrong gender pronoun? Is my base mad at me for being too mean?"

His base thrives on the transgressive, offensive, ignorant, and linguistically incoherent sewer outflow of his Twitter feed. It binds them to him. It is a secret handshake, and the outrage from anyone outside the cult only makes the bond more powerful. They're all members of the same juvenile, shitty little club, but it's their club, and it's all they've got.

As noted above, there were some signs by the summer of 2019 that Trump's Twitter account was reaching a point of diminishing returns, yet it's still the most powerful weapon in his arsenal, and no Democratic candidate has anything close.

And of course, he gives no fucks. He will lie. He will mislead. He will incite fear, hatred, and violence. He will burn down norms and sanity. He is an unconstrained political force. It's his best weapon, and he's going to use it.

DIGITAL AND DATA

Campaigns have evolved in the last decade from digital being just one element of the campaign to digital *is* the campaign. Until 2004—the dawn of modern, digital campaigning—campaigns were built using the same model they'd followed for generations: money, media, and message delivered by the modality of the time, first human contact, then print, then radio, then television, then cable, and lastly, digital.

Like every other thing that collides with the power of software and the Internet, politics has become mediated by digital analytics and online communications media. It doesn't matter if the message is in your Facebook feed, a YouTube video, a text on your phone, or a snap. Digital campaigning is platform-agnostic.

Before George W. Bush's 2004 campaign's micro-targeting operation, campaign data was largely list management: slow, cumbersome, and limited in scope and power. Bush's team combined commercially available consumer data with polling, voter history, and interest data to build big typologies of American voters. Today, that seems clunky. Then? That was some rocket science.

Obama's 2008 campaign seized the moment when Facebook penetrated society, and they leveraged it beautifully. The GOP scrambled to reverse engineer it, and though it didn't quite make the cut in 2012, they clawed and scraped to the point of extinguishing the Democrats' digital advantage.

In 2016, Russia, Steve Bannon's Cambridge Analytica, and, in their punch-drunk way, the Trump campaign hammered in messages to Trump-friendly audiences using Facebook and other targeting data. The RNC had their own data operation and, once they got on board with Trump, turned it on for him. Speaking of Cambridge Analytica, they're back with a new name and still working for the Trump reelection effort via the RNC. Data Propria, CA's new cover name, is the same suite of software tools and many of the same people, with all the same spooky tiebacks to Russian investors and coders. What could go wrong?[2]

Trump may not understand data, but he will have some of the smartest humans on this planet behind the scenes. Most of the campaign will be invisible to people outside their very narrow target set. The messages will be tuned and timed to keep his base aroused and fevered, and to try to normalize and tribalize his behavior for softer Republicans.

He'll have help. Facebook had reps in the room for both the Trump and Clinton efforts to help them maximize Facebook data in 2016. They'll still be there for Trump again in 2020. Silicon Valley's personal politics may be hard progressive, but their corporate politics are raw capitalism.

It's vital the Democrats get their data and digital warfare in order. They have every element at the ready, and a bigger talent pool, but don't underestimate the commitment of people down the chain in Trump's digital consulting universe; they either win or spend a decade in the wilderness. They'll fight, and they'll fight hard.

PAID TV ADVERTISING

Paid television ads are still a killer app in politics because—and pay attention here, because this is the tenth time I've told you this and there will be a quiz on November 3, 2020—old people watch television and old people vote. Trump was outspent on TV and cable in 2016 because he thought he would lose and didn't want to spend money he could keep for his own uses.

But 2020 will be different. The campaign will spend, and spend big, on television in the targeted states. They'll have the money and the targeting tools to do it effectively this time. Their creative work will be backed by the ability to put Trump in settings that are tailor-made for politics. Even this shaved ape can look presidential standing in front of the Lincoln Memorial, as he made sure he did on the Fourth of July in 2019, though a just God would have struck Trump dead for besmirching the memorial of a president who saved the nation.

Here is a preview of what kinds of television ads the Trump team will run and why the Democrats should take them very, very seriously. The definitional ad of the 1984 presidential campaign was the "Morning in America" spot produced by the great Hal Riney. It's a famously powerful, positive ad for an incumbent president about whom the nation was divided, even in the face of a strong economy. Sound familiar? The narrator's message went like this:

It's morning again in America. Today more men and women will go to work than ever before in our country's history. With interest rates at about half the record highs of 1980, nearly 2,000 families today will buy new homes, more than at any time in the past four years. This afternoon 6,500 young men and women will be married, and with inflation at less than half of what it was just four years ago, they can look forward with confidence to the future. It's morning again in America, and under the leadership of President Reagan, our country is prouder and stronger and better. Why would we ever want to return to where we were less than four short years ago?[3]

Democrats greeted it with howls of derision. The "Yeah but what about . . ." screeching was deafening, and utterly ineffective. No matter how much they yelled, "Morning" connected with voters. Since nothing is new under the sun, expect Trump's Morning in America to be even more over the top.

Prepare yourselves for claims from Trump on the economy that fly in the face of the reality on the ground, that elide the weak spots, pain, distress, and inequality in America, and that feature Trump claiming credit for everything good and right from sea to shining sea. His sole pillar of strength—though undeserved—is the strength of the economy, and this will be the core of his paid advertising. He'll deliver this message to the same people who held their nose and voted for him in 2016. It doesn't matter if it's accurate in every detail. No amount of "But it's Obama" or "But it's the Fed!" will change his use of ads with this powerful framing.

He'll shamelessly lard his ads with the faces of African American, Hispanic, Asian, LGBTQ, and disadvantaged Americans of all stripes. It will be a fucking Benetton ad of soft-focus close-ups of diverse and beautiful American faces. It will have a gruff-looking steelworker. A pretty but tough female soldier. A young, happy, suburban mom with her adorable moppets. A pair of handsome gay men. A sharp, urbane African American professional couple. Asians! A Hispanic farmer! See, they'll say, we love diversity. Pay no attention to the racial arson.

Hell, I could write the ad in my sleep. Here's the script to make your brain melt:

Under President Donald Trump, America is great again.
Stock markets and 401ks are at all-time highs.
More people are at work in good jobs than ever before.
The middle class is doing better than ever.
The Trump tax cut is working for families.
We have record African American employment.
Wages for women are breaking records.
Respected judges sit on the highest courts.
Our military is tougher and stronger.
Our vets are cared for at last.

We're safer and respected in the world again.

Our borders are protected from drugs, disease, and human trafficking.

President Donald Trump: Keeping America Great, forever.

You'll nitpick the details. It won't matter. The ad will look and feel polished as hell, featuring lots and lots of American flags, rolling landscapes, and glowing sunrises. It'll be Main Street, farm country, and prosperous towns. It'll be church steeples and glittering skylines. Newspapers and media will play it over and over as they tear it apart, only reinforcing the airings and the message. Fact-checkers will spurt blood from their eyes.

The campaign will seek to dial back the threat of Trump's instability, the crazy tweets, and the rampant corruption to convince America that Trump is a determined president with a record of success in the economy, the one area that decides most elections. Because Trump's team knows this is a referendum on him, they'll shore up this economic message as often as they can, seeking to reframe the election as their own referendum of prosperity versus godless socialism.

As for the negative ads, expect a frenzy of claims that will, again, make Democratic eyes bug out. The Democratic nominee will be cast as a dangerous socialist, an open-borders traitor, a coastal elite liberal snob, a killer of babies, and a taker of healthcare. Negative ads are very on-brand for Team Trump, and expect many, many millions of dollars behind them in the swing states.

When Democrats see the ads running in Michigan, Wisconsin, Ohio, and Pennsylvania, they need to pay close attention to the cultural context embedded in the negative messages. For all their pretense as the party of working folks, there is a long-established GOP playbook to divorce voters who might otherwise vote Democratic from the party because it misses cultural, religious, and regional cues.

I know. I helped write it.

Liberal activists have a repeated pattern we've often exploited: Their desire for national ideological conformity is boundless. That's why there are virtually no pro-life Democrats; the normative power of the party means a Democrat in a conservative Catholic district must still be as pro-abortion as a Democrat in Brookline, Massachusetts. Democrats in the rural South must still be as anti-gun as Shannon Watts and Michael Bloomberg.

Twitter has made this problem worse, but for a generation my old team rolled up Democratic seats with ads that hammered that cultural divide. "San Francisco Democrats" was poison for a lot of formerly Democratic voters in the South and Midwest. Expect more than you've ever imagined of that flavor of cultural warfare in 2020.

Objectively, Democrats will know the game he's playing. Emotionally? Not so much. Trump's negative ads are going to drive Democrats not just to defend but to *hyperbolically* defend late-term abortion, a full ban on guns, single-payer government-run healthcare, higher taxes, and all the cultural signifiers of the elite coastal cities in which the Democratic political and media machines reside.

Very few campaigns understand the first fundamental rule of responding to negative ads: Don't repeat the charges. The second fundamental rule of negative attack ads? Never, ever let an attack go unanswered. The only way to respond to a negative ad is to hammer home with a different negative ad of your own. You can never explain or correct; you must simply nuke them back with more. The first person on the campaign who says "We're not doing negative attacks" needs to be shipped out to the yard-sign department and never heard from again.

Every political generation seems to learn these rules the hard way, through painful experience. The trick for Democrats in 2020 is to prepare—knowing that Trump has previewed these culture-war attack ads, and that the Fox mode of politics depends on them—and have pushback ads in the can and ready to roll. Make them ugly. Make them hurt.

FUNDRAISING

"Really fucking huge" is the number of which you're thinking. Really, really huge.

Every day from now until Election Day, Donald Trump's online cash machine is going to pump out hundreds of thousands of appeals, all carefully market-tested to stoke the rubes, raising $5 here, $25 there, a $1,000 from time to time. He's going to have repeat donors, and he's going to scare them into giving until it hurts.

Never mind that Hillary Clinton outgunned Trump financially in 2016, for all that it mattered. If you underestimate the power of an incumbent president to raise all the damn money in the world, you're mistaken. Lobbyists will be lined up outside the RNC with pickup truck beds full of bearer bonds.

Every president takes care of his donors, in large ways and small, but in the Trump administration, there's everything but a price list. Corporation after corporation has seen how effective donations to the RNC, the Trump campaign, and the constellation of super PACs and joint committees have been. Industry groups and leaders know rewards come—damn the consequences—for people who play ball in this new, utterly transactional Washington.

Even companies that posture like they've got progressive corporate values are going to stroke Trump, the RNC, and their allied super PACs with metric tons of money. Democrats have, thus far, been terrible at trying to freeze these corporate donors and their lobbyists from sending a tidal wave of cash to Trump. Ahem, Nancy—did you forget you control the House? The old, politically incorrect rule in fundraising of "be the pimp and not the whore" when it comes to donors still obtains, as horrible as it sounds.

Mere incumbency gives any president a massive financial advantage. Trump's position is not one of mere incumbency. He's a warlord president, both utterly bribable and utterly capable of turning the mechanism of government against his political enemies. Corporations that give to the Democratic nominee will face his Twitter wrath, and that of his horde.

One of the better Democratic fundraising consultants told me in July 2019 that she expects Trump to be able to raise $700 million for the campaign, the RNC, and the combined committees. That's a lot of zeroes. That's real money.

Trump's small-donor suckers also believe this is the fight of their lives, an existential challenge between Trump and mandatory abortions fortnightly, the razing of every evangelical church, and forced Arabic lessons at their grandchild's elementary school from the local deep-state MS-13 representative. Trump will drain every single dollar from every single Social Security check to survive, and his people will happily give it.

Democrats will be at a financial disadvantage in 2020. The primary is going to be a long, costly slog through hell, leaving the campaigns bankrupt. This is always the challenge party's problem, but in 2020 it will be far more marked than ever.

Small-dollar donations on the Democratic side will be vital, and will be there in big numbers, but only if you make this election a referendum on Trump. No one is sending in donations because of the nominee's infrastructure plan. They will send in donations by the billions if you promise to crush Donald Trump, see him driven before you, and hear the lamentations of his women. The Democratic nominee needs to outline to donors in the usual Silicon Valley, Hollywood, and Seattle enclaves that the checks need to have seven figures, not six. Trump's corporate cash advantage, driven by the lobbyists who manage their interests in D.C., will be significant. Don't be shy.

FIELD ORGANIZING

Democrats used to have a monopoly on field organizing. They were good at it, and all the hot girls volunteered for the Democratic candidates (if you think I'm sexist, this was a truism in politics until the late 1990s), so off the lads went to knock on doors with Betty Sue Holyoke.

Though not the first modern, hypertargeted field operation, Obama's 2008 field operation was famously effective and organized. They faced up against a field team on the GOP side that could fit in a midsized high-school auditorium. It was a far cry from the GOP volunteer efforts run for George W. Bush's successful reelection campaign. In the post-Obama era, the commitment on the right to data-driven, direct-contact campaigns grew, funded by folks like the Koch brothers. The GOP vowed never to get caught short again on field and data in races from dogcatcher to president.

I should know. I was part of a secretive effort to reverse engineer the Obama model after 2008. It took a while to trickle out, but like building nuclear weapons, only the first time is hard. Now the Trump team (and more important, the lifers at the RNC and in the consultocracy) have the blueprints, the materials, and the money to put it together.

You might have a shock coming in 2020. Trump, a man devoted to television like it's religion, likely couldn't give a damn, but the RNC, the state parties, and the various victory committees will be working their asses off to deploy MAGAs into the field. They have a unique selling proposition: The GOP is no longer defined by the old divisions of social, economic, and foreign policy conservatives. GOP activists are now all one with the Trump borg, and the RNC is moving quickly to turn the cultists into door-knocking, voter-registering, tweet-posting automatons.

They're investing in training, with more than one thousand sessions held across the country in the week before Trump's June 18, 2019, campaign kickoff.[4] Trump's base may be many things, but above all they are motivated, even if their motivations are in service to the worst president in our history. Democrats take the Trump/GOP's 2020 field operation lightly at their peril.

OPPO

The Democratic candidates may not be paying attention to the Trump/RNC's opposition research wizards, but those wizards are most certainly paying attention to them.

The RNC has access to a horde of smart, eager, and talented oppo nerds who will drill down into the most granular details of the lives of the candidate, the candidate's family, the candidate's dog, the candidate's business associates, and every person on the plane the candidate took to the last rally.

Remember, the power of their oppo is their ability to provide a stream of information to feed into the maw of the Trump–Fox–social-media machine to keep the rubes angry and terrified. Most oppo folks, especially the professionals, will give you an objective road map for attacks that will and won't work on your opponent. Some stuff is simply too much of a reach. Some of it is unethically obtained. In those cases, the so-called silver bullets turn out to be the opposite.

Trump's orbit is also filled with folks who aren't standard opposition research professionals. They're dirty, dark, and will pay money for dirt. The kinds of things that you silly Marquess of Queensberry types think are off-limits, aren't. Trump can and will use unverified, untruthful oppo, and no matter how many times it's debunked, a fraction of his audience will believe every word.

THE RUSSIANS, PART DVA

Donald Trump's first election was a triumph for Vladimir Putin, the Russian intelligence services, and the model of special warfare the Kremlin is pursuing in a world where the hyperpowers of the United States and China will always outgun it economically and technologically. This model uses things the Russians are really good at to launch asymmetric attacks against more powerful opponents, and if 2016 was a proof of concept, it was a great success.

The Russians never, ever walk away from equity. They never let an asset, either willing or unwilling, leave their embrace. They're already back in the fight in 2019 to help ensure Trump's reelection. Their propaganda model has been refined, their audience is more credulous than even they can believe, and the target of their operation does everything but take long steams with Vova at his dacha.

The Russians will be hard at work running a repeat of their 2016 operation because it was cheap, it was effective, and it worked. Expect more of the same propaganda, more of the same manipulation online and off, and more active measures designed to reelect Donald Trump. It's one hell of an in-kind contribution, from a man who operates from ego and venality rather than ideology. Money and pride are always more certain to produce the outcomes the Russian kleptocracy desires. They're really, really good at this, and they've picked a side.

White House Diaries: Melania Trump

So, typical day.

I gets up, does the Peloton until you know, am sweatings like same way Donald is sweating when he climb maybe two stairs. No, diary. Not two flight of stair. Two stairs. No, is not mean. Is real!

But Peloton is good. You see this body? Work, bitches.

Anyhows, typical day. I don't has to see him on typical day, which is you know, good. Prenup is points system; go to rally, 50 points. Go to press conferencing, 100 points. Don't ask what get 5000 points, but I would rather doing so with Justin Trudeau, if you know what I am meaning.

So he is saying to me, "Why you no look at me as you look at Justin and Macaroon?"

One day, creepy Jared see me texting Justin, so I am telling him, "Snitches get stitches." (Is better in original Slovenian.)

Please gods, don't lets him be releect. Please. I am beggings you.

NEVER UNDERESTIMATE
INCUMBENCY

The Trump White House may be Bedlam on the Potomac, but the power of the presidency to draw cameras—where the president goes, cameras follow—and move headlines is enormous. Trump's team understands this, and they will use the power of the government as a rapid-response tool to keep Trump in the news, to make news, and to step on Democratic events.

As a showman, Trump has a gut-level understanding that the audience is always hungry, and they will eat up the things he does that are outside the usual spectrum of presidential behavior. During an otherwise painful G20 Summit in Japan, Donald Trump called an audible and decided he wanted to spend some quality time with his BFF Kim Jong-un. In a hot scramble, the Secret Service and the Air Force spun up the jets, set the scene at the border between the two Koreas, and voilà, instant media roadblock.

Trump's meeting with Kim, and his symbolic crossing into North Korea, were just that—symbolic.[5] It meant nothing. It didn't move the ball on denuclearizing a nation led by the last remaining Stalinist on earth. It didn't further U.S. interests. Oh, it helped *Kim* dramatically, further legitimizing him in the eyes of his starving people as he made the leader of the free world come to him, but that wasn't the point.

The point was that Trump wanted a picture, and he got it. He got it on short notice, and he got it regardless of the costs. Expect this in

2020 in foreign and domestic scenes when Trump uses the tools of the presidency—White House advance teams, the Secret Service, Air Force One, and government facilities around the country and the world—to do "government" events. These events will cost the campaign nothing because they're, um, cough cough, official business.

Both the White House itself and Air Force One are powerful visual campaign props, and presidents of both parties have used them for their political ends. As we're painfully aware, Donald Trump lacks the genes for shame, modesty, and discretion, so expect the AF 28000 and AF 29000 to get a lot of air miles clocked in service to his campaign. Expect to see one of the two Air Force One planes parked behind him during speech after speech at airport hangar rallies around the country.

Most presidents would instantly draw a sharp, clean line between campaign operations and the use of military force. This is the proverbial "wag the dog" scenario where a president in trouble seeks to bomb his way out of it by hitting a target overseas. With no adult supervision in the Pentagon—just who is the acting, provisional, temporary, staffing-agency, drop-in SECDEF this week?—no one should put it past Trump to escalate conflicts with China, Iran, or elsewhere when some part of his lizard brain tells him that some boom-boom will goose his polling numbers.

Some of my former GOP colleagues will whisper, "How dare you accuse the American president of ever using the military for . . ." and then drop the subject, because no matter how deep they are in the Trump hole, they know who this man is and what he'll do. Trump proves time and again that morals, laws, norms, traditions, rules, guidelines, recommendations, and tearful pleading from his staff mean nothing when he gets a power boner and decides he's going to do something stupid. President Hold My Beer comes from the Modern Unitary Executive Power theory, where there are no limits, no laws, and no right and wrong. I'm not saying it's a matter of if Trump will wag the dog in 2020. I'm saying that anyone who thinks he wouldn't is a damn fool.

One other powerful weapon in Trump's incumbency arsenal is his addiction to executive orders and unilateral executive action from the White House. Sure, it'll be mostly a nonsensical mass of unconstitutional, incoherent piffle, but it will be directed at swing states.

You should certainly expect him to fill the air with executive orders that feed the base—"All immigrants must have a PhD!" "Ivanka will now be addressed as HRH Ivanka!" "Eric will be my viceroy for Greenland!"

You should also expect counterintuitive plays like suddenly declaring an interest in the Flint water system, or disaster relief in the Florida Panhandle. Watch for Kellyanne Conway to talk him into doing orders on feel-good but substanceless items like childcare, job training, cat adoption, and literacy.

Incumbency is always powerful, but in Trump's case it is even more imposing as a political asset. His ability to utterly dominate the political discourse for his first term isn't always a positive for him, but he knows the showbiz rule: All PR is good PR. He is the best-known brand on the planet, a singular character in a nation where people often kinda sorta maybe know their elected representatives. (We test this frequently in focus groups, and the number of people who know their congressional representative and U.S. senator is disheartening, to say the least. The number who know their state reps and senators is even lower. Everyone knows Donald Trump.)

Other presidents felt bounded in their behavior, obligated to respect the office of the presidency even if it meant forsaking political advantage. If you think that's Trump, I have some prime swamp-front lots to sell you in the Everglades.

White House Diaries: Melania Trump

The Donalt is telling me, "Erection Day is coming." He thinks is funny joking. Me, not so much.

Do not like.

This is why I should have given old Gypsy woman dollar in subway.

TRUMP'S MESSAGES
AND STRATEGIES

The surface level of Trump's 2020 reelection campaign will be crafted to look like Reagan's 1984 reelection: the Big Show, a patriotic extravaganza contrasting Morning in America 2.0 with every cliché of the Democrats of old; good economic news versus stodgy centralized state planning; sunny optimism versus doom-and-gloom. This campaign will frustrate Democrats because it will appear superficial, phony, and laughable in comparison to Trump's actual record.

Here's the irony: For his target audience, it will work—really well. For the media, it will work because it will be accompanied by big, staged events, monster flags and monster trucks, a picture-perfect group of 'Mericans behind him. They'll look surprisingly diverse, surprisingly female, and surprisingly reasonable.

Don't be fooled. The real Trump base is still there.

No, the lock-her-up, send-them-back crowd will be well and truly in the cooler, always on the back side of the cameras, and with their manias, conspiracy fantasies, sputtering rage at the media, and crazy-uncle-on-Facebook personas.

The real Trump campaign just below the surface will be pure, vintage Richard Nixon. Trump can't stop himself because his mindset was formed by his early exposure to politics with Roy Cohn and Roger Stone. Factor in the cruel tutelage of Roger Ailes, from whom Trump learned much of his media-battering techniques, a man who validated Trump with the right as well as, you know, invented the Nixon playbook.

Add to that his own demonstrated history of inflammatory racial views and actions, and the reward he gained in 2016 by activating the alt-right, the old-guard racists around David Duke, and the slurry of neo-, crypto-, and actual Nazis, and the preview of the 2020 campaign is easy to see.

For his base, and like Nixon, Trump will replay 2016, portraying himself as the tribune of the silent majority, the oppressed working man, and the downtrodden white middle-class American facing a changing culture and a changing country. He may flip "MAGA" to "KAG," but the top-level message is still "I'm with you against the elites and the scary brown people."

REVENGE

With distance comes clarity, and I'm going to own up to something about my old party's behavior. For years, it tweaked at the edges of my dislike, but now that it's become a central defining characteristic of Trump Republicanism, it makes my skin crawl.

It's grievance culture. Trump has brilliantly exploited it, and 2020 will see the grievance, paranoia, and self-loathing of the GOP blossom into central themes. It's profoundly pessimistic, and fundamentally un-American.

Everyone is coming to get you. The immigrants. Black Lives Matter. Antifa. The deep state. Silicon Valley. The godless homosexers. Academia. Women. Sloths. Atheists. Muslims. Jews. Zoroastrians. Who knows what else will be added to the catalog, but the Fox media programming will always give you a clue. War on Christmas? Atheists. Sharia law? Muslims. Drag queen story time? Duh.

"ALL HAIL ME"

"Me, me, me, me, me" will also be central. Trump's personal-message branding strategy is the 2016 playbook writ large, with two big thematic stories:

First, the hero narrative.

Trump, the iconoclast hero of America's forgotten working class, has delivered unparalleled prosperity and finally made America Great Again. He has built the wall, kept every promise, and told the truth at every point. He is the smartest, handsomest president in history, not of the United States, but of the world, and we are lucky to have him give up his valuable time to serve as our leader. His royal family beside him, he will lead us to greater heights.

This will make eyes roll and earn fact-checkers overtime, but it's irresistible to a natural-born con man like Trump. This is the brand as it has always been and shall always be. Gold-plated. Top-notch. Luxurious. The biggest. The best. A walking superlative.

Then, the fear narrative:

Après moi, le déluge. Without me, the economy will collapse. We'll be taken advantage of by world powers in both trade and security. Murderous immigrant criminals will kill your families and take your jobs. There is a conspiracy of elites ready to crush your church, your community, and your values. You will be punished for not believing the right things. Also, immigrants. And Muslims. And immigrants.

His polling and strategy team desperately wants to make this a base-only election about a core package of issues, not a referendum on his personality, leadership, or accomplishments. The Trump base has demonstrated time and again that they're not exactly sticklers for the little stuff like facts, truth, and consistency. Democrats can and must make this race—as I'm sure you're sick of me saying by now—a referendum on Trump.

White House Diaries

DEPUTY ACTING ASSISTANT PROVISIONAL TEMPORARY CHIEF OF CABINET OPERATIONS STAFF LELAND BOB SNIPES, JR.

Well, I made it. All the way to the White House. It seems like just yesterday I was working at the Waffle House in Weeping Sore, Arkansas. As fill-in night manager, I had plenty of responsibilities, I can tell you, but here at the White House it's a whole new level.

How'd I get so lucky? Well, I'll tell you, being at that rally with my QAnon sign made all the difference. The President finally understood that people like me, and JFK Jr., are his real supporters.

I get to deal with the President almost every day when he comes out of the Oval and screams at me because the Secret Service won't let UberEats in with his second KFC order of the day.

When I got here, they said they had to do a background check on me, which is fine. I knew Q would protect me. My President needs all the help he can get to fight off the Deep State. On the Q Discord channel last night (too bad 8chan is gone. I loved 8chan.) they were saying that term limits are a Deep State fraud, and that this election is being manipulated by the Illuminati Reptilian Overlords.

NO HEROES IN THE GOP

As a rule, I'm not a man given to a rosy view of the nature of politics and politicians. Thirty years of experience electing them has demonstrated that even the "good" ones have a gnawing desire for love and adulation that is essentially boundless. "Don't fall in love with the meat" was a lesson I learned watching a few great, some good, and a lot of average pols live down to my lowest expectations. (Yes, Rudy, I'm looking right at you.)

The Republican defenses of Trump have evolved slightly since I wrote the number one *New York Times* bestseller (sorry, but that's never going to get old) *Everything Trump Touches Dies.* When that book hit the market, Republicans still had enough members of the Republican branch of the Republican Party to occasionally speak up about Trump, even if it was in the furrowed-brows and deep-concern mode.

Now? The GOP is sunk even deeper into the muck of Trumpism, slowly losing its ability to think, move, or respond to even the most obvious moral questions surrounding this president. The resemblance to a cult becomes more pronounced with every passing day. Many of my former friends and clients who served as a silent resistance in Congress and in elected offices across the nation are gone now, either retired or defeated in the 2018 beatdown.

The wipeout in the House increased the percentage of true believers in Esoteric Trumpism. Centrists and moderates simply quit or lost in blowouts across the suburbs. Before 2020, the last few moderates—Will Hurd of Texas, most notably—pulled the ejection handle, knowing there was no place for them in Trump's GOP.

Fox News has amply rewarded the opportunists—particularly former Trump-skeptics and hustle monkeys like Matt Gaetz and Kevin McCarthy, now favorites in the Fox lineup. These are men (and they're almost all men—the jury is out on Ann Coulter) who live and breathe for the positive tweet, the ride on Air Force One, and the pat on their blocky heads from Trump. Remember, opportunists can work without moral consistency, and these folks prove it every day.

The king of this soulless class is Lindsey Graham. Graham, who in May 2016 tweeted "If we nominate Trump, we will get destroyed . . . and we will deserve it"[6] has become Donald Trump's attack lapdog and is among Trump's most eager Washington cheerleaders. He spent decades as John McCain's political wingman and as a center-right Republican. Graham now routinely shits on the late senator's legacy with his every waking action in service to Trump.

Graham does everything but beg to shave Trump's back in his public statements, all for the sweet connection to a man who consistently and revoltingly insults the memory of an American hero. Graham argues it's to influence the president, but we all know who wears the gimp suit in this relationship. His obedience to Trump is so abject, so complete, and so cringe-worthy that when Trump inevitably fucks him over, the national supply of schadenfreude will instantly run dry.

The Trump-world Javerts like Devin Nunes, Mark Meadows, Matt Gaetz, Jim Jordan, and Doug Collins engage in performative deep-state dipshit japery every time a camera is nearby. This fake deep-state panic has become essential for the continued maintenance of the myth that there is a massive conspiracy inside the Justice Department and intelligence community against Trump. The people behind this Big Lie continue to stoke the corrosive strategy of protecting Trump by shattering America's faith in the people on the front lines against hostile foreign powers. Expect many, many more Fox stories about Hillary's goddamn emails, imaginary deep-state villains, and lurid conspiracies by the evil Never Trump establishment (hey, that's me!) against Donald Trump.

Mitch McConnell is, as always, Mitch McConnell. Love him or hate him, McConnell spanks Chuck Schumer and the Senate Democrats on the daily. He is now without question the most powerful and effective Senate majority leader in history. He's dethroned Lyndon Johnson, and that's saying something.

My Democratic readers are reaching for their smelling salts, but I'm giving you nothing but the truth about Mitch; he's better than you at all of this. He's better at Senate business. He's better at elections. He's better at shamelessly raising fucktons of money. He looks like a turtle, and he behaves like a great white shark, constantly prowling, feeding on the dreams of the Senate Democrats.

His desire to protect Trump will lead him to be a powerful ally of the president in 2020, and if you're not watching that flank, Mitch can and will leverage his unparalleled power to devour you. His deal with the devil took a simple form: President McConnell would be in charge of the federal judiciary from top to bottom. When I asked a McConnell aide how a pending federal judicial appointment of a Bush-friendly nominee could have possibly emerged from the Trump White House, he responded, "Oh, he's one of ours, not theirs. They're almost all ours."

The reasoning according to some close to the majority leader is simple: Trump is a reality congressional Republicans must accept, and they fully expect an apocalyptic political backlash to follow him. The only way they see to secure the gains of the conservative movement from before and during Trump is to flood the federal bench with Federalist Society hard-ass constitutionalists (is there any other Federalist Society type?).

The shame elected GOP leaders feel about Trump is generally about one inch behind their bluster on his record. The combination of fear and ambition will make them even more determined to defend Trump until the bitter end. His power over the mob has broken them, even in the wake of the spanking they received in 2018. It's Trump's party now, and the postconservative moment rewards obedience over ideas, ass-kissing over principle, and forelock-tugging deference even to Trump's most egregious behavior.

Heroism should be its own reward, but in Trump's Republican Party it is punished, and swiftly.

For congressional Republicans, it doesn't matter what happens in the 2020 election. They will lose their seats before they cross Trump, so great is their terror of his mob. No revelation will split them. No behavior will stop them from towing Trump's line. It is now well beyond the typical partisan loyalty we've seen in the past. They will not stand up. They will not speak out. Expect no heroism. Don't even expect passive-aggressive asides. Lyndon Johnson always sought his opponents' abject submission, and he got there by intimidation, threats, power plays, and horse-trading. The GOP lined up to give Trump full control of their destiny without so much as a fight.

Trump could say "Yeah, the Russians are going to elect me again and the payoff is I get to build a tower in Moscow when I'm done. What about it?" and they'd praise him like the second coming of Lincoln. He could admit every conceivable sin, and his elected GOP cohort would redefine them as virtues. "Well, adultery is a problem, but a man as virile and powerful as Mr. Trump needs . . ."

The Party of Lincoln is now the Party of Trump, a weak, cowardly, amoral, and faithless husk of a once-great party of ideas and leadership. They'll follow him into a political graveyard, red hats, tawdry nationalism, dumb policies, cruel tweets, and all. Their cult-like obedience to him has consumed their honor, and their souls.

White House Diaries

DEPUTY ACTING ASSISTANT PROVISIONAL TEMPORARY CHIEF OF CABINET OPERATIONS STAFF LELAND BOB SNIPES, JR.

The great thing about the Qmunnity (Hey, I like that! I'm going to use that more!) is that we really back each other up. I'm not very busy right now, so I've been spending a lot of time looking at the evidence the Deep State is still trying to take out Our President.

This election looks bad, I'm not going to lie, but I've seen the real truth. All those polls are fake news run by Jeffrey Epstein (you don't really think he's dead, do you, sheeple?) and his pedophile army.

Mr. Trump is the winner already, and we know it.

This election is a big fake news lie. Someone has to do something about it.

And that someone is me, Leland Bob Snipes, Jr.

HIS FUCKING TWITTER
FEED, FAKEBOOK, AND
FOX AGITPORN

Fox.

I know, I know. I can hear it in your head. "Rupert's propaganda network." "Faux News."

Hate Fox all you like, but don't underestimate its power to cement the views of your candidate in the minds of the Republican base voters and beyond. With their various personnel's role as Donald Trump's chief fluffers, enforcers, cheerleaders, policy advisors, and image launderers, Fox has a massive, almost unrivaled media reach. When you're tempted to dismiss them, have your media consultants give you the earned-media value of the airtime Trump receives on their network every single day.

More important, and for the first time in history, the largest news outlet in the country isn't just ideologically simpatico with a president; Fox is in daily coordination on message, targeting, and strategy with the president and his campaign.

No, this isn't normal. It isn't cool. It isn't American. But it is the reality of the most powerful cable news outlet in the nation.

Their bond is driven both by the network's understanding of its audience (old, white, and pissed off) and by the president's addiction to their fellating coverage of his every move, word, and thought. He supplies them with an audience who follows his every utterance. They keep his numbers up with his base.

Fox has 1.39 million views a day. Its rivals CNN and MSNBC are at 622,000 and 1.04 million, respectively.[7] Fox is an unmatched weapon in Trump's arsenal, and you'd better be ready for it. Pick the most damaging thing in your defensive oppo file and turn it up to 11, then add a big dose of insane. Overcoming this media ecosystem is going to be one of the Democrats' singular challenges in 2020.

An impassioned speech about the challenges and glories of America? Lost in the static when Trump tweets out some incoherent tripe. Your brainy essay for *The New York Times* on climate change or gun control or worker retraining will get a few thousand smart people nodding, but Trump's angry tweet will be read and retweeted by tens of millions of followers not known for critical-thinking abilities and shared by hundreds of thousands of boomers on their Facebook pages.

Democrats still don't seem to have a serious approach to the massive, organized Facebook infrastructure on the far right. Grassroots groups and pages created by one person can take on a life of their own, and their utility to spread political propaganda, misinformation, overseas propaganda, and deceptive messages and images was abundantly demonstrated in the 2016 election. Democrats need constant monitoring of these sub-rosa, powerhouse propaganda arms of the Trump effort; they need the infrastructure and teams to push back with countervailing messages and, when they identify that "Real Americans for America" has an IP in Macedonia or Moscow, to work with Facebook to kill them off.

Fact-checking doesn't work with these folks. Politifact, Snopes, and the rest aren't a remedy for Facebook information warfare; in fact, the Trump fan base views refutations of Trump's lies based on facts and evidence as confirmation Trump is right.[8]

Fake news is a problem almost exclusively on the right. The people driving it can't be shamed, and the only people who could make them play by the rules—at least at this point—won't. Mark Zuckerberg has a wee bit of power at Facebook but can't seem to rouse himself to meaningful action. Democrats will face stories that make the worst excesses of the *National Enquirer* look like the pages of *The Paris Review,* and the social-media giants won't do a damn thing about it unless they're under market and social pressure. Get to know their board members, folks.

Democrats are running against a party and a constituency who not only view the president's loose relationship with the truth as tolerable, but who see any lie or conspiracy theory that accomplishes their beloved goal of owning the libs as acceptable and, in fact, desirable.

Crazy Facebook pages pushing fake news to the Trump right are here to stay. If the Democratic campaign isn't staffed, trained, and ready to push back on these stories instantaneously, expect a meaningful fraction of the American people to buy into characterizations of your candidate's life, morals, finances, religious practices, and sexual appetites that are lurid, crazed, and utterly false.

I know. I saw it on ConservativeDailyEagleNewsHubSuperMAGA TruthWarriorQAnon.com.

Donald Trump's Twitter feed is the very maw of hell. It is the crapulous wellspring of his endless river of bullshit, polluted and polluting. It is like a biblical flood of divisive mendacity, a shameful example of dementia, sociopathic behavior, foot-stomping rage, Adderall-babble, and a window into the hideous, Lovecraftian landscape of Trump's id.

For all that, his Twitter feed has been, and remains, an asymmetric political weapon of unparalleled power. You wish you had one-thousandth of that power.

His Twitter leverage can reshape the day's media coverage, move attention from one crisis to the next, detonate massive explosions in the political sphere, and turn the most egregious, obvious lies into rock-solid gospel truth for his 60 million followers. The temptation to dismiss his tweeting as trivial, as a mere online embarrassment or amusement, and to believe that it won't be his main tool in the 2020 earned-media war is a profound mistake.

The Democratic nominee will never have the Twitter following or power Trump enjoys, but it's time to learn the ancient art of tweet-fu. The Democrat needs to use swift replies with a video or graphic component to increase the reach of every response. They need to be fast, funny, authentic, and cutting. Don't hesitate to go to the vaults to hurl out Trump's triggers and insecurities—his business failings, his taxes, his payoffs to porn stars, his terrible polls, his physical appearance, his friends in jail, his D-grade celebrity, and, of course, his tiny, tiny hands.

White House Diaries

DEPUTY ACTING ASSISTANT PROVISIONAL TEMPORARY CHIEF OF CABINET OPERATIONS STAFF LELAND BOB SNIPES, JR.

My God. The Fake News Libtard Antifa Socialists are claiming they won. They're saying President Trump lost the Electoral College.

Save us, Q. Please. You're the only thing standing between us and socialism.

We can't accept a fake election where the fake news media lied and said Mr. Trump lost. I didn't take the Greyhound from Weeping Sore, AR to see Mr. Trump get taken out by Deep State Sharia Sleeper Agents.

UPDATE: Just had a really interesting meeting with "the alumni" group. It looks like Mr. Trump and Mr. Bannon have a plan. #TrustThePlan

THE MAINSTREAM MEDIA

Donald Trump has a powerful media ally.

It's not Fox.

It's not Rush Limbaugh.

It's not Mark Levin or Ann Coulter or Breitbart, or any of the rest of the shill-caliber Trump-centric right-media enterprise.

No, Trump's biggest media ally in 2020 is the media itself. The mainstream media. You know, the enemy of the people. The Washington–New York media axis. They're not ideologically in line with Trump. They find his behavior, attitude, actions, and policies largely as revolting as do the 60 percent of Americans who dislike Trump in degrees ranging from distaste to apoplectic rage.

The American media is under constant attack from Donald Trump. They are put at physical risk by the edge cases of his wild-eyed minions. They are insulted by his staff. They are lied to by his most senior advisors with a frequency and intensity that boggles the imagination even as they themselves are routinely cast as liars attacking the only font of truth and wisdom, Mr. Donald J. Trump.

But they just can't quit him.

Trump knows it, and they know it.

He is the human train wreck from which they can never look away. He is the evidence the dog isn't house-trained. He is every addiction, wrapped into one package. He knows that no outlet will truly punish him for lying. No outlet will bust the "senior administration official" who makes calls from the White House residence at midnight.

The Democratic campaign will struggle every day to overcome his brighter-than-the-sun media presence. For 2020, they have to build a smart, media-friendly team of surrogates who can get on television—the only place attacks are real for Trump—and follow his rule: Punch back twice as hard. The key is to recruit, train, and inform surrogates early, and tune them to one key point: Always bridge back to making the race a referendum on Donald Trump. Skip the senior statesmen or people with their own ambitions and agendas; get quick-thinking, sharp surrogates with social-media amplification powers. Set them free to "commit news" every time they're on camera.

Democrats need to dramatically up their earned-media game. It's no longer "Lemme email you this press release."

Some of the Democratic campaigns in the primary running up to 2020 seemed a bit . . . old-fashioned. I was born the week JFK died, so I'm in that bridge between boomers and gen X, but some of the campaigns seem to be ready to embrace the telegraph and that newfangled faxin'. The Biden, Sanders, and Warren campaign operations on the press side weren't exactly full of digital natives.

Trump is an earned-media machine who depends on his opponents to be on defense, and to respond to his cues. If they spend the day only pushing back on Trump's tweeted outrages, lies, and bullshit, they're not pushing out their own messages, and they're not on the attack.

The media wants war, fire, loud noises, alarums, and explosions. Democrats need press people who are aggressive as hell and don't need much sleep. It's better for them to move fast, break shit, and cause trouble than it is to be too cautious. The idea of campaign-ending gaffes by staffers died when Corey Lewandowski grabbed a reporter by the arm so hard it left a mark.

Trump feeds the media, practically every minute of the day. If the Democratic campaign isn't launching messages at reporters every one of those same minutes, they're fated to get swamped by Trump's social-media-powered flood.

The tone of the earned-media efforts needs to get off that snippy, shame-function tone so much Democratic messaging seems to display. You cannot shame Donald Trump. You can put his excesses and evils front and center to the American people to keep your base motivated and to address the targets in the Electoral College swing states. It's about the damage he's doing to everyday Americans. It's about his corruption, vulgarity, dishonesty, broken promises, and failed policies.

Be angry. Be aggressive. Be American. Voters want to see some fight from the Democrats, a return of the happy-warrior ethos where you don't duck a fight and you're ready to take on bullies. Stop with the "deeply disappointed" tone—hoist the black flag and commence cutting throats.

The press and media operations of every presidential campaign are always top-down and top-heavy. In 2020, the national campaign needs to put aggressive press operatives on the ground in the top fifteen targeted states. They should be folks who understand the media in Florida or Michigan or Arizona or Pennsylvania. Spend the money; it'll be worth it. Those operatives need to feed the state press corps in the target Electoral College states stories of real people who have been hurt by Trump's policies—talk about agriculture in Iowa, trade disasters in Wisconsin, the Puerto Rican hurricane relief failure in Florida, and so on. The national press, with few exceptions, won't chase or find those stories. Why bother when the Trump twitter feed spews stories that write themselves?

You want a story about that Iowa soybean farmer weeping because she supported Trump and now she's losing her farm. You want one about that union worker in Michigan or Wisconsin who hated Hillary and held his nose while voting for Trump. Now the trade war has cost him his job.

The great thing about this is that television wants it also. You're committing news, and you're spreading a message to local television viewers, news consumers, and social-media junkies that Democrats give a damn about the swing states as much as they care about the coastal blue kingdoms.

What about the big blue states, you ask? Assign one intern to them at HQ. They'll take care of themselves. Honestly. I know Democrats hate this idea, but the election is already over in thirty-five states. Fight where the fight is.

White House Diaries

DEPUTY ACTING ASSISTANT PROVISIONAL TEMPORARY CHIEF OF CABINET OPERATIONS STAFF LELAND BOB SNIPES, JR.

We've got a lot of people ready to back the President's play, and it's only fair since we all know the election was invalid. Mr. Bannon is positive the American people will be with us. Mr. Hannity and Mr. Tucker are on board. It was such an honor to meet them.

The Q forums are popping with real news.

Did you know no one has ever seen Hillary Clinton and the President-elect at the same time? DID YOU? It's probably her in disguise, which makes our mission that much more important.

Also, since the President-elect would be "46" it's so obvious. 46 divided by 2 is 23. Benjamin Harrison was the 23rd President. "Benjamin Harrison" is an anagram for "Major Brains In Hen" which is obviously Hillary Clinton. It's all SO CLEAR NOW.

We have to stop her.

DEEPFAKE NATION

I f you have a creeping sense that what you read, hear, and see online these days might not be the exact truth, you're not alone. From Photoshop in the 2000s to highly convincing digital imitations and manipulations of video today, the arc of technological progress to produce convincing fakes is riding the same Moore's Law curve like everything else. Even the uncanny valley effect of fake video and audio a few years ago has passed. The use of faster AI, GPUs, and hella processing power, even on desktops, means that amateurs can produce decent-looking fakes, professionals can hit near-perfection, and nation-state actors can generate work so sophisticated it takes AIs and other nation-state actors to detect it.[9]

If our civic and media cultures were healthy and relatively sane, this would be a more tractable problem. If the largest American cable television network acted in good faith, and we had an agreed-upon standard of truth, this would be more manageable. If the largest social-media platforms moved aggressively against fakes and outright propaganda, we would be in a better position to protect our republic from this threat.

If you haven't been paying attention, our current political culture isn't sane, Fox is Trump's pet outlet, shared truth is a memory, and the social-media platforms seem both uninterested in and conflicted about finding a solution to the problem. After all, they monetized the propaganda efforts of the bad guys in the last election, and while they've said the right words, their actions are lagging, badly.

Given bad actors at home and abroad, Trump's willingness to cheat, and the eighteen- to twenty-four-month cycle of technological innovation in this country, by the time the fall of 2020 arrives, you should doubt your eyes, your ears, and the truth of any video you see.

Profoundly convincing deepfakes will enter the political bloodstream in this election. The first are attacks on your candidate, and they'll be real enough to blow the news cycle to hell. Deepfake attacks are an existential threat to the Democratic nominee. They'll seek to wreck the message and media cycle, take attention off Trump, fire up his base, and divide the Democratic coalition.

Here's a scenario for which you'd best prepare because it or its cousins are coming:

First, some trolling account on Twitter will post an "Oh My God have you seen this video of Joe Biden using the n-word??" tweet with the usual #MAGA #KAG #QANON hashtag crap. (The surest tell of a Trump social-media hardliner is a serious hashtag fetish.) The link to the YouTube video will be to a brand-new account, of course.

The clip will look *so* damn real. It'll be Biden (for the purposes of this example; stay in your damn seats, Warren and Bernie fans) on video, saying something to the effect of, "Well, I thought Barack was OK, for a nigger politician from Chicago. Oh, did I say 'nigger'? Sorry folks, keep that one between us."

You're thinking, "Too much, Wilson. That's ridiculous. No one would buy that."

Really? A meaningful fraction of the Republican Party bought into a conspiracy theory that Hillary Clinton was the center of a global ring of child-predator cannibals based in a D.C. pizza restaurant. You really think they won't bite on this one?

Here are the next steps in the deepfake laundering cycle, not based on speculation but on observation of the Trump-right media ecosystem, and of the mainstream media.

Over a couple of hours, the video will go viral on Trump-right Facebook pages, Twitter, and Instagram. At this point, the scummiest elements of the Trump media—for example, InfoWars, Gateway Pundit, or Conservative Whorehouse—sorry, Conservative Treehouse—will blast it out to their readers and social-media followers. The ball is rolling now, and mainstream reporters are pinging the Biden campaign for a response.

Thousands of bot accounts will start posting and reposting the video, driving the view count from a few hundred to a few hundred thousand in a matter of hours. Facebook and Reddit groups for conservatives and Trump supporters are flooded. Every damn second-, third-, and fourth-tier social-media platform is pumping the video.

At the same time, a bot army on Black Twitter starts posting furious, outraged comments, like "Do you believe this shit? Fuck Biden." Jesse Jackson and Al Sharpton, ever keen for a chance to be on camera or to profit from Biden's agony, begin concern trolling.

The Biden campaign is readying a response, but hoping this cancerous little nugget doesn't spread. Inside his staff, a few people are quietly sending one another messages on Confide and Signal, asking "Wait, did he say that??" Their hope of keeping it pushed down fails when Don Jr. tweets out a link to the video. Drudge pops it onto the top of the page, siren GIFs flashing.

The monster is loose. The views climb rapidly before YouTube takes it down, but it's too late. The relatively respectable conservative media starts pounding out the story: "While this video is unconfirmed, it has added to existing concerns about Biden's gaffes. . . ."

It's been two hours, and the Biden campaign's war room has finally found the video from which the fake was made. They're posting it as fast as they can, but Biden's legal people and senior staff have their hair tangled in the spokes of this crisis and are talking through how to handle it.

One group wants Biden in front of live cameras, *now,* to call it a fake. (In this fucked-up Choose Your Own Adventure story, that's the right choice.) The lawyers want to put out a typical weak-ass twenty-paragraph statement couched in language about his record, his love of Barack Obama, his personal history and . . . oh fuck, it's breaking news on Fox.

This will be their coverage for the next four hours. Hannity parachutes live into the studio, sucking on a Juul and pissing in a bucket under his desk to not miss a single, glorious second of this. In the first fifteen minutes, he's called for Biden to leave the race.

The mainstream media now has to—kill me—"cover the controversy" of the Biden N-Word Tape. As they start breaking in live, the Biden campaign has been contacted by a deepfakes researcher in Silicon Valley who has watched the video, broken down the clever editing, and told them in broad strokes how it was done. They finally race out a better statement, but now it's way too late, because the worst is already happening.

Trump tweets it—because of course he does.

"I LOVE THE BLACKS UNLIKE N-WORD JOE BIDEN. #KKKJoe should leave the race! #MAGA #KAG"

Trump doesn't include the YouTube link to the video. No, he pops a link to the video on an RNC server, where it won't get pulled down, as YouTube and Facebook would do in the next twenty-four hours.

That's right. Twenty-four long, painful hours.

YouTube pulls down the original video, then spends twenty-four hours playing human and AI whack-a-mole as other copies pop up, their new links amplified by the Russian- and MAGA-bot hordes. Facebook, being Facebook, will hem and haw as it spreads the lie and generates all that lovely, lovely click traffic across its network, feeding the data maw.

The takedown attempts will spawn two new waves of instant stories in the Trumpian clickservative media, both beloved tropes of the whiny right. The first will be some variation of "The liberal media won't report on the damning Biden N-Word video." It's a beloved flavor of horseshit that the deplorables scarf down.

The next story and message wave firewalls the sense of Trumpian grievance and keeps the story rolling. "Why are Google and Facebook trying to hide the truth about Joe Biden? Even if the video is a fake, this shows how the biased tech giants are trying to suppress and de-platform conservative speech." Now the respectable(-ish) conservative class weighs in, repeating the smear as a bank shot.

The chan-children join the fun, posting memes of Joe Biden in a Klan hood with #OurGuy memes. Richard Spencer will let it be known that if Biden stays on this path he might vote for him over the cuck weakling Donald "No Border Wall" Trump. David Fucking Duke will slither out of his hole and tweet (or post something on Gab or some other social-media darkhole), "Finally Joe Biden speaks to white, working-class America in a language they understand."

Six hours have passed. The nightly cable lineups are set, with defenders and opponents of Joe Biden on deck. About 4:00 P.M., the analysis starts to hit, proving the video is fake. The cable-news tone everywhere but Fox immediately turns, hard. They try to start making the story about how the Trump campaign is promoting the attack and is to blame, but it's a heavy lift. They stop showing the clip, at least. Headlines blast, "Trump Promotes Fake Viral Attack on Biden."

Slowly—very, very slowly—the *Daily Caller,* Breitbart, and the rest append tiny corrections in itty-bitty type at the bottom of their stories: "Some sources now allege this shocking video of Biden's racist racism is fake. We will update this story as it develops." Drudge takes down the siren and headline and replaces it with "Trump Tweets! Biden N-Word Tape Rocks Campaign."

The nightly cable bloodbath is one for the record books. Everyone is screaming, including me. I leave a Trump surrogate choking in a pool of his own blood and get six beeps from the seven-second-delay guy in the control room.

Trump tweets out the link a few more times that night. The morning editorials are full of disappointed words about how the media got taken for a ride. Biden's campaign loses a full 4 percent of African American support in the tracking polls.

On Election Day, 40 percent of Americans will go to the polls believing that Joe Biden used the n-word on a video and that Donald Trump is the real champion of the civil rights battles of the last fifty years.

A good deepfake can click its way around the world before the truth has time to fire up its browser.

White House Diaries

**DEPUTY ACTING ASSISTANT PROVISIONAL TEMPORARY CHIEF OF
CABINET OPERATIONS STAFF LELAND BOB SNIPES, JR.**

It's Inauguration Day.

I snuck in the last of the guns with the KFC delivery. Luckily, two of the Secret Service guys are Q, and that made it easy. They know this is the end of America unless we stop Killary's plan. We're going upstairs into the Residence now, and I hope I survive this.

Maybe I'll be something important, like Ambassador to Greenland.

YOU HAVE NO SECRETS

Opposition research has been with us as long as politics: Cicero was killed in 43 B.C. over what was essentially an oppo dump on Mark Anthony. Campaigns that won't do the work to understand their own record deserve to lose. I'm begging you, Democrats, please get three or four opposition researchers who are working for different firms to scrub every single aspect of your nominee's life, even if you think he or she is an open book. Spend the damn money. Tell them nothing, and I mean nothing, is off-limits. Pretending that there are areas that are off-limits in this day and age is as foolish as it is absurd. Just ask Hillary Clinton.

After over forty years in the public eye, Hillary Clinton was an absurdly rich opposition-research target, and not just the stupid conspiracy "Arkansas body count" and Rose Law Firm claptrap. The deep unwillingness of people around her to bring her bad news about research findings and public perceptions was hideous malpractice. All the old material that her staff decided she didn't need to review again got dredged up. Steve Bannon, Roger Stone, and Team Trump went all the way back to Arkansas to unearth the Clinton family's skeletons, and she seemed shocked by it.

Campaigns that won't look in the mirror will wake up to discover that a story they haven't heard about is suddenly front-page news. When Rudy Giuliani was running for U.S. Senate, we were ordered not to research the girlfriends, including the one who would eventually be a part of his very messy, very public divorce from Donna Hanover. Of course, we did so in secret and were vastly more prepared than we would have been if we'd followed orders and averted our eyes from the obvious. I've been on too many races where the candidate presumes there are secrets the other team won't discover.

This invasive political examination is something no one escapes. The Internet remembers everything, and the old formulation of "That was a long time ago" has disappeared in a cloud of hashtags, outrage, and amplification mechanisms.

If Joe Biden's forty-year-old tapes on busing, Al Franken's surfaced USO tour photo, Ralph Northam's yearbook, and other stories of recent vintage didn't teach Democrats this lesson, they're not paying attention.

And because the people around Trump know how to turn oppo into messaging, amplified in the form of his Twitter feed with backup from the conservative media, *National Enquirer,* and his Russian friends, expect oppo drops from the Trump world to have an explosive public impact, often disproportionately so.

There are some simple oppo survival rules for 2020.

First, presume that nothing will remain hidden. The girl you knocked up. The one time you took X. The bounced check. The time in college you woke up with a hangover and a burning sensation when you went to pee. The time you padded your expense report. It's all coming out. The trip to Tijuana. (That's in my oppo file, and let's never speak of it again, except to say bribery works to extract people from Mexican jails, and I'm good at it. "How many American dollars, right now, for my friend to walk?") Every dumb email joke. Every retweet of someone you barely noticed but turns out to be sketchy.

Second, don't look at the dirty laundry your researchers discover as a normal, nonpolitical person might. Look at it and ask, "How would the most vicious, amoral, cruel operative of the Trump campaign pitch this to Fox? How would Fox turn it into a campaign attack against me? What's the worst-case TV spot a bastard like Rick Wilson could make based on this attack? What's the least charitable explanation for this story?"

Third, there will be moments when you are exposed on the hot

mic or the hidden camera video. These instances might be spontane-
ous or carefully, deviously engineered. It might be the candidate
speaking far too candidly at a time he or she thinks is private—"Of
course we're going to seize every gun in America"—or a joke gone
badly, badly wrong—"We're called the Aristocrats!" Some are
public—"Corporations are people, my friend"—and some are
private—"People who cling to their guns and religion." In the era of
HD camera phones, expect the worst. Even moments you believe are
innocent, public, and aboveboard will be repurposed as political attack vectors.

Fourth, the best defense is an endless, aggressive, chain-saw offense.

Finally, don't expect to be able to pitch great dirt on Trump to
national reporters. They've become so jaded and so deeply cynical
about the tidal wave of revelations about this shitbird president that
you would take them solid evidence he's a serial killer and they'll
largely shrug. Don't try to silver-bullet just Trump himself—be constant and wide-spectrum. Tie the failures and scandals your research discovers—and those that are already painfully in the public
domain—to Trump's personal failures and scandals. Make it about
his low character, shallow intellect, and bad judgment.

Build the picture for reporters of the corruption around him, and
if it touches on his family and close associates, all the better. There are
no civilian targets in Trump's orbit.

Frame stories on how embarrassing it is that Trump didn't know
that Cabinet Member X was in trouble for Issue Y. Your goal is to add
friction and internal trouble, and to force him to focus on defense.
He's actually quite bad at playing defense, and you won't get him
there without a constant attack tempo.

The private made public has a powerful attraction, which is why
high transparency, quick reactions, and deep self-knowledge are es-
sentials in your defensive arsenal on this front. People will perceive it
as a politician talking about average Americans behind their backs—
no matter how incidental.

Next, secrets are political sores. They fester. They become worse
for the hiding. Why are Trump's taxes such a compelling mystery?

Because he seeks to keep them hidden. If you work from the knowledge that the Trump-right media ecosystem can pitch any story and launder it from a bot tweet to RealTruEagleFreedomMAGANewz2020 .ru to Infowars, then Breitbart, then Fox, you'll know that there's one thing you can do to even the odds: Beat them to the punch.

The old rule of politics is "Hang a lantern on your problem." If you set the narrative, you retake control of the story. Identify the problems, then wargame the hell out of your responses. Tell the lawyers in the room to fuck off; their caution will kill you when it comes to messaging.

The old cliché was that the worst thing the oppo could discover was a candidate with a dead girl or a live boy. In this more woke age, that's hardly politically correct, but unless you murdered your gender-fluid nanny and made a skin suit from xir remains, there are very few things that you can't manage or defuse if you move fast and deflate the bubble before it bursts.

Know your history, have a full inventory of your dirty laundry, and be ready to own it before the bad guys own you.

White House Diaries

DEPUTY ACTING ASSISTANT PROVISIONAL TEMPORARY CHIEF OF CABINET OPERATIONS STAFF LELAND BOB SNIPES, JR.

(WASHINGTON, DC) Special to *The New York Times*—Today four former Trump White House officials were arrested and one killed after a shootout that echoed across the nation as President Donald Trump attempted to retain power following a crushing Electoral College defeat last November. It was the first time in modern American history that the transfer of presidential power was accompanied by violence, and serves as a grim bookend to the Trump administration.

The day began with a break with tradition that foreshadowed the shocking events of the afternoon. As President-elect Joseph Harris-Warren was waiting in the White House to depart for the swearing-in, the 45th president refused to accompany the group to the Capitol. When the motorcade departed without him, it is alleged former Trump aides Corey Lewandowski, Stephen K. Bannon, Sebastian Gorka, Stephen Miller, and Leland Bob Snipes, Jr., began to use furniture to barricade themselves in the White House residence along with President Trump.

After the swearing-in, Washington was beset with rumors that Trump would refuse to vacate the White House, and a series of tweets from the @realDonaldTrump account soon became national news.

> **@realDonaldTrump:** *Fake News. Election results wrong. Your favorite President will serve three more terms. #KAG*

Secret Service and FBI Hostage Rescue Team agents were dispatched to the White House, where gunshots were then heard. The agents who ended the armed standoff were shocked to find Lewandowski, Bannon, Gorka, and Miller manning the barricade.

"They were wearing what looked like mall-ninja tactical gear they ordered off eBay," said an HRT member who spoke on the condition of anonymity. "We knew it was Gorka and Bannon because they were wearing

'Husky'-cut plate carriers." Gorka fired repeatedly and inaccurately from cover.

Previously obscure White House aide Leland Bob Snipes, Jr., was the sole casualty in the White House gun battle.

Digital forensics are continuing, but sources tell the *Times* that Snipes was found with his phone in hand, an unsent tweet as a last memorial to his odd, lost cause of an eternal Trump presidency: "Taking fire. Q will save us though. Any minute JFK Jr. will lead the QArmy through the gates and we'll . . ."

QAnon is the widespread conspiracy theory embraced by many Trump supporters.

Former president Trump was uninjured in the battle and has been taken to a private mental health facility for observation. He was extracted from the White House residence master bathroom holding his ubiquitous "Twitter phone" and an extra-crispy drumstick from Kentucky Fried Chicken.

In the last hour of his administration, Trump issued multiple pardons via Twitter, and legal scholars are already debating their validity. Ivanka Trump and her husband, Jared Kushner, are rumored to have fled the country. Former First Lady Melania Trump was seen boarding an Air Canada flight to Ottawa and declined comment.

As the smoke cleared, former Trump senior advisor Kellyanne Conway was seen whispering to President Harris-Warren on the White House lawn. Sources indicate she is in line for a senior position in the new administration.

THE DEATH OF TRUTH

Donald Trump broke something fundamental in our politics: the value of facts and truth. He alters the truth based on whims, and spreads both accidental and deliberate misinformation. His more cynical followers view this as part of his five-dimensional chess game, but America is now a post-truth republic, to our detriment.

In 2020, Trump is counting on his ability to lie his way to a second term. He will do so shamelessly, constantly, and even proudly.

Trump's endless, torrential outpouring of outright bullshit has become a primary feature of American political life, a Colorado River of mendacity slowly carving itself into a Grand Canyon of lies. This corrosion of the value and power of truth is a political weapon in the hands of a man with so little regard for it.

Trump has always been, to put it mildly, a lying liar who lies. His business empire was built on lies—lies to customers ("This is the most luxurious condo tower ever built in the history of the world, and every world leader and all Fortune 500 CEOs have apartments here"), lies to his contractors ("The check is in the mail, in full"), and lies to his bankers ("I'm really, really rich, lemme hold your wallet").

What should concern Trump's opponents in 2020 is how readily voters have abandoned honesty and truth as necessary to a healthy society. In fact, many revel in the transgressive thrill of knowing the president of the United States is spouting bullshit. They wink back at him about how fun it is to own the libs with lies bordering on pathological.

Two quotes have been rattling around in my brain since the first focus groups we conducted on Trump in late 2015.

The first is from Eric Hoffer in *The True Believer,* his study on mass political movements:

> It is the true believer's ability to "shut his eyes and stop his ears" to facts that do not deserve to be either seen or heard which is the source of his unequaled fortitude and constancy. He cannot be frightened by danger, nor disheartened by obstacle, nor baffled by contradictions, because he denies their existence.[10]

The second is from my dog-eared copy of Hannah Arendt's 1951 *Origins of Totalitarianism,* in which she writes something that could map so perfectly onto the Trump voter it's as if she had a time machine:

> The ideal subject of totalitarian rule is not the convinced Nazi or convinced Communist, but people for whom the distinction between fact and fiction . . . and the distinction between true and false . . . no longer exist.[11]

In the 2020 campaign, Democrats need to plan to combat the effect his lies have had on the media, and on Americans. Trump has conditioned them to a quick-cycle pattern of behavior: He tells an outrageous lie, media condemnation rains down, he repeats the outrageous lie, and he blames lying libtard failing fake news outlet X for daring to call him a liar.

Major news outlets have wrestled mightily with calling the president of the United States a liar. They are complicit in accepting his lies—often delivered personally, late at night from his own cellphone—and in amplifying them, at most times uncritically. Trump, a creature born in the fever-swamp New York tabloid media culture, understands the awesome power of the access journalism addiction. He's not bothering with "John Barron" any longer; now, he's a "senior White House official."

Second, while fact-checking is both meritorious and necessary, it's also almost completely ineffective for Trump voters. You can't and won't move them with facts. The defense of Trump's lies has become a core tribal signaling function inside the hollowed-out husk of the GOP. Of course, elected officials still keep getting away with the Washington game of whispering to reporters, "Well, that's just Trump being Trump. It's not hurting anyone. It's just his style."

No, folks. It's not a style. It's a pathology, and in 2020 the Democratic candidates need to prepare for a picture of America painted by this president, both the fake good and the fake bad. They'll see it as the equivalent of a madman smearing the walls of his padded cell with his own feces, but the framing of the 2020 campaign will look much more like the 1984 campaign than they currently care to admit. Trump will paint the picture as one of unparalleled economic success, and the lies will come down fast and furious.

On the negative side, fear is one of Trump's few weapons, and the GOP and the conservative media apparat have weaponized and monetized fear based on ludicrously overdrawn lies. Expect the 2020 campaign to feature breathless lies about the millions of criminal gang members forming armed caravans to storm the borders. Expect more stories of how immigrants are bringing smallpox, Ebola, and the plague over the border. You'll hear stories about the mythical Antifa army sweeping the nation, Black Panthers outside every voting booth, and the terrifying scourge of godless homosexuals luring preschool children into sex-change surgery. He'll paint the Democrats' technocratic semi-, demi-, hemi-socialism as the second coming of Stalin, with deplorables in the place of kulaks.

He'll lie about the scope and intent of the culture war, because Trump understands how deeply conditioned his base is by Fox, talk radio, and the grievance culture of the right. Trump's framing will be apocalyptic: It's me or sharia law. It's me or the scourge of government death panels. It's me or godless communism (and/or Muslim theocracy) in the dark future.

All the golden oldies are coming back! The war on Christmas.

Kneeling NFL players. Taquerias replacing the local diner. You know, all the *real* threats in the minds of Facebook boomers with Fox News on 24/7.

Rather than disputing the lies, it's crucial to keep up the fact pressure to discredit the liar, and get back to what's real and relevant to the targeted voters in the swing states. All the economic happy-talk in Trump world doesn't fix the devastation Trump's trade war has wrought on Midwest farming communities.

Trump's 2016 win relied on suburban Republicans, many of whom voted against Hillary Clinton rather than for him. In 2020, he'll offer both a tribal and an economic choice to those same voters—that's why we'll hear all the "Look at your 401k!" rah-rah reaching a fever pitch. He'll be working very hard to present a false but compelling case that choosing the Democrat means a quick slide in the markets, the destruction of John and Jane Suburbanite's retirement fund, and a future not in a luxury condo in Del Boca Vista but one of living below a highway overpass, scrounging for roadkill.

No matter where the economy goes in the next year, he'll argue that the tax bill—arguably the biggest legislative action of his presidency—helped most Americans. Democrats must make the case that the Tax Cuts and Jobs Act of 2017 was not a bailout for America but a monster payday for a small number of hedge funds, banks, and tech billionaires. As of this writing, Elizabeth Warren has come closest to working out a solid message on this, but it's not rocket science, and it solidly falls into the category of making the election a referendum on Trump. His hallmark legislative accomplishment was a lie.

America knows by now that he lies, but no one is really prepared for a body of deception so large it's like the meteor that crashed into the Yucatán and killed the dinosaurs, only instead of a Texas-sized rock it's a mass of Trumpian bullshit that will plunge through the atmosphere.

Trump's strategy is the mirror image of what the Democrats' should be; he wants to make this a base-only election about a core package of issues relying on horseshit. He's going to lie both to the American people and about the Democratic candidate, every day.

Democrats still harbor some faint hope that they can shame him into telling the truth, or that the media fact-checkers can do it.

Whoever the nominee for the Democrats is, he or she has a magnificent opportunity to repeat the famous "Where's the beef?" moment in which Democratic candidate Walter Mondale wrecked his competitor Gary Hart. Driving hard on Trump as a liar, a discredited and weak man dependent on a curtain of absurd deceptions to maintain his fragile self-image and political status, can be a striking, viral moment, and the Democratic nominee should be practicing for it, every day.

PART 4

HOW TO LOSE

Donald Trump, as I'll say until I'm blue in the face, cannot win this election.

The Democrats can sure as *hell* lose it.

Once again, my Democratic friends, in the spirit of tough love—and honestly, do I have any other kind?—you have every advantage, and yet how often you blow it. A previous part of this book looked at a lot of the myths you love so deeply, and how those sincere beliefs have left you open to repeated political spankings.

The demographics keep shifting your way, but you keep missing elections that should be layups.

You win the White House only on the backs of fluke, generational candidates who silence or ignore the chattering claques of highly specialized micro-interest groups inside the Democratic machine. You rush forward into obvious traps set by political morons.

You think you sound compassionate, but it often scans as hectoring. You think you sound righteous, but it too often comes across as one long scold from the political correctness commissars. They may sometimes deserve it, but when you lecture the rubes in flyover country, damn are you condescending jerks.

Even now, your singular advantage in the 2020 election is staring you in the face, and yet as a party you seem entirely unable to convert the fact that 60 percent of Americans loathe Donald Trump into a coherent referendum on whether America will be led by him or a sane person.

Trump's approval ratings, overall polling numbers, and the polling in key states point to a position of political peril of the highest order.

The only thing that can save him is you being you.

FLYING BY THE SEAT
OF YOUR PANTS

When I'm not busy writing *New York Times* number-one best-selling books and overthrowing governments, I like to fly. I like to think I'm good at it, a reasonably skilled and safe pilot. There's a lesson from flight training that I need to impart to Democrats.

I started out as a solid pilot in the kind of blue-skies stick-and-rudder Visual Flight Rules piloting we get in Florida much of the year. But the first time I was "under the hood" in instrument flight training I was mostly just irritated. When you train to fly on instruments, the "hood" covers your vision so you can't look outside the cockpit to get your bearings. This simulates flying in fog or bad weather. My flight instructor popped the hood on me and started demanding I fly by instruments alone. No problem. Then he started taking my instruments offline and asking me to tell him if we were in a climb or a dive, a left or right bank. Since I couldn't look outside to check, I learned quickly that you can't rely on your body and senses to guide you. What felt like level flight was a slow spiral down.

When he brought my instruments back online, I could fly perfectly well, even if I couldn't see out of the cockpit.

It was a revelation. The rule of trusting your instruments is there for a reason; in bad weather, reduced visibility, and the dark of night, your senses lie to you, and dangerously so. You think you're in a climb when you're plunging to earth. You think you're turning slowly when you're moments from a spin. Your eyes, sense of balance, and mind are contingent and unreliable. Aviation history is replete with people flying into bad weather, trusting their eyes and senses over their instruments, and ending up in a smoking hole in the ground.

The only way to fly safely and survive in those conditions is to rely on your instruments.

I've explained this rule to candidates before, and I'll tell you now, the only safe flight plan through 2020 is to trust your instruments. Trump's team is counting on you to put your ideological inclinations, emotions, and policy wish-fulfillment fantasies front and center in this election. They're praying you run a campaign based on what the edges of your base demand, and not what a serious, bloodless analytical campaign based on polling, data analysis, and turnout models tells you.

They want you to play for the cheap seats in California, not the tougher targets in Wisconsin, Pennsylvania, Florida, and Michigan. They want you to buy into a read of the political map where the fantasy of a massive, hidden progressive vote is lurking under the surface in the handful of decisive states.

They're desperate for you to tell the truth about what you believe on issues like guns and abortion, because they're watching the numbers on those issues in the swing states. They want you to engage in magical thinking about who is up for grabs in this election, to chase electoral unicorns ("Hey, let's spend money in Texas!"), and to operate on impulse, not intelligence.

They want you to trust Twitter over polling, and Resistance Facebook groups over data analytics.

You don't have to fly blind. The ability of campaigns to turn polling and underlying social-media analytics into actionable political intelligence has been proven. You have the ability to target and segment messaging to a degree of granularity and power that was unobtainable two decades ago, and cutting-edge ten years back. Voters are telling you things every day, and Facebook, Instagram, Google, Snapchat, Comscore, Rentrak, and a hundred other firms can tell you how to weaponize those opinions. But listening and taking action based on those streams of data and information (there is a distinction) takes a willingness to subsume political *desires* for political *practicality*.

When I was doing political ads for a living, I was good at the work of creating and producing those ads, but despite my rep as an amoral madman, the secret was that I built these ads with my pollsters, my researchers, and, as the science developed, my data team. We didn't just whip out spots based on witchcraft or mystic auguries. They were tools, calibrated to move the hearts and minds of voters. They were tested, crafted, and deployed to hit targets we didn't have a right to persuade, but we found ways to do so. Often it meant making spots with a message or ideological polarity that our base didn't love but that the targets did.

In politics, the weather is always foggy. The clouds are always bad and getting worse. Nobody knows nothin'. You're in the cockpit and you can either trust the numbers, technology, and analytics in front of you, or you can fly by the seat of your pants.

One decision results in a win. The other? A smoking hole in the ground and a political funeral.

Fox News Election 2020 Special Alerts

Two Fox reporters are walking through crowds, a rare walk-and-talk live shot.

KIP: I'm Kip Karson, reporting live from the Democratic Convention, where in a surprise move, the president of the United States is parked outside in his presidential limo, "The Beast."

KASSIE: I'm Kassie, but does that really matter? I'm just one of several dozen interchangeable news bots who came from a mid-tier j-school with great hair and big . . . oopsie. *(Giggles.)* Was that my out-loud voice?

KIP: It sure was, Kassie. Folks, we're here in Milwaukee, Wisconsin, for the 2020 Democratic Convention, and well, it looks like we're going to break some news. Kassie, I think that's the president standing up in the sun-roof of his limo. I think he's—what's the word, Kassie?

KASSIE: I think it's heckling, Kip. He's heckling passersby. Mr. President! Kip and Kassie from Fox!

TRUMP: Hillary needs to come out and fight me. *Fight me, she-witch!*

KIP: Mr. President, Mrs. Clinton isn't going to be the nominee. I'm not even sure she's here.

TRUMP: YES SHE IS. She needs to be locked up.

KASSIE: Sir?

TRUMP *(incredulous)*: For murdering Jeffrey Epstein.

(Trump looks down into the limo from the sunroof.)

TRUMP: Bill, can I do a citizen's arrest? Can I?

BILL BARR: Of course, m'lord.

(Trump begins clanking three beer bottles together and starts a singsong chant.)

TRUMP: HILLLAREEEE HILLLAREEEE. Come out to pl-ay-ay. HILLLAREEEE HILLLAREEEE. Come out to pl-ay-ay.

KASSIE: Thank you, Mr. President. This is the kind of leadership that makes a second term inevitable. My producers are telling me we're going to cut away briefly for a special on the upcoming War on Christmas. It may be August, but it's never too soon for atheists to hate America!

PLAYING THE CAMPAIGN, LOSING THE REALITY SHOW

The 2020 campaign is the biggest, most dangerous, most expensive reality-television show of all time, and the only stars are the Democratic nominee and Donald Trump. The stakes are, you know, the fate of the republic and possibly the world. This game is gambling with the lives of 350 million Americans and the future of our country.

Both the Republican and Democratic campaigns will run, well, campaigns. They'll be fought by both sides with all the usual tools: digital and physical organizing, online and broadcast media, press relations, coalitions, and so on. They'll look and feel like campaigns. All of those things matter on some level, but in the end they're not the real battle of 2020.

In this reality show, the host is also a contestant. Even worse, he is a master of the form and understands the audience with a kind of feral cunning few others share.

In this show, policy loses to personality every time. Brain loses to heart, every time. Stunts, joking asides, dumb nicknames, and lowbrow pranks beat substance and gravitas.

Here's how to win this reality show.

BE GREAT ON TELEVISION

Democrats who think this whole battle will be fought and won on social media have another thing coming. This campaign will be waged on television. Social media is necessary but not sufficient for victory in 2020. One of the gifts Roger Ailes gave the GOP was to beat into the heads of three generations of candidates that looking like the winner on television, that great wasteland in which reality is mediated, wasn't the only thing—it was everything. You have to be great on TV.

Media training, speech training, debate training, and authentic presence are all vital. For the love of God, hire the best speechwriters money can buy—it's infinitely worth it—but training is what makes a great television presence. Beto O'Rourke, who is seemingly nine feet tall and consists of one gesticulation after another—almost has it, but somehow he comes across as one Decemberists lyric reference short of parody. The nominee needs to practice, mindful that Trump's natural instinct for the camera and his showmanship have been developed over decades. He is a creature of television. Even those with longtime exposure to the camera need to keep tuning up, and keep practicing. It's a skill like any other.

Being able to post up against Trump visually is central to success. With his height, his absurd hair, his gigantic booty and belly, Trump stamps around the stage like an ogre. You, on the other hand, should look fit, perfectly dressed, and polished as hell. That's what the audience wants and needs.

BIG TV MOMENTS MATTER

Campaigns usually come down to big television moments. (And no, kids, I'm not a Luddite; when I say "television" I'm agnostic on what kind of screen you watch it on.) The camera catches the hangdog Nixon versus the poised Kennedy. Ronald Reagan, prepped and sly, promises not to take advantage of his opponent's youth and inexperience. Mike Dukakis blows a question on whether he'd want someone who raped his wife to face the death penalty. Bill Clinton, feeling the audience's pain, connects with millions.

The Democratic nominee needs to connect with TV audiences on big nights like primary wins, clinching the nomination, and at the convention by framing the race as a choice between flawed good and perfect evil—otherwise, they'll leave Trump to define the next episode of the reality show on his terms. The big moments matter; after all, about 65 percent of the electorate doesn't even start paying attention until the last thirty days of the campaign. When they're watching, the nominee has to deliver.

DEBATES

The most important forum for delivering the big moments is debates. Trump will work his hardest to intimidate, embarrass, and demean the Democratic candidate both before and during the debate. Hey, no pressure, but the whole election will come down to those moments. Let the bully win, and the campaign is over in an instant. Punch the bully, hard in the nose, and it's a whole new ballgame.

Trump's skill in the 2016 GOP debates was simple: They were politicians; he was a performer. They were driven by policy; he was driven by celebrity. They came with jokes written by speechwriters; he came to mercilessly destroy them.

RULES FOR DEBATING TRUMP

Trump will distort, mangle, and mischaracterize any real policy the Democrat brings to the debate floor. So don't bring policy. If Trump is playing to the camera, and you're playing to the *New York Times* opinion page and Woke Twitter, hang it up.

Physicality is an unappreciated element in presidential debates. The debate stage isn't merely an ideological arena. It's also an arena where Americans judge if you look the part and play it well. Anyone who fails in their physical presentation fails the test.

Trump, ever mindful of the staging and television picture that mediate politics for audiences, knows where every camera will be. He knows how to use his size as a visual marker. He quite deliberately stalked around the stage in his debates with Hillary Clinton, hovering behind her, mugging and japing in his apelike way. The Democratic candidate on that stage with Trump needs to be ready for his power moves.

We've seen a few examples of candidates trying to physically intimidate an opponent in the past. In 2000, Vice President Al Gore and Texas governor George W. Bush appeared in their October 17 presidential debate at Washington University in St. Louis. As host Jim Lehrer asked Bush a question, Gore had three inches on W, and tried for a visual power play. He rose from his stool and took four strides toward the governor as Bush was in mid-answer.

The trick flopped. Instead of pulling back, Bush cocked his head, waited for a beat, nodded, and dismissed ManBearPig with a curt nod. I was standing offstage watching the moment, and it was perfect debate-fu, leaving Gore looking awkward and dorky. It was how you play the game when someone else is looming over you onstage, and Trump, with his massive throw weight, lifts, and four inches of hair fluff, comes across as a large presence on the stage. The Democratic candidate needs to be more ready than Hillary was in the 2016 debates.

If he gets too close, touch him. A hand rested on his arm should do it.

Interruptions and asides from Trump will be constant, as they were during the 2016 debates, and since he's less in control of his faculties now, the Democrat needs to be ready to keep talking and not let Trump's jibes take her off-agenda.

TWO ENTER, ONE LEAVES

In 2016 Trump left Republican candidates gasping on the mat after their battles with him. They had an inability to rapidly punch against him, fought him on the wrong grounds, and never showed righteous anger.

Jeb Bush, the most accomplished Florida governor in decades, raised a shitload of money and lost to Trump before the fight even got going. When Jeb would poke at Trump, Trump never blinked; he punched back and kept punching. Jeb would run through one zinger and be left with Trump talking. And talking. And talking.

Marco Rubio, once considered one of the most gifted rhetorical stars in the GOP, made one of the few power moves against Trump in the 2016 race when he punched Trump hard in the mouth with a cutting set of jokes about Trump's nanoscale raccoon-paw hands. Marco's consulting team panicked even though he had finally entered the actual arena where the campaign was being waged: a reality-TV show battle of disses and insults. They freaked out, imagining that the American people were crying out for dignity, stature, and probity when what they clearly rewarded was the knife-fighting, dick-joke politics of Trump. We're a country that loves hair-pulling reality TV.

What was Marco's mistake? He pulled back. He looked at the audience and blushed, ashamed that he was fighting for his own political life. Once he broke, Trump had him, forever.

Trump broke Ted Cruz mentally from the jump. Even when Ted finally got angry, he came across as impotent for not having brought the pain sooner. It was a manhood test, and Cruz failed.

What rule did we learn from this?

When you start hitting Trump, never, ever let up. Never blink, never blush, never pull back. Trump's ego is delicate, his skin is thin. His boasting about his good looks, stamina, physical and sexual prowess, and intellect are of course laughable in the extreme. His sensitivity to having these called out remains a great psychological weapon in the 2020 battle . . . if the opposing candidate is strong enough to keep punching.

Your spouse will hate it. Your consultants will hate it. Your do-gooder friends will hate it. But in the words of my beloved and now-departed grandmother, "If you cut the hog, you better finish the job."

No one in 2016 understood that once you cut the hog, you're committed.

Trump fights dirty. There are no rules. There are no boundaries. You cannot make him feel regret, or shame, or embarrassment.

The only rhetorical tactic that will work on Trump is to hammer his ego and his personal narrative. Call him weak. Call him poor. Call him a failure. Call him fat. Call him impotent. Say he overpays for sex. Pity him for having to lie to make himself feel better. When he rolls into one of his attacks on you, take a beat and tell him he looks tired. Ask if he wants to rest or take a break. Point out that he's sweating like an unrepentant sinner in church.

You already hate this. I get that. Hillary Clinton won on points in the debates of 2016. Trump was a boob during each of the GOP outings. It doesn't matter. The voters were scoring these debates on the Trump Reality Show scale, not some polite speech-and-debate-club scale.

Most of the candidates for president on the Democratic side aren't exactly rough-and-tumble barroom scrappers. I get that too. But whoever ends up as the nominee, you'd best get really tough, really fast when it comes to debating a man with no conscience and no sense of shame.

JUDGE JEANINE PIRRO: Tonight, I'm deeply honored to have a once-in-a-lifetime special guest in the studio with me. I'm joined tonight by Ri Chun-hee. You know her as North Korea's Pink Lady, the Songbird of Pyongyang.

RI *(via translator)*: Thank you, Comrade. I bring fraternal greetings from the Democratic People's Republic of Korea, the one True Korea, the rising sun, the scourge of the imperialist running dog Western degenerates.

PIRRO: For me, you represent what a real journalist looks like.

RI: I believe our audience shares my respect for the brotherly love between your Great Leader and our Great Leader.

PIRRO: Ri, you're so right. Both men are strong . . .

RI: Masculine . . .

PIRRO: . . . Powerful

RI: Athletic . . .

PIRRO: Does Chairman Kim have the same powerful musk President Trump exudes?

RI *(giggles)*

PIRRO *(husky)*: Desired by all women, envied by all men . . .

RI: I have but one regret.

PIRRO: I think it's the same one I have . . .

RI: Yes. Sadly, we are both past the age where we could bear these men many sons, and populate the earth with a race of giants.

PIRRO: Ri, you are welcome here anytime.

RI: May I please take all the food from what you call the "Green Room"?

ASKING THE WRONG
POLLING QUESTIONS

Democrats in 2020 will poll a hundred questions and probe a thousand models, variables, and regression analyses when it comes to determining their pathway against Trump. Yet there's a high likelihood they'll miss the most important set of questions to determine Trump's actual strengths and weaknesses in the field.

Polling contains a known artifact called the "socially desirable response." SDR, in the words of a noted pollster friend with almost forty years in the field, is what leads people "to lie their fucking asses off."

If you ask a polling question like this, "Are you a racist who thinks people with other skin colors are genetically inferior to whites?" you're going to get an affirmative response somewhere around 1 percent. Sadly (and, obviously, in the era of "both sides"), the true percentage who would answer yes if it weren't for SDR is much, much higher.

SDR also works on positive questions: "Do you recycle?" "Do you donate to charity?" "Do you volunteer?" All yield positive responses in the 75 percent range, when the truth falls sadly short on all of those.

In 2020, SDR and its corollary "shy Tory" effect loom large. "Shy Tory" voters were afraid to say they were voting for Margaret Thatcher as prime minister, but vote for her they did. The Labour Party spent years trying to identify and woo them back.

Donald Trump is the ultimate socially undesirable candidate, particularly among soft- and leaning-Republican voters, male independents, and educated women.

There was an iceberg out there in 2016 that Hillary Clinton's pollsters didn't spot, and on Election Night the Democratic campaign ran into that iceberg when shy Trump voters in Pennsylvania, Wisconsin, Ohio, and Michigan put Trump over the top in the Electoral College vote. Shy Trump voters weren't secret Trump fanatics. They were shaky Trump voters who rationalized his candidacy, wincing as he talked of John McCain, pussy grabbing, and a host of other pathologies. They told themselves that judges and tax cuts would be worth it, that the behavior was just an act. They now rationalize his presidency the same way, telling themselves the corruption, criminality, and self-dealing are "just Trump being Trump."

The Trump campaign will message to them—largely via digital advertising—in ways that portray Trump as a regular Republican who is getting things done. They might even wink and nod that Trump is "rough around the edges" or "not a politician" but that he's the only one who could accomplish what those voters want.

There will be a secret polling battle, a midnight set of skirmishes to identify and target those voters. Democrats should hit them in that same invisible digital realm with a greatest hits of Trump's outrages. As much as outright Trump voters are largely intractable, shy Trump voters are in play. But if you ignore them in favor of stoking the progressive base, they're likely to drift back to Trump.

For shy Trump women voters, messages about his history of sexual assault, dalliances with porn stars, and pussy grabbing need another workout. Reminding them that their daughters will grow up in a world defined and shaped by Donald Trump's values is a powerful message. These women voters were part of the swing away from the GOP in 2018, but their importance for 2020—particularly in the suburbs of Philadelphia, Pittsburgh, Detroit, Milwaukee, Tampa, Orlando, Charlotte, and Atlanta—can't be emphasized strongly enough.

Shy Trump voters have a corollary: the shy Dem voters. Democrats must ask themselves the right questions to examine these voters closely. The shy Warren or Biden or Harris or Buttigieg voters, driven from the GOP by Trump and Trumpism, aren't wearing pink pussy-hats and demanding Medicare for All. They're looking for an American who's more normal than the extremes of Trump, but they're not ready to greet Comrade Bernie when he steps off his sealed train from the Finland Station.

These shy Democrats fled the GOP because of Trump's affect and actions, not because of ideology. They ran because they're disgusted by rampant cruelty and Twitter dick-wagging. It's a game of margins, where a few tens of thousands of votes in a few key counties in a few key states decide the election.

As for Never Trump Republicans, Democrats seem as lost as the GOP as to what to do with us. Often, we're seen as dangerous saboteurs, particularly when we tell Democrats—as I'm doing in this book—how to beat the machine we helped build and run. Democrats often fear that asking for the political support of Never Trump Republicans will infect their party with some strain of dangerous moderation. Some Democrats don't want us and are more concerned with relitigating old battles than in winning in 2020.

The Never Trump demo members are, by and large, educated, suburban, more affluent, and more politically engaged. They're accustomed to voting. The outspoken few of us hear from other Republicans who live in terror of being exposed for having left—or never boarded—the Trump train. The right nominee who focuses his or her message as a referendum on Trump can and must win them.

These shy Democrats and Never Trump Republicans aren't going to be easy to poll and identify in some cases, but given the importance of suburban votes in Florida, Michigan, Ohio, Pennsylvania, and Arizona, maybe—just this once—the Democrats should try to find a way to bring them into the fold of the 2020 coalition.

Fox News Election 2020 Special Alerts

SHEP SMITH: Good afternoon. It's one month before Election Day, and the president has had a hell of a day. At a campaign stop in Orlando, Florida, President Trump brought a young woman from the audience onstage and . . . well, there's a term you don't hear much on cable news, but he dry-humped her onstage.

With us is Kevin Lackey, the 31st White House communications director.

Mr. Lackey, thank you for being with us. Today at a campaign rally, the President of the United States grabbed a female audience member and . . .

LACKEY: Shep, this is just more of the liberal fake news your communist network is famous for. The president did no such thing.

SMITH: Mr. Lackey, I'm going to stop you right there. There is live video, from this and other networks . . .

LACKEY: So you admit the conspiracy.

SMITH: . . . and we're going to roll the tape.

(Trump, wild-eyed and gesticulating onstage, pulls a young woman out of the crowd. She's blonde, gorgeous, and thin. Her MAGA shirt is clinging to her, and Trump leers. After a long whisper in her ear, he paws at her. With an arm wrapped around her waist, he drags her to the podium.)

TRUMP: "You're done, Melania. I have found my next wife."

(The President of the United States simulates a sex act with the woman.)

LACKEY: That's fake, Shep. That video is obviously fake. That's not him.

SHEP: No, Kevin, it's him.

LACKEY: Fake News. Fake, fake, fakety fake.

SHEP: Mr. Lackey, my producers are telling me you're taking my job now and I'm to leave the building. *(Tearing off his IFB)*: This is Shep Smith, signing off. Fuck this noise. You can't fire me. I quit.

MAGICAL THINKING

I have never met a group of people more inclined to magical think-ing than Democratic operatives and politicians. If I had one skill in politics apart from my ability to recite huge blocks of Elizabethan poetry and rap lyrics, it's that I tried to never fall in love with a speech, an ad, or a message or tactic for too long. I always did my best to fol-low the numbers, not just the art.

Magical thinking in campaigns is deadly. It's dumb. It's all too common. The coming election is a time to focus on the real world, and it's not a pretty picture. Donald Trump takes advantage of human weakness like few other people in the world. He's predatory, amoral, and a dark, shitty monster of a person. This chapter is meant to help you identify and face your weaknesses, and to cauterize your soul sufficiently so he doesn't wreck your campaign.

DEPENDING ON DECENCY

You want to believe this is a just and good world. You want to believe that good guys win, liars never prosper, and righteousness is its own reward. You want to believe you can run a campaign and a nation along principles that reflect the better angels of our nature, and not our most base desires.

Are you new here? This is a fallen world, and decency is dead.

I've said this before, but if your campaign ever for one moment believes it can shame Donald Trump over an action, a statement, a tweet, or a policy, quit now. You cannot. Decency and gentlemen's agreements in campaigns aren't unknown—hell, I'm good friends with Democratic consultants where our candidates tried to politically slaughter one another—but they do not exist in Trump's world or this era.

You will never get the MAGA tribe to back down, apologize, or go forth and sin no more. Their cult and culture is performative dickishness, of never-back-down fuck-youism. Trolling triumphs over argument, and shitfits are their version of a reasoned discourse. This will increase in pitch as the campaign is engaged.

Everything they say to you, back channel or publicly, is a lie. Every second of weakness or indecision will be exploited. Every assumption is a trap. When you're across the table from Brad Parscale or Jared Kushner or Matt Schlapp or whoever they delegate to deal with the Democratic campaign, realize that evil can wear a nice suit and have a firm handshake. They'll wink at you to signal they too understand that Trump is crazy, but we're all just professionals, amirite?

They're not. Trump surrogates, spokesmen, and staffers aren't punished for lying, for racism, or for whatever flavor of MAGA scumbag behavior they display. They're not punished for stealing from the campaign, as long as the Trumps get a cut. They're not moral, or honest, or accountable. Think of the worst things you could do in a campaign. Ponder criminality, incompetence, assault, harassment, or using the fruits of hostile foreign powers to win.

Those are part of the incentive structure for working for Team Trump.

I'm not saying you need to emulate them. I'm just warning you that their campaign is life-or-death, and they'll act accordingly. You are not dealing with your father's Republicans. You are not dealing with rational actors. They are in service to an utterly amoral man, and by both inclination and necessity they will mirror his behaviors.

DON'T BELIEVE NATIONAL POLLS

It's not simply that they're often wrong. It's that they make you focus on doing the wrong thing. The national polling pretty closely reflected the results of the 2016 race: Hillary Clinton was predicted to win the popular vote, and did.

That wasn't the ballgame, though, was it? I will continue to beat this message into you until understanding dawns: You need to build your models, your expectations, and your strategy around a basket of states where you will win the Electoral College vote. National polls give you false confidence. They give you the sense that a single, national message or strategy works when you're not really running a national campaign. You're running fifteen state campaigns.

Trump's narrow skate past Hillary in the handful of Electoral College states wasn't even entirely unexpected in some quarters. I'm told Clinton's campaign watched the Wisconsin numbers in their own trackers—not from the pollster, but from their data folks—plummet in the closing week. So they took swift action—deploying the candidate, ad money, and a tidal wave of digital ads and phone banks into Wisconsin, racing thousands of volunteers into the state for a final push to victory . . . Oh. Wait. That's on the Earth 2 timeline where her campaign wasn't complacent and insular.

They did nothing. They sat around planning where they would sit on Inauguration Day.

Do not make the same mistake of taking comfort in national polls. Have your numbers nerds build whatever dashboard for your data operation keeps you hungry, aggressive, and paranoid in the target states. Watch it like a hawk. Prepare to die broke; spend whatever you need to spend to move those numbers. Fuck sleep. The candidate can sleep when she's dead.

National polls are useful. They are fun. They can be illustrative as hell, and they're great for understanding sweeping typologies and trends. They tell us Americans mostly dislike Trump, and they do. They tell us Americans think he's a lying liar who lies, and they do. They tell us his job performance outside the economy is considered, at best, mediocre. They tell us a lot of the things you love are popular.

The polls don't tell us what the issue trade-offs are in the key states. They're not a solid window into the demographics you'll be targeting. They don't tell us what the hot buttons are that could take an issue that's popular nationally—and with your activists—and turn it into a millstone around your neck. Get into the states with polling and data collection, spend the money—and it's going to be spendy—and rely on that, not big feels from big polls.

BANK SHOTS DON'T WORK

One of the most absurd magical thinking behaviors in politics is the belief in the bank shot. It may work in pool, but it doesn't in politics. Bank shots are ideas that depend on the electorate to think through complex policy options . . . hell, any policy options tend to result in eyes glazing over and a quick scroll through their text messages.

The voters don't think through tactical voting options or complex policy alternatives; they don't understand the implications of this or that policy proposal. For them, it's about love versus hate, hope versus fear, good versus evil.

That bank-shot idea of "We'll do A and then Trump will do B and we'll do C and then we win!" is the Underpants Gnome theory of politics. It doesn't work. What works is a move from A to B, not A to Q to G to T to X to B.

In 2008, desperate to reset a flailing campaign and find some way, any way, to interrupt the narrative that Barack Obama was running away with the election, John McCain suspended his campaign. Hit the brakes. Full stop. The idea seemed to be that McCain's willingness to put the country and the raging financial crisis first by returning to Washington would send a signal that the senator was a serious leader for a serious crisis. It was a bank-shot play—high stakes, high risk, high reward.

He stopped making a case either for himself or against Obama, and hoped Americans would take the time to watch, learn, and react to his leadership in the crisis. His numbers dropped.

Bank shots don't work. Referendum on Trump. Electoral College states. End of sermon. (Who am I kidding? I'm going to keep on the Electoral College thing until you hunt me down with dogs.)

THE BASE IS ENOUGH

Bless your hearts. No. No, it isn't. It's never enough in any national contest. This contest is going to be waged in places where the base is really short of enough. This is why I will continue to lecture you on not scaring the shit out of Republican squish voters. There are a lot of them in the Florida, Wisconsin, Michigan, Ohio, Arizona, and Pennsylvania ring suburbs who voted Democratic in 2018 because the Democrats ran center-left candidates for Congress. I know you want to fire up the prog warriors, but they're already with you. Obama won suburban votes from independents and soft Republicans because he wasn't a firebrand; he was a technocrat. He wasn't ideologically hot; he was cool to a fault, reasonable, a TED Talk in human form.

Base plus. Say it with me: Base. Plus.

DO NOT EXPECT MIRACLES

Donald Trump has the devil's own luck when it comes to getting out of things that would have doomed any other candidate or elected official. I've been as guilty as anyone of believing that some issue or outrage would finally destroy Trump. Because I believe we are being tortured by the cruel and capricious gods of politics, he slithers away from crisis after crisis, never tested fully, never held to account, and always ready to detonate a wave of more news to escape the problem of the moment.

People hoped insulting John McCain would derail him.

They hoped Iowa or New Hampshire or Florida would derail him.

People hoped that a floor fight at the convention would derail his nomination.

They hoped pussy grabbing would derail him.

Then they hoped the Electoral College wouldn't vote for him.

Then they toyed with the idea of removing him through the Twenty-Fifth Amendment.

Or that impeachment would be a thing even with Mitch McConnell running the Senate.

Some hoped that the Mueller Report would lead to his removal from office.

Some thought Jeffrey Epstein would reveal Trump's penchant for teen girls.

Some believed that, facing terrible legal trouble, Trump might simply resign or, at the very least, not run for reelection.

We do not live in a world of miracles.

I fully confess that I let myself get carried away with bank-shot scenarios of "If x then y then profit" as Trump shit the bed over and over in 2016. That was before I realized that Trump shitting the bed had a market with enough Americans to win. Sure, it's a niche product, but it's a product nonetheless. Obviously, the whole shitting-the-bed brand has continued in the White House. He's continued this pattern in office, engaging in a portfolio of stupid, shameful, backward dumbfuckery, but his dumbfuckery is not entirely sufficient to defeat him.

This election is a test of Trump's opponents to exist in the real world of actual politics, not the hope-as-strategy bubble. It's why the messaging and strategies against Trump have to be grounded, smart, and simple.

It's why the campaigns against him—the Democratic, Republican, independent, and citizen efforts against him—must be effective, accountable, and professional. Inchoate anger isn't a strategy, even though he deserves every iota of fury we can muster. Every decision needs to be grounded in data, targeting, and return on political investment. Democrats won in 2008 by using this exact model and walked away from it in 2016.

Outside of the spectacle of Trump's 2020 rallies and deliberate provocations, serious, professional, and dangerous people are building a massive, sophisticated, well-funded campaign from hell. Democrats who think hatred of Trump alone can compensate for building the greatest campaign effort in the world are accomplices in Trump's reelection. GOP guys like me beat Democrats pretty frequently because of the simple, nuts-and-bolts operational things, not just message mojo.

If you stop believing in miracles, your campaigns and your lives will be better off. There is no substitute for organization, planning, discipline, data, metrics, and accountability. In campaign after campaign, the grinding power of those dull things isn't cinematic; it's not the genius guru, the insightful pollster, or the witty, dissolute ad man (hey, that's me!) who's the real star. It's the grinding organizers who get volunteers to make the calls, send the texts, knock on the doors, and do the shit work.

Those folks work outside the Twitter bubble or the N.Y.-D.C. horse-race media coverage club. They work in shitty, temporary offices in shitty, temporary strip malls. They're the last mile in the campaign, and likely the only real-life contact a voter will ever have with the national election.

Teaching them that this election won't be easy, and that no one is going to hand them Donald Trump's head on a platter, is vital. The campaign rule of God helps those who help themselves proves out time and again, and this will be no different.

Fox News Election 2020 Special Alerts

RANDOM BLONDE GIRL: Mr. President, welcome back to *Fox and Friends*! It's such an honor to have you here for the 418th time! With three weeks to go before the election, how are you feeling?

TRUMP *(call-in)*: Well, I'm feeling great. Since the Democrat candidate wants open borders, Satanic child sacrifices, mandatory sex-change surgery, sharia law, and they're going to bring back Zima, I feel confident we're going to win bigly. They also want to take away your doctor and replace them with trained raccoons.

STEVE DOOCY *(chuckles)*: Now, Mr. President. We've seen some polls from the swing states like Michigan, Florida, and Pennsylvania that show you're not doing as well as we—I mean, you—had hoped.

TRUMP: Well, you and your failing network are poopy, Steve. Poopy doo doo liars.

(The hosts share an uncomfortable glance. Trump seems . . . off.)

TRUMP: Here's the real news not your fake news, Steve. I'm winning in Pennsylvania, bigly. The last poll had me (papers shuffle in background) at 118 percent to 6 percent against the Democrat. The numbers are even bigger in Florida, Ohio, Michigan, and Ivanka. The people who took those polls will be arrested.

BRIAN KILMEADE: Ivanka, sir?

TRUMP: Yes. Since I bought Greenland, we needed to do the right branding for the newest state, so I've used my executive power to name it Ivanka. She has 37 electoral votes, which many people are telling me is only fair.

RANDOM BLONDE GIRL: Ivanka is a beautiful state. I went to camp there.

DOOCY: Well, that about wraps up all the time . . .

TRUMP: Oh, no you don't, Steve. I'll call Roger Ailes about you.

DOOCY: Sir . . . uh . . . Roger is . . .

TRUMP: Try me. Now, let's get on with the second hour.

THE CULTURE WAR: WHERE DEMOCRATS GO TO DIE

Trump's campaign team desperately, passionately wants 2020 to be about socialism, abortion, gun control, left-wing anti-Semitism, gender pronouns, the news media, and identity politics. It's their safe space, and Democrats who get lured into playing the Social Justice Olympics of Political Correctness are going to lose forty-plus states.

The 2020 election is a once-in-a-lifetime chance to break bad habits, rebrand the party, and win seats that looked off-limits before Donald Trump. The Democrats won forty-two seats in 2018 in large measure because they stayed out of the culture-war quicksand.

Bill Clinton's 1992 presidential race is the perfect example of this winning approach. Clinton understood that the Ted Kennedy flavor of Democratic politics was hopeless as an electoral strategy, so he wisely became a champion of both job creation and deregulation. Even more wisely, he adopted a line on abortion that defused the cultural potency of it with a large fraction of the Republican base. The line was simple, brilliant, and devastatingly effective: "I want abortion to be safe, legal, and rare."

Compare that to the flailing, blazing political stupidity of Virginia governor Ralph Northam and other Democrats swinging for the fences to defend abortion in the last moments of pregnancy. Of course Trump turns that into vivid tales of doctors killing newborns. Why?

Because you let him. Because you are so determined to never, ever let any question about the morality of the pro-choice stance get in the way of ideological purity. Because today, "safe, legal, and rare" is too far to the right for you.

I'm not trying to change your minds on the moral question of abortion in the last trimester, but I am trying to tell you that the vast majority of Americans disagree with you, and that there are political consequences. Get this number in your head: 13 percent. That's the percentage of Americans who think abortion in the third trimester should be legal. Legal, not acceptable.

Sixty percent think it should be legal in the first trimester, and 28 percent in the second.[1] This is part of America's uneasy truce on a painful issue; the nation is split down the middle on abortion, with equal numbers saying they're pro-life versus pro-choice. (And please, don't quibble over the terms. No matter how you cast it in the surveys, the results end up in the same band of 50-50 percent.)

Donald Trump's greatest culture-war victory will be the Democratic nominee on camera making excuses for something only 13 percent of Americans approve of. Expect Trump to talk about late-term abortion. This will be an electoral tentpole for his messaging. He understands that a solid evangelical base is mandatory for reelection, so more tweets like this one won't surprise anyone: "Democrats are becoming the Party of late-term abortion, high taxes, Open Borders and Crime!"[2]

Because it's Trump, you should know that he'll cast it in the most vivid, dishonest light possible, just as he did at a rally in Green Bay, Wisconsin, on April 26, 2019: "The baby is born. The mother meets with the doctor. They take care of the baby. They wrap the baby beautifully. And then the doctor and the mother determine whether or not they will execute the baby."

Execute the baby. I am not shocked that he said it; Northam made it easy for him by conducting a radio interview that sounded more like ideological-purity-check idiocy. Trump has a keen appreciation for the things that rev up his base, and this was a slow pitch over the plate.

Would it kill you to talk about third-trimester abortions in a better framing? Even in the third trimester, a majority approves when the "Bush rule" conditions apply: the life of the mother, rape, or incest. Would it kill you to say, "For women whose pregnancies are in the third trimester, outside those rare and narrow conditions, we hope they'll also at least consider adoption, and we should give them the help they need to do so"? Generations of pollsters have studied this question, and try as the pro-choice purists like, there's still a stubbornly pro-life element of the population, and it's not all old white dudes.

I know you're mad reading this. Good. Because the lesson is about to get even more pointed.

You know those swing states Trump stole from you? Ohio. Michigan. Wisconsin. Florida. Pennsylvania. Remember those? The pro-life movement in each of those states is organized, and relies on their large Catholic and evangelical populations. Oh, you know who else isn't as far to the left on abortion as you might think? Hispanics. And African Americans.

Trump may be wildly exaggerating on abortion, but those voters are listening, and Democrats ignore them at their peril.

Fox News Election 2020 Special Alerts

LAURA INGRAHAM: It's a week to go before the election, and I'm joined by two very special guests. Tonight, the lovely Ann Coulter is with us, and on Take Your Fascist to Work Day, she's brought along her youthful ward Tammy Laurent.

LAHREN: It's Tomi.

INGRAHAM: Right. Tumor. My apologies.

Now, ladies, with a week to go, can you tell me how you feel about this campaign? Is it looking good for the only president who ever promised to maintain the ethnic purity of our gene pool?

COULTER: Honestly, Frau Laura, it's not. Trump should have followed my plan for slaughtering and butchering immigrants for food. Mexican: the other dark meat.

INGRAHAM *(nervous laugh)*: Well, Ann, that sure is an interesting metaphor but . . .

COULTER: It's not a metaphor.

INGRAHAM: Well, I mean . . .

COULTER: I really do think the only way to stop the browning of America is to eat illegals. Trump cucked out on the wall, so it's the only logical choice.

LAHREN: Like, um, like, am I supposed to, like, be, like, mad now?

(Glares at Ingraham, is directed to stare directly into camera)

INGRAHAM: Though I suppose if President Trump won't build the wall in his second or third term, we'll have to start eating the caravans. Would you try immigrant meat, Ann?

COULTER: Well, hypothetically, but I haven't eaten solid food since 2011. My diet is Marlboro Reds and diet pills washed down with the tears of immigrant children. I had a gummy bear at Christmas.

LAHREN: Can we talk about my athleisure clothing line now?

REVIVING THE CLINTONS

He was a giant astride the political landscape for a generation. A once-in-a-lifetime, Electoral College lock-picking genius of politics, policy, and human connection. She was his brilliant, put-upon wife and a political force in her own right.

For all that, it's time to put Bill and Hillary into a cryo-chamber for the 2020 election. No more tweeting. No more speeches. No convention role. I know some Hillary fans and staffers will look at this recommendation with a bit of a scowl, but hear me out.

For as much as Republicans disliked Barack Obama, his natural poise and steadiness—almost to a fault—meant even his harshest critics were often disarmed. Not so with Hillary. The 2016 election was in large measure a referendum on Her. In Hillary, Republicans had a villain who'd checked every damn box for decades, and a media apparatus to reinforce it, every damn day. It doesn't matter if it was fair. It matters that it was real.

Why on earth would you give Donald Trump a chance to make the 2020 election about Her again? Why on earth would you let him turn this race into Crooked Hillary Part Deux? Jesus, people . . . do I have to do all of this for you?

No more tweeting. No more speeches. No convention role.

This election must be a referendum on Donald Trump.

If I'm a Trump "strategist" (it's hard to call them that, since for most of them "strategy" is standing in front of a TV camera saying things like "Donald Trump did not shit the bed on Issue X, and if he did shit the bed, it was the most amazing bed-shitting in history"), I want nothing more than to see Hillary Clinton's mug on TV. It's a callback for the Trump base to the person they hate more than Hitler. Hell, in this current iteration of the GOP, some Trump fans (and Steve King) are muttering into their anime waifu pillows, "What's wrong with Hitler, cuck? Hitler did nothing wrong compared to Hillary."

For God's sake, follow where the numbers lead you: Barack and Michelle Obama need camera time at the Democratic Convention, not Hillary Clinton. Keep her away from 2020, but should you win, park her on the podium on Inauguration Day in Trump's sight line. He'll know she got the game, at long last, and had a hand in his demise.

Fox News Election 2020 Special Alerts

TUCKER CARLSON: With less than a week to go before the most important election in history, I have a vital message for America. If you're a white-leaning . . . pardon me . . . right-leaning voter who hasn't gone to the polls, I encourage you to gather your Klan . . . if you know what I mean . . . and get them out to the polls tomorrow. The Fuh . . . President needs you to help make America white . . . er, great again. Fox has had reports today of brown people voting early around the country. I don't know if they're black, or Hispanish, or some other race. I don't see color . . . We'll be right back after a word from our sponsor.

(90 seconds of Fox show promos run back-to-back.)

TUCKER: This election has seen the hateful brown horde who have washed up on our shores since 1619 refuse to acknowledge the good Donald Trump has done for them. The man who lives in the Big House . . . I mean, the White House . . . is a master. Some of these ingrates have even refused to stand in the colored lines at their polling stations, to take their literacy tests, or to pay the required poll tax. Is that the America you want? *(wild-eyed)* Is it? A taco truck on every corner?

If we fail to stand by President Trump now . . . now of all times . . . we're doomed to a future of miscegenation, uppitiness, and sassy back-talk from the help.

As an American and a multimillionaire heir to a frozen-food company that sells processed fish as prole chow, I vow to you, this will not stand.

Thanks for tuning in tonight. Catch my new column at *The Daily Stormer* and my one-man show at the German American Bund Hall in Babylon, Long Island.

THE DANGER OF
DEMOCRATIC TRUMPS

This election has two stars. Only two. Trump and the Democratic nominee.

One of the meaningful dangers of the Ambition Cohort in the Democratic Party comes from people who aren't in the 2020 race or who will have lost the primary. Many will sit on the sidelines, cynically convinced Donald Trump will inevitably win and that their time is coming in the 2024 cycle. Some of them will try to sandbag the nominee for not fitting their exact ideological test set.

For the right, Alexandria Ocasio-Cortez is straight from college-dorm-Marxist central casting. She combines incandescent social-media skills and a patent hunger for attention with a lack of policy credibility. Sorry guys, I'm calling balls and strikes here. Every moment she does anything other than be a surrogate for the prog base, Trump is winning. Her polling numbers outside the Democratic base are well in the negative range. But she can, and should, be useful playing the role of progressive rah-rah with groups who question the nominee's far-left bona fides. The GOP and Fox have elevated her because they are masters at creating a villain, and Trump's instinct to play against her is part of his feral genius with his base voters.

Ilhan Omar has given Donald Trump a gift-wrapped package. She's so fucking tone-deaf she can't understand that her flirtations with anti-Semitic tropes and themes are one step short of a Pepe meme; she lets Trump off the hook by projecting the anti-Semitism of his alt-right fan club back on them.

The self-styled Squad of progressive freshmen who spent the early summer of 2019 taking Nancy Pelosi off-message and off-agenda and thus depriving the Democrats of messaging opportunities against Donald Trump were elevated by Trump's attacks on them. He's a crafty animal, and he knows that four women of color who aren't pure 'Mericans like the MAGA base are a fantastic foil.

The ambitious Squad are riding the Trump attacks to more prominence. They're also buying the eventual nominee no end of trouble. Expect the Democratic presidential candidate to have Pony-Tail Guevara and the others tied around his or her neck and to have to continually play defense on socialism and anti-Semitism when they could be hammering Donald Trump. Presidential politics is a team sport.

We've talked previously about Bernie and his proven pattern of wrecking the party when he doesn't get his way, but some of the other candidates may be so cynical as to hope for a Trump victory on some level to clear their path for 2024. The party, the nominee, and the donor class need to keep folks like Beto, Booker, and Buttigieg (it sounds like a great law firm—think about it, boys) in the game and on the team.

Fox News Election 2020 Special Alerts

HANNITY: It's Election Night and I'm Sean Hannity, bringing you live Fox coverage of the vote. Tonight, the deep state, Jim Comey, and the cabal of Satanists decided to end the reign of our God-Emperor President who has led America into an era of glorious prosperity and stability. Our nation and civilization will now plunge into an epoch of darkness and despair.

(Hannity is visibly weeping now.)

Why, Mr. and Mrs. America, did you betray Donald Trump, this paragon of leadership, this tall, handsome—so, so handsome—man of compassion, grace, and poise? *Why?* You elected a ravenous, deadly Antifa sleeper agent eager to burn our nation to the ground.

PRODUCER *(off-camera)*: Wrap, Sean.

HANNITY *(wild-eyed)*: You wrap, you lefty sonofabitch. I'm staying on the air live until Donald Trump is named president for life or my bladder fails.

PRODUCER: Sean, we need to go to break, and you're saying that live.

HANNITY *(begins removing his jacket and shirt)*: Donald Trump isn't our best president. He's our only president. There was no America before Trump and there will be none after. Don't you people see? Can't you see his aura?

PRODUCER *(off-camera)*: Sean, what the fuck?

(At this, Hannity leaps onto the desk, peeling away his tie, shirt, and Spanx girdle. Moments later, the Fox feed cuts to footage of a waterskiing squirrel, but for a brief, indelible moment America saw that a florid Sean Hannity's jiggling, barrel-like torso was covered from neckline to waist with a tattoo of Hannity and Trump in a passionate embrace.)

HANNITY: There is a place for all of us on the Trump comet! Join us and live forever!

(Broadcast ends.)

TAKING THE
INFRASTRUCTURE WEEK BAIT

This chapter is for you, Nancy.

The rules, mores, and traditions of the ancient regime of Washington are a smoking hole where Donald Trump's presidency landed, but Democrats in Congress still persist in a set of beloved traditions that are the political equivalent of standing outside a monkey cage at the zoo. Unless your objective is to be splattered with monkey feces (hey, I'm not judging your life), you're going to get the inevitable, shitty result every time.

Nancy Pelosi keeps repeating variations on a remark that sounds like it was expelled from the bowels of some interminable focus group: "The American people sent us here to do X," and for X insert healthcare, infrastructure, education, or any other pet issue.

No, they didn't, Madame Speaker. The election of 2018 was about one thing, just as the election of 2020 is about one thing.

Donald Trump.

The midterms were a bloody, raging, furious burst of energy and anger to deprive Donald Trump of control of the House of Representatives. The era when people think of their elected leaders as tribunes for good policy is over. This is a brutal, Darwinian struggle.

Every time Nancy drags the hapless Chuck Schumer to the White House and pretends it's happy-family time, they're giving Trump an edge. They're helping to normalize the abnormal and giving Trump leverage to push back against the oversight and investigations the American people elected forty-one new Democrats to conduct.

Besides, my Democratic friends, by now you should know that in addition to Donald Trump . . . what's the word . . . oh, yes . . . fucking you on every policy question, Mitch McConnell is going to get his turn at bat to humiliate you, either before or after you sit in the Oval Office with Trump. Democrats consistently underestimate just how good McConnell is at his job, and how much he has riding on Democrats getting trapped in transactional moments that always end the same way.

I know, you're thinking, "That unassuming, soft little man with the turtle face doesn't look the part of a blood-soaked political killer." That's part of his power; Democrats spent decades missing the fact, in legislative fights large and small, that Mitch was the Patrick Bateman of the Senate, ready to party with his fire axe.

If Mitch McConnell has a polar opposite for courage, competence, and ice water for blood, it's Chuck Schumer. He's a proxy for the weakness of the Senate Democratic caucus, and it's because he's a transactional liberal of the New York School. "Fuck you, let's make a deal" may be fine with rational actors, but I think we understand by now that Donald Trump is a hundred miles from rational.

Democrats go to the White House, Trump throws a tantrum and sends out a batch of shit-talking tweets, and we end up with neither legislative action nor any improvement in President Oppositional Defiant Disorder's behavior. While Pelosi irritates and baffles Trump, Schumer believes in so very little that even though he's known Trump for thirty years, he still seems inclined to fall for the con.

If Nancy Pelosi and Chuck Schumer trot down to the White House one more time to make a deal with Trump over an infrastructure plan or anything other than his constitutional surrender of office, they should be slapped. For anything short of a national military emergency, stop playing nice with the monster.

EXTERNALITIES ARE A BITCH

No battle plan survives contact with the enemy. Everyone has a plan until they get punched in the face. Your hidden porn folder is labeled "Taxes." She'll never guess the PIN code to your phone. No one expects the Spanish Inquisition.

Welcome to the world of the October surprise, 2020 edition. I've been in politics for something like 1,500 years now and I've seen a few October surprises in my day. Hell, I've caused a couple October surprises in my time, and I honor the form.

There are two kinds of October surprise. This election will add a third type for our mortification and dismay. The first kind is, well, engineered by assholes like my evil opposition-research minions and me. (Shout-outs to G, J, D, and M. Y'all know who you are.) They are legitimate, though stinky, attacks. They're the hits on the opposition candidate's voting record, campaign finance, friends and allies, personal life, business dealings, and taste in clothes from the 1980s. Both sides play it, and play it hard. The long-fostered relationships with reporters on the campaign trail come into play with a fake-frenzied call or email, "You won't believe this shit!"

The second kind of October surprise is the external event: the sweeping crisis, international incident, or financial meltdown that no one plans for when they're doing their calendar of the campaign's end. The financial crisis of September 2008 was a shock that sent McCain's effort into a stall. In 2012, Mitt Romney couldn't have planned on Hurricane Sandy giving Barack Obama a chance to play the Serious Leader in a Time of Crisis. (Or Chris Christie's photogenic, viral bro-hug of Obama.)

October surprises generally influence folks making up their minds late in the game. And, by and large, voters traditionally are not that highly engaged in the minutiae of campaigns until the closing weeks of October, if then. (Lower-propensity voters don't pay attention until the final days of the effort.) These surprises are a final, gift-wrapped opposition-research hit to bloody the water and set the mood before people march into the booth and dimple their chad. These days, as early and absentee voting rise in popularity, campaigns should plan for a number of stories in the closing weeks of the campaign.

Are you ready for the October surprises this time around? Hillary Clinton most certainly wasn't. There's no doubt that FBI director James Comey's October 28, 2016, release of a letter announcing the FBI was reopening the investigation of Clinton's use of a private email server drove her White House bid into a ditch. It didn't matter if the story was turned, flipped, distorted, or misinterpreted; by the time Comey walked it back with an awkward retcon, the damage was done. This October surprise was a classic of the genre.

The Trump campaign—which, it is rumored, had been given a steady drip of intel on this matter by the New York Field Office—reacted as if they knew it was coming. They were so ready to exploit the opening that it seemed dissonant with their usual level of incompetence and dumbfuckery.

After weeks of blasting Comey, Trump turned on a dime, saying, "I have great respect for the fact that the FBI and the DOJ are now willing to have the courage to right the horrible mistake that they made."[3] (That respect wouldn't last, but it showed how Trump's feral media brain understood the opening.) A gloating Kellyanne Conway tweeted, "A great day in our campaign just got even better. FBI reviewing new emails in Clinton probe."[4]

The Clinton campaign's reaction was a kind of bemused "What fresh hell is this?"

They could not process the power this externality would exert. It meaningfully shifted the discourse and allowed the Trump (and Russia's, but I repeat myself) efforts to amplify the "Hillary is corrupt" message they'd been blasting into (wait for it) targeted Electoral College states.

I've drilled down on this story for you for a reason: If you think your candidate could never face something absurd and manufactured in the last two weeks of October 2020, think again. You are about to be enrolled in the 2020 master class in engineered crises for the Democratic nominee. Expect to see both the Trump campaign and the government engage in political dirty tricks. Nixon was a piker.

In 2018 we saw repeated attempts by the Trump White House and their allies at Fox News and elsewhere to turn the alleged "caravans" of deadly migrants streaming north into a political weapon in the closing days of the election.[5] The president tweeted: "We are a great Sovereign Nation. We have Strong Borders and will never accept people coming into our Country illegally!"[6] But caravan fearmongering was ultimately a flop; the caravan's members were more tattered, exhausted women and children than hardened, bloodthirsty, rapey MS-13/ISIS.

Just because it didn't work as well politically as the administration expected on Election Day 2018 doesn't mean you won't see the caravan and its parallels trotted out in the hit parade to come. Even though a series of Trump-inspired killers have swept America, there's nothing Trump loves more than to double down on being a shit-tier human, so this season's caravans will be bigger, more threatening, and more imminent than ever.

Hell, in the summer of 2019 the Russo–Right Wing alliance was trying to sell a story that Ebola-infected Congolese migrants were trying to sneak across the southern border to take our jobs and infect us with a deadly hemorrhagic fever. Bonus!

As with damn-near everything, Trump's dominant—some could argue only—style as president is creating a crisis, declaring an emergency, blowing things up, then either dropping the subject or pretending it never happened. "Aren't you happy I didn't nuke Omaha? Because I could have and they deserved it."

With traditional October surprises and last-minute hits, the attacks generally have something to do with a candidate's record. It may be shocking, but not insane. These hits are grounded somewhere in reality. A conflict of interest. A DUI. An affair. Because the Fabulist in Chief has been a strong influence on his campaign staff, surrogates, and advisors, expect the last-minute accusations about the Democratic nominee to blow your damn mind.

Remember, Trump campaign surrogates like Ratfucker in Chief Roger Stone, bloated conspiracy jihadi Alex Jones, wee alt-right strategist Jack Posobiec, and flounder-eyed lunatic Mike Cernovich were aggressively pushing stories that no sane person would touch with a fifty-foot sterilized pole. The unsubtle line between the Trump campaign and this collection of douchebags was former caddy but now Twitter factotum for the president Dan Scavino. They also—largely through Steve Bannon and former alt-right boy wonder and now professional Internet beggar Milo Yiannopoulos—had a strong communications channel to the dregs of the white-supremacist, neo-Nazi, and neo-fascist elements of Trump's base. Bannon also loved having these alt-right ass-kissers serve as a feeder element for stories that were too over-the-edge for Breitbart. (I know, let that sink in.)

This cavalcade of malicious dipshits worked tirelessly and successfully to market outright lies, asserting that the murder of Democratic National Committee staffer Seth Rich was ordered by Hillary Clinton's campaign as revenge for the WikiLeaks release of her emails. They jumped in feet-first with the ludicrous Comet Ping Pong/Pizzagate smear, which came damn close to costing innocent lives.

This was all when they weren't too busy pushing the stories that Hillary Clinton was suffering from Parkinson's, gout, heart failure, stroke-related vision loss, and rickets. The thin veil between reality and fantasy has been pierced for most of Trump's voters; they've been conditioned to buy into stories because the Gresham's Law of douchey Trump-right media is that bad coverage always drives out good, and insane coverage always drives out sane.

The system for disseminating Trump's conspiracy horseshit is built out now, a mighty machine well-practiced at laundering conspiracy nonsense into the eyeballs of 90 million Fox viewers every day and then shoving it down the gagging throats of mainstream viewers.

Sure, whatever crazy conspiracy that infects the political bloodstream this time was first posted on QanewsMAGASiloEagleVision .ru, but then it showed up on Gateway Pundit, Breitbart, and Fox. Rush Limbaugh said he couldn't confirm it, yet. Sean Hannity is just asking questions, y'all. By the end of every cycle, even *The New York Times* is covering the story about the story. "As conspiracy rumors swirl on Biden's cannibalism, Washington waits." This is part of the social engineering of the extremes and propagandists; they know the story's very absurdity makes it newsworthy, driving more coverage, more clicks, and more repetitions of the initial lie.

Expect the very worst from these jokers—and the worst will border on unimaginable. They'll bet big, and late in the game. The story will tweak all the hot buttons the audience loves: criminality by arrogant elites, conspiracy, sex, and power. This is the kind of tabloid-meets-QAnon conspiracy fuel that reminds the incoherent Trump voter that some amorphous "they" are trying to stop the Golden One. (For "they" insert the Illuminati, the Bilderbergers, the Jews, the Muslims, the gays, the lizard people, Hillary and Huma's coven, the Gnomes of Zurich, the Jews, various alien species resident at Area 51, time travelers, and also, the Jews.)

The first way you face these things is to prepare. You need to be prepared with responses to legitimate attacks, including statements, social-media posts, talking points for surrogates, digital and television advertising, and countervailing messages.

The second, and vital, discipline on these questions is to laugh. Out loud. To the camera. Not a nervous "oh dear" laugh, but a big, hearty belly laugh. Call bullshit. Defuse the bomb. They want you to come across as angry, outraged, and demanding an apology they will never give. That feeds their power.

Say it right out. "This is bullshit. It's ludicrous, absurd bullshit from Donald."

Don't ask for an apology. They thrive on denying you one. Don't be disappointed. They love tears and sadness. Don't craft some lofty rhetorical gem to call down the judgment of history. They're meme-tards, not true rhetorical equals.

A simple "Fuck you, Donald" will often suffice.

None of that can prepare you for the fantasy-based attacks. It's not traditional campaigning, I know. Voters hate the poise and polish of the too-calm politicians. They view it as fake and deceptive. When the crazy comes, it should be met not with hand-wringing or "woe is me" responses, but with a passionate, serious, fuck-you attitude back. You need to blame it all directly on the president himself, and remind voters he is a persistent liar and barking conspiracy loon.

Anything else that can happen to fuck up your campaign gener-ally will. Weather, natural disasters, economic downturns, emer-gent scandals, Russian interference, terrorism, Chinese interference, plague, pestilence, and Guilder invading Florin.

Strap in, because the last two weeks of the 2020 campaign are going to be lit.

PART 5

HOW TO WIN

2020 Debate Fact Check no. 1

During the first of three presidential debates last night at Bryn Mawr College, just outside Philadelphia, Pennsylvania, President Donald Trump made the following claim:

"Every American knows I am the tallest, healthiest, most attractive man to ever hold the office of the president. At 6'6" and 175 pounds, my body is a temple. Greek gods are jealous of me. I have the only 12-pack of abs in the world. My blood pressure is 7 over 2. My opponent is a 96-year-old woman with bad knees and body lice."

FACT CHECK

While attractiveness is subjective, many presidents before Trump have been considered attractive men, notably Barack Obama, Ronald Reagan, and John F. Kennedy, to name just a few from the modern era.

Donald Trump's medical records and annual health reports contain numerous unverifiable claims about his personal health.

Photographic evidence comparing President Trump to other men of known heights indicates he is not 6'6".

Donald Trump weighs 175 pounds from the waist up.

The only 12-pack Donald Trump possesses is the KFC 12-pack of boneless chicken wings.

That's not a blood pressure measurement from this world.

Donald Trump's opponent is not a woman, not 96, has no record of knee difficulties, and no sign or history of body lice.

ONLY FIGHT THE ELECTORAL COLLEGE MAP

I've mentioned this a time or two in this book, but I want to emphasize once again that the only fight in 2020 is a fight for the Electoral College win, and nothing more.

Don't bullshit yourself that you're going to win deep-red states, no matter how much time and how many resources you put into it, or states that you'd like to imagine might, if you squint, turn kinda sorta blue someday soon.

The election is already over in roughly thirty-five states. California, Washington, Oregon, New York, Massachusetts, and other big, blue powerhouses aren't going to change this election cycle. Don't go there, except to raise money. Don't spend a penny there on advertising or get-out-the-vote efforts. You must engage in brutal political triage.

I know how hard this will be for you. Everything inside you rebels at the thought.

First, there's your typical conceit that the entire country is one single political and ideological entity. You really want to think of the United States as a democracy, and not as a republic. Tinker with the definitions all you want, and the Constitution and the law still end up with the reality that fifty states use electors to decide the president. Those fifty states still display meaningful political, economic, and cultural differences that you'd imagine the party of diversity would embrace but instead loathes.

There's a part of you that hates flyover country for resisting the inevitable tide of liberal groupthink, for their higher religious participation, and for their clingy hold on their guns and religion, but there's an even worse inclination that Democrats display: the idea that the South and Midwest are just filled with eager AOC types, yearning to breathe free.

Bless your hearts. The idea that these states are rife with a sense of populist anger on the left just isn't backed up by history.

As in all things, we can also blame social media for much of your problem with the Electoral College. With its most woke voices screaming the loudest, it tricks you into believing that your edges are the center of the ideological spectrum, and that everyone, everywhere is as progressive as the average resident of Brookline, Mass. As we've covered elsewhere, this isn't true even in your bluest states. Yes, the coastal kingdoms are more liberal, but there's still a meaningful fraction of your party that's either moderate, or simply tribally Democratic.

Here's the 2020 battlefield, as of this writing. Sure, it can change a bit by the election, but the voting history, demographics, and polling tell us where the fight will take place in the coming contest. Your advantage is that Trump has broken his promises in many of these states—his trade war is an economic wrecking ball—and the novelty of Trump has worn a bit thin. The bad news is that in many of these places your favorite issues are alien, offensive, or political poison.

Once again, this isn't a value judgment. It's just observed political experience; we stole seats from you in these places because of the differential between your national political reality on one hand and the state and local realities on the other.

Both sides come to the fight with a bit over 200 Electoral College votes in the bag. I don't need thirty years of experience to tell you Alabama is going red and California is going blue. We may debate the details—and the details of these states would be a book in itself—but the real map of 2020 is as follows:

THE REAL MAP OF 2020

There are some arguments about which swing states are, well, swingy, but for the purposes of this exercise, I'm basing it on a Cook Partisan Voting Index of fewer than 10 points in either direction, a history of party-switching at least once in the last five presidential contests, and some ground-level common sense based on thirty years of experience in the field.

The outliers—states so partisan that they have no impact on a tightly contested EC equation—can be pulled out right away; these are states with a Partisan Voting Index of more than 10 in either direction.

On the Republican side, that means Alabama, Arkansas, Idaho, Indiana, Kansas, Kentucky, Louisiana, Mississippi, Missouri, Montana, Nebraska, North Dakota, Oklahoma, South Dakota, Tennessee, Utah, West Virginia, and Wyoming are out of the fight for Democrats. Just stop. You're not running a fifty-state campaign. States with a PVI over 10 in favor of Democrats are fewer in number: The Democratic Death Star for Republicans includes California, Hawaii, Maryland, Massachusetts, New York, and Vermont, as well as Washington, D.C.

Some states are *technically* under the 10 PVI but still don't count as swing states simply due to voter performance history or other demographics. Washington State is only a D+8 PVI, but any Republican who spends a dime there is a damn fool. Texas is only an R+6 PVI, but again, a graveyard of Democratic ambitions, for now at least. Opposite is my list of the 2020 swing states. Many of these states are changing and becoming more Democratic over time, but remember, kids: This is 2020, and the "Someday state X will be solidly blue" argument is a bad bet.

STATE	ELECTORAL VOTES	2016 WINNER	PARTISAN VOTING INDEX
Florida	29	Trump	R+2
Pennsylvania	20	Trump	R+1
Ohio	18	Trump	R+5
Georgia	16	Trump	R+4
Michigan	16	Trump	R+1
North Carolina	15	Trump	R+3
Virginia	13	Clinton	D+2
Arizona	11	Trump	R+3
Minnesota	10	Clinton	0
Wisconsin	10	Trump	R+2
Colorado	9	Clinton	D+2
Iowa	6	Trump	R+6
Nevada	6	Clinton	0
Maine	4	Clinton	0
New Hampshire	4	Clinton	R+1

Trump's triumph in the Upper Midwest should scare the hell out of the Democrats. No false bravado, please; the region has a PVI of R+3 and is culturally *far* more conservative than *any* of the Democratic candidates. In the South, Democrats face two hard targets: Georgia, which is still a reach, and Florida, which demands massive resources and effort . . . and has a regional PVI of R+7.

This analysis is necessarily brief and superficial, and any Democratic campaign worth its salt will be running a massive set of multivariate scenarios trading off polling, resources, and media costs, and planning their message, strategy, and expenditures accordingly. I *assure* you, the professionals in the Trump campaign are doing just that, backed up with data scientists and pollsters who are focused like the proverbial laser on victory.

Here's a very brief tour of the Electoral College swing states.

ARIZONA: 11 ELECTORAL VOTES

Democratic Arizona is trending blue after being a solid GOP strong-hold for decades. Clinton's narrow loss in Arizona is belied by the GOP's troubles there in 2018 and problems to come in 2020. A prime state where the GOP's clown-show candidates like Joe Arpaio and Kelli Ward are great foils for a smart campaign. Immigration lords over everything in Arizona politics right now.

COLORADO: 9 ELECTORAL VOTES

Breaking hard into the blue side, Colorado is an obvious double-bang target for 2020. Senator Cory Gardner, a GOP incumbent, is in trouble, and Trump's numbers in the state have been consistently poor. Colorado was Libertarian Party candidate Gary Johnson's best performance in this list. Weed and the energy sector are big stories in CO, and with the majority of Colorado's votes coming from the Denver-Boulder suburbs, it won't be a swing state much longer. It's a ripe, easy target, and Democrats need to wrap it up fast for the 2020 cycle.

FLORIDA: 29 ELECTORAL VOTES

Florida is the biggest, baddest, face-eating white-hot center of na-tional crazy in the race . . . and the biggest prize in 2020. Trump man-aged a narrow win (all wins in Florida are narrow). Here's some savage real talk for the Democrats: Florida Republicans are *really* good at winning statewide races. The state Democratic Party is noto-riously ineffective and disorganized. Floridians love low taxes and a clean environment, and our love of guns is rivaled only by the tribes of northwestern Pakistan.

The Orlando metro area is trending blue because of a massive in-flux of Hispanic voters, but Democrats failed to capture them in 2014 and 2016. It was a classic Potemkin village Democratic Party effort both times: all talk, few deliverables. Rick Scott spent time and money talking to new Puerto Rican voters who hate Trump and won them over in numbers sufficient to ensure a narrow victory for U.S. Senate. There's a lesson there, and it's a grim one for Democrats who are complacent about minority voters.

Florida is bigger geographically—it's got *ten* media markets—than most candidates realize, and one-size-fits-all campaigns don't fly. Prepare to become Florida Man (or woman; we don't discriminate) in 2020.

GEORGIA: 16 ELECTORAL VOTES

Georgia is slowly—very slowly—trending blue, and despite the flutter over Stacey Abrams, it's still a damned red state outside the "donut" of twenty-three counties surrounding Atlanta. Winning Georgia would be a coup. For a Democrat to capture Georgia, it's going to take someone willing to butt up against a lot of pressure from their left on guns and abortion, both of which are make-or-break issues with the roughly 55 percent of voters who live outside Atlanta.

Underappreciated fact: African Americans in Georgia living outside the Atlanta metro are much more conservative than their urban counterparts. The formerly Republican suburbs to the north are squishy Rs; a Democrat who doesn't scare them off by being too far to the left could win their votes in 2020.

IOWA: 6 ELECTORAL VOTES

Iowa has long been a state that defies expectations. I place it on the swing list because while Trump captured it in 2016, Barack Obama won it handily twice, and John Kerry came within a few thousand votes of capturing it in 2004. Culturally conservative outside the metros, Iowa is now a very ripe hunting ground for Democrats; the trade war has given them a singular opportunity to crush Trump in the heartland, and the simple referendum question of "Is your farm doing better or worse because of Trump?" is an easy framing mechanism with an obvious answer. Don't mistake Iowa for a progressive hotbed, though. It's still culturally conservative, rural, and so very white . . . and we know Trump plays that demo to perfection.

MAINE: 4 ELECTORAL VOTES

Maine is tricky because it's one of two states that splits its Electoral College votes by congressional district. In 2016, Trump captured

Maine's 1st congressional district. Since then, Maine's timber and lobster industries have been hit and hit hard by Trump's trade war, and, like Iowa, the referendum question to Mainers involved in the state's two key industries is "Has Trump made your business better or worse?" Maine voters also respond strongly to environmental questions in polling, and to a slightly lesser degree to economic matters. Maine's population is aging fast, and shrinking faster. This is a state where very focused efforts in the 1st CD can pay big dividends.

MICHIGAN: 16 ELECTORAL VOTES

Michigan was a perfect target for Trump in 2016. After the state suffered decades of industrial decline, Trump became an avatar of their fury over both parties promising miracles and delivering shit. The state had become older, whiter, and less educated due to the flight of one-third of its population to the Sunbelt. Michigan is dying, and Trump told them revenge was to be theirs.

The promised return of the auto sector and heavy manufacturing to Michigan was the usual Trumpian nonsense, and Democrats who fail to make a real case—not "We'll build windmills"—against Trump are missing the march. The suburbs of Macomb County—home of the famous Reagan Democrats—and Oakland County are the make-or-break ultimate swing counties, and attention must be paid there to ensure the state flips back in 2020. Michigan is going to be bloody, no matter how you slice it.

MINNESOTA: 10 ELECTORAL VOTES

Minnesota's electoral performance in 2016 pointed to the Upper Midwest slowly trending more Republican, even in a state considered to be a progressive breeding ground. The last Republican to win Minnesota was Richard Nixon in 1972, but Trump came very close to defeating Clinton there, losing by just 1.5 percent. Democrats have also faced a slow march by GOP candidates in the state legislature over the last few years. It's still a blue state at heart, but expect Trump to push hard there. Media is cheap; Minnesota's rural non-college male Democrats are prime targets in his demo, and they can swing the balance if Democrats aren't smart and careful.

NEVADA: 6 ELECTORAL VOTES

Hillary Clinton won Nevada, though not with the sweeping margins of Barack Obama. The state is clearly shifting into the blue column in presidential races. A massive influx of Hispanic voters in the past decade, and the California diaspora, have transformed the state and its politics. It's a hot battleground, and with its relatively small voter pool, both sides will be hip-deep in trying to move the voters in booming Las Vegas.

Nevada's politics are particularly tuned to the overall economy, and when the overall economy gets a cold, Vegas gets Ebola.

NEW HAMPSHIRE: 4 ELECTORAL VOTES

One of the classic swing states, New Hampshire is a wee battleground, and Hillary Clinton's razor-thin margin there means Trump will view it as amenable to spending big to wrap up votes there. One Trump ally told me he views it as a place where his rally-style politics is particularly effective. Famously crusty and cranky, New Hampshire voters are a weird mix of far-right politics on taxes and guns and far-left on healthcare, often in the same voter. It hasn't gone Republican in a national election since 2000, but with former Trump enforcer Corey Lewandowski potentially on the ballot for U.S. Senate, Democrats shouldn't take their eye off the ball in the Granite State.

NORTH CAROLINA: 15 ELECTORAL VOTES

A microcosm of a bigger trend in American politics, North Carolina's metro areas are turning very blue, very fast. Its rural areas are moving more Republican at the same rate. Despite Democratic gains, North Carolina is still a tough target; even Mitt Romney's 2012 effort posted a win there, and Trump won the state handily in 2016. North Carolina should be early on the triage list if the Democratic nominee needs to focus resources elsewhere. As with Georgia, North Carolina's African American voters tend to be less flamingly progressive than the national Democratic average.

OHIO: 18 ELECTORAL VOTES

I have some bad news for Democrats. Ohio is the hardest target on this list. Yes, Obama won the state twice, but this is a red state, trending more red from the grassroots up. Can a Democrat win it? Yes. Will they? Not without a massive, costly fight. Alongside Florida, this is one of the most expensive states in which to run advertising.

The case to be made in Ohio is simple: Trump's lies over the economy and the disaster of the trade war are a twin hit. He lied about the return of steel and coal jobs, then put the manufacturing economy at risk with pointless trade decisions. In Ohio, it's an economic and cultural challenge for Democrats as well. It's still a state where pro-life Democrats at the grassroots will cross over to the GOP on abortion, as many did in 2016. The right candidate can win them—Obama did it, twice, but Ohio is a tough nut to crack.

PENNSYLVANIA: 20 ELECTORAL VOTES

If there was a real shocker in 2016, it was Pennsylvania, a state Hillary Clinton and her campaign very much took for granted. Another part of the arc of Rust Belt victories that Trump racked up that year, Pennsylvania—like Ohio, Michigan, and Wisconsin—is a state where the industrial glories of the past are fading quickly, and his promise to restore the coal and steel industries was particularly resonant, especially in rural and western Pennsylvania.

The famous Philly suburbs may be blue and trending bluer, but the Reagan Democrats in the rest of the state are now Trump Republicans, and he's a master of playing their cultural resentments. Democrats will need to maximize African American turnout statewide and boost female turnout in Bucks County and the suburbs to be competitive.

Pennsylvania is hellishly expensive for advertising and operations, so get ready to spend, and spend big.

VIRGINIA: 13 ELECTORAL VOTES

Virginia barely makes the list as a swing state these days. Donald Trump single-handedly destroyed the GOP there in the last two years, and the wipeout is starting to have massive political repercussions. Don't bother campaigning too far outside the "Big Six" Northern Virginia suburban counties (Fairfax, Arlington, Prince William, Loudoun, Stafford, and Fauquier counties) in the 2020 race; Virginia was the home of soft-Republican votes and a more genteel style of politics now sadly out of fashion, and Trump has killed the party there. Still, the state will be a risk factor if Democrats take their eye off the ball: Everywhere outside the Big Six and Richmond, the place is as red as Alabama on a hot day.

WISCONSIN: 10 ELECTORAL VOTES

Wisconsin is another Rust Belt case study on how a narrowly targeted campaign focused on economic resentments can squeak out a win. The Democratic nominee has a massive opportunity to capitalize on the sweeping gains the party made in the state during the 2018 midterms. For three decades, Wisconsin's rising GOP tide came from an organized party farm team, strong grassroots work, and a flood of donor money, much of it from folks who saw Tommy Thompson, Paul Ryan, Scott Walker, Sean Duffy, and others as the glowing future of the GOP.

Trumpism is stronger here than it looks, even though his numbers have slipped and the GOP paid a heavy price there in 2018. Wisconsin agriculture, from dairy to corn to soy to Christmas trees, has taken a trade-war hit, so get ready to spend a lot of time eating cheese curds. Hillary regrets not doing so in 2016, believe me.

SPEAKING AMERICAN

I love words. I love rhetoric. I love the ringing cadences of a fantastic speech by a great orator before a rapt or raucous audience. It was the power of words that elected men from the time of the Greeks, and words still hold power and magic in the human mind. Watching great presidential speeches is my nerd hobby.

Then there's Donald Trump, for whom chanting "Lock Her Up" is the MAGA equivalent of Demosthenes. Sure, some days Trump will grunt and stumble his way through a teleprompter speech saying the words that Kellyanne and his speechwriters cut and pasted together at the last minute while praying Mr. Bigbrain Bestwords would, for once, stick to the script. (Spoiler alert: Anything Trump reads from the teleprompter is the lie; the truth is always in the asides.)

He gave one of those speeches on the Fourth of July in 2019. He will give one of these speeches at the 2020 GOP convention. He will give one of these speeches at his next State of the Union. In this era, these exercises don't really change minds, or hearts, because this country knows what Trump is. The teleprompter, far from guiding him, reveals his inauthenticity. He staggers and struggles through every line, because he believes in none of it.

The real Trump is impulsive, crude, ignorant of America's long traditions and of human decency. The tweets, the throwaway lines, the insult-comic shtick is the real rhetorical legacy of Trump. His fans are ravenous for it. His enemies loathe it. Most Americans think it demeans the nation.

But it's the genuine, seedy, shitty Trump. The authenticity of his awfulness is palpable. His lies and hideous nature are the product. In focus groups, even today, people who oppose him and consider him a chronic liar admit that he's awful, and that awful person is the real Trump. America's political cynicism is so deep that they still have a grudging respect for the worst president in history because he's not a contrived politician.

Democrats need to dig up a slim volume by former Bill Clinton speechwriter David Kusnet called *Speaking American,* published in 1992. I'll update it for you here.

As for the rhetoric of the 2020 campaign, below I'm going to teach you how to lie. This is where I do some of that amoral consultant shit y'all hated when it was directed your way.

Political rhetoric is about selling people on your ideas, even when the true face of those ideas repels voters. For the major points below, I'm not reflecting my ideological preferences, but the polling, research, and experience on how voters in the targeted swing states behave. Readers should bear in mind that the language, messages, and policies that work for California don't play in North Carolina or Michigan in the same way.

Some Democrats will read these and think that it won't motivate their base voters sufficiently. Your base is already motivated, and they don't need the nominee to put on a show of performative progressive values to believe he or she will be better than Trump. Since this election is a referendum on Trump in purple and red states, the words that work for the base aren't the words you need.

ABORTION

What Trump will say: "Democrats want abortion on demand, for any reason at any time, all paid for by the taxpayers. Right now, abortion doctors are taking infants from the womb and killing them. Democrats' support for abortion is support for infanticide."

How Democrats should respond: "Abortion is a difficult, personal choice, and it's a choice we firmly believe should be between a woman and her doctor. We believe states that pass laws giving women no options in the cases of rape, incest, or where the life of the mother is in danger are taking us backward from where even conservative courts have ruled on this question. We're grateful that late-term abortions are very rare, and usually are performed only to save the life of the mother." (Grit your teeth; I told you I'm teaching you to lie.)

GUNS

What Trump will say: "The Democrats want to end the Second Amendment. They will take all of your guns, and you will be helpless to defend yourself from criminals. They don't just want to ban assault weapons; they want to ban hunting rifles and all semiautomatic weapons."

How Democrats should respond: "After all we've lost in mass shootings, we want to make America safer by closing loopholes that put guns in the hands of people who are criminals, terrorists, or mentally unstable. We believe in strengthening the background-check system and in requiring guns to be stored safely so no child can access a firearm. We believe in the Second Amendment." (Yes, you have to say that.)

IMMIGRATION

What Trump will say: "Democrats are for completely open borders. Immigrants bring crime, violence, and disease. Immigrants will get free healthcare from you, the taxpayer. Immigrants are taking away your jobs, and only the Wall will stop it."

How Democrats should respond: "President Trump puts children in filthy cages without blankets, adequate food and water, or medical attention. His policies are killing people who want to come to America to seek asylum or legal status. America is a better country than this, and we have always welcomed immigrants to our shores. We believe immigration reform will make our borders more secure, and our nation more prosperous." (If you can't nail this one, no one can help you.)

THE WALL

What Trump will say: "The 3,000-mile Trump Wall is a wonder of modern engineering and is already mostly completed. The Wall is 400 feet tall, made of solid gold, with laser turrets, robot Dobermans, and a lava moat. It stops approximately 50 million tons of meth per day, as well as the entire population of Guatemala, Honduras, Costa Rica, Nicaragua, and Mexico from crossing the border in their relentless quest to dominate our job markets and park their taco trucks on every corner."

What Democrats should say: "The choice isn't between a wall and the dreaded 'open borders.' The choice is how to deploy resources and assets that actually reduce the risk to American families of drug smuggling, human trafficking, and terrorism. We're not stopping the real threats, because this president is too busy pretending to build a wall that won't work and that we don't need."

THE ECONOMY

What Trump will say: "The economy has never been better. I am responsible for all the growth and employment because I deregulated and passed a middle-class tax bill. The stock market is breaking records because of me, and your 401k is doing great."

How Democrats should respond: "The tax cut is working great if you're a billionaire, a hedge-fund manager, or a big bank. For average people, their costs keep rising, the trade war is bankrupting farmers across the country, and the promises of new jobs have been nothing but that—empty promises. Donald Trump promised he'd make your life better, but he's put the donors and lobbyists in Washington first."

THE MEDIA

What Trump will say: "The media is the enemy of the people. They are all lying liars who hate me, hate you, and hate America. Never trust their fake news, because only I tell you the truth."

How Democrats should respond: "Mr. President, you took an oath to uphold the Constitution. In case you missed it, in this country we care about freedom of the press, and no amount of whining about fake news will change that."

JUDGES

What Trump will say: "No one has named more conservative, highly qualified judges to the federal bench than I have. Gorsuch. Kavanaugh. You must reelect me because Ruth Bader Ginsburg and Breyer could go at any time, and you can't afford to have a liberal Supreme Court." ("I like beer!")

How Democrats should respond: "We believe in appointing highly qualified judges to the federal bench, judges who will uphold the law, protect the rights of every American, and respect the Constitution." (Leave *Roe v. Wade* out of it; the GOP already thinks all you care about is abortion.)

NO COLLUSION

What Trump will say: "I never conspired or colluded with Russia. I did not obstruct justice. It was all a witch hunt, and now we need to punish the real culprits—the deep-state coup leaders who tried to take out a president."

How Democrats should respond: "Robert Mueller uncovered hundreds of contacts between your campaign and the Russians. The only reason you're not charged in this case is the Department of Justice guidelines. Two of your former aides are in prison. Donald, the way you behave toward Vladimir Putin is so deferential, and the way you trust him over American intelligence and military officials has people wondering about you. If Putin doesn't have something on you, it's hard to tell."

SOCIALISM

What Trump will say: "Democrats are socialists who want to take away your freedom, your money, and your property."

What Democrats should say: "Donald, the only one here who wants to pick winners and losers in the economy is you. We want the winner to be the American workers and American businesses. Socialism is your administration paying farmers who lost everything because China beat you in a trade war you started and we didn't need. Socialism is propping up dead industries and dead companies. Socialism is feeding the elites a massive tax cut that screws workers. If that's socialism, Mr. President, you're awfully good at it."

HOW TO TALK ABOUT IMMIGRATION

We need to spend some extra time on this one.

Immigration is the killer app of Trumpism. For his supporters and true believers, it is a symbol of Trump's imaginary strength at confronting an imaginary problem. And it is a permission slip for millions of Americans to Make Racial Animus Great Again.

With its sister issue the Wall, Trump's immigration obsession motivates the rally crowds and a handful of high-profile Trump fellators like Lou Dobbs, Ann Coulter, Mark Levin, and others. But the Wall is one of his most meaningful vulnerabilities and needs to draw as much ridicule as Democrats can muster.

Say it with me: There is no wall. There will never be a wall. The border wall is a Trumpian construct, a confection of horseshit and marketing that still tricks the rubes but isn't changing anything on the border.

Don't bother arguing the positive economic externalities; a 2017 focus group we conducted showed Trump voters are utterly convinced that all immigration—including legal immigration—should be ended. Not reduced. Ended. It's a contemptible sign of their commitment to the post-rational Trumpist desire to Make America White Again, but you ought to understand that it's real and it's pervasive on the right.

On immigration, your audience includes a broad demographic that, you know, doesn't like kids in cages. Here is your case:

Under Donald Trump, deportations are down; Barack Obama deported more people than Trump, and had a more serious plan to control the border.

Don't take his bait. Remind voters that immigration isn't about MS-13 or drugs or human trafficking. Those are symptoms, and ancillary symptoms at that.

Kids. In. Cages. The deliberate theater of cruelty designed by Trump henchboy Stephen Miller that led to the forced separation of families and detention of immigrant children was one of the most morally and politically damaging episodes in the Trump administration, and it led to measurable drops in Trump's approval ratings across the board, even from Republicans.

Get back to America's superhero origin story: As imperfect as our founding may have been, we've staggered and stumbled our way into being the most diverse nation on earth, a landing ground for men and women from every point on the planet. Be proud of immigrants, and tell their stories.

Speak American. The stifling language of campaigns too often seems designed to avoid appealing to Americans' emotions, to feeding that appetite for inspiration that abides even today. Too much campaign talk comes across as contrived, crafted, a lifeless litany of barely there ideas. It doesn't have to be the lowest-common-denominator war grunts of a Trump rally, but it does have to be vernacular, colloquial, and relatable.

Don't build a watch; tell voters the time.

Don't describe policy; tell stories of how you'll be better for them, their kids, and the nation.

Don't stay locked in a doom-and-gloom, we're-all-gonna-die message; Americans are a relentlessly, passionately optimistic people who show resilience and determination. Be a happy warrior, not a doomsayer. "We're all gonna die" is a Trumpian, negative frame that you can, and must, reject.

Speaking American isn't tricky. It isn't secret. It isn't an act. It's a recognition that leaving the confines of Washington and New York shows you a world where voters curse, fart, spit, love their dogs and their kids, play sports, drink beer, talk shit, recycle, pray, work, sing bad karaoke, and worry about the future but push on every day. It's a social-media cliché that authenticity sells, but it's not wrong.

They hate politics, but they love leadership. They hate partisanship, but they love passion. They're flawed and frail and uncertain much of the time, but they still imagine a bigger, better life. Tell them you're listening. Tell them they matter. For once, tell them it's not about you, or the party, or some book of policy proposals but about *them*.

2020 Debate Fact Check no. 2

During the first of three presidential debates last night at Bryn Mawr College, President Donald Trump made the following claim:

"The trade war is amazing. It's been so easy to win. China is paying us over a bazillion quatloos per minute because they love me. Because of the trade war, we've been able to force Naboo to give us many, many concessions because I am the world's greatest negotiator."

FACT CHECK

The trade war initiated by President Donald Trump with China and other nations has not, in fact, been easy to win. American industries from agriculture to manufacturing to raw materials have lost markets in China and elsewhere. Bankruptcies are rising across the Midwest, and the federal government has spent billions in farm support payments in a desperate attempt to stave off financial disaster.

"Bazillion" is not an actual number. "Quatloos" are a fictional currency from the 1960s television series *Star Trek*.

No evidence exists that anyone, anywhere loves Donald Trump.

Naboo is a fictional planet first mentioned in *Star Wars: The Phantom Menace*.

We can find no evidence of concessions to President Trump, or evidence to back his claims of being the "world's greatest negotiator."

THE FIRST RULE OF
TRUMP FIGHT CLUB

When you start attacking, never, ever stop. Ever. Not for an hour, not for a moment. This is a lesson in military history that Democrats would do well to study. Any time you pause to let an enemy rest, replenish, or regroup, you've lost the vital momentum of the battle. Once you attack, you must press on. Once you break the seal, there's no going back. Cry "Havoc!" and let slip the tweets of war.

This is particularly true with Trump.

Trump fills the political ether with a constant background radiation of tweeting, shit-talking, madness, and lies, using it to corrode both his political and his media opponents. He knows that the media and political ecosystem is trained and primed for one shitstorm to devolve into another shitstorm at his hands, feeding the ravenous but shallow attention economy with wave after wave of tweets and clicks.

Every Republican who faced Trump in 2016 failed to learn this lesson.

Ted Cruz, Jeb Bush, Marco Rubio, Rick Perry, and a dozen others weren't temperamentally able to swing and keep swinging. Decency held them back. Their willingness to observe boundaries and norms kept them from landing the deepest cuts. Trump knew from the start that the opponents he faced in 2016 were unable to sink as far and as fast as he could.

This fight won't be pretty. It won't be easy. It will make you feel bad. It will make you wonder if it's all worth it. Your friends and family will tell you that America really wants you to be nice. That they're looking for normal. That you can set an example.

Have they been in a coma? If you believe that, even for a moment, you're toast. Donald Trump secretly loves the decency of normal people because he knows it to be a weakness. Every woman he ever sexually harassed or assaulted, every business partner he screwed, every contractor he stiffed got to know Trump's style of predation and mistreatment: He finds a weakness and bullies and intimidates you into silence at best or obedience often, and at worst forces you to become an accessory to his continued bad behavior.

Trump is a man without a single ethical scruple. He is without compunction when it comes to breaking the letter of the law. Hell, he'll crack the spirit of the law just for fun.

Democrats must not be shocked by the depths to which he and his campaign will sink. Your father will become the latest Rafael Cruz, noted assassin of John F. Kennedy. Your husband or wife will become a figure of ridicule for his or her looks and weight. He will attack your children. Your successes will be portrayed as abject failures, your pinnacle moments as mere nothings. Ever had a medical issue you'd rather not discuss in public? How about your spouse? Your kids? They'll use it. For Democratic candidates who have had an extramarital affair, you'd better have the come-to-Jesus talk with your spouse and your staff, because they will find it, they will use it, and Trump will have no shame or self-awareness about how hypocritical he looks attacking you on it.

Mentally prepare your family for this, because it's coming. It will be amplified by a social-media machine that is vicious, relentless, and overwhelming.

I'd leave Barron out of it, but the minute Trump goes at your kids, everything is fair game. He talks shit about your spouse, you hammer the soft-porn mail-order bride currently serving as First Lady. He hits your kids? Fredo, Big Gums, and Fascist Barbie are fair game. Trump voters will be angry, but no candidate ever laid a glove on his family even as he went after theirs in the 2016 race. Decency is your enemy.

Ted Cruz did everything but cut his own balls off on television when he endorsed Trump after what Donald said about his father and wife. If I'd been in Ted's shoes and heard Trump go after my family like that, I would have walked across the debate stage and left that punk bitch eating through a straw for six months.

Maybe fisticuffs are out, but you must hit back, in Trump's own words, twice as hard. You will gain nothing with the American voter by letting Trump make you into the latest doormat for his shit behavior. The Democratic base will be judging you not on policy, but on your ability to take on Trump. If you're strong, you win. If you're weak, he wins. Zero sum.

Michelle Obama is wrong when it comes to fighting Donald Trump. "When they go low, we go high" is easy for a popular, talented, charismatic First Couple to say. No. When they go low, you bring out the goddamn flamethrower. You show real passion, real heat, and let people see you're not taking one fucking iota more of his bullshit . . . and that no one else should either.

I know you will still hesitate. You will still wonder if you can win this with love and not combat. You can't. I wish we lived in a perfect world where all this would be settled by a scholarly discourse, but this is a chain fight in a biker bar in Frogsass, Alabama.

You cannot shame him. You cannot correct him. You cannot hope he will reflect on his actions and words. He is the Douchebag Terminator, a bullying, demeaning thug until you raise the pain level. His audience thrives on seeing him attack with impunity, like the hangers-on around every bully in history.

His insults are projection, and you can and must use that. In fact, you need to get ahead of that with constant, personal, targeted attacks on the three softest points in Trump's psyche.

First, he's not rich. He's poor. He's—to use the famous words of my hedge-fund friend—"a clown, living on credit." The billionaire image was a powerful marker for 2016 voters, but the pettiness and greed of his campaign to monetize his presidency is a great vector for attacks. Remind him that eventually we'll know everything about the serial business failures in his hidden tax returns. The truth about his finances won't move many in his base, but taunting him on it is known to make him lose his mind in spasms of tweeted defensiveness.

Second, his self-image is that he's handsome, sexy, and athletic. (Try not to laugh.) Trump's obvious obesity, sloth, and indolent lifestyle are hanging off him in rolls. Call it out. Tell him he's not physically well enough to hold the office. Hit him hard on his creeping dementia: "Donald, you've lost a step. It's sad and I'm sure your family is concerned. I know you don't have a real doctor, but we're worried about you." One wag suggested to me that the Democratic nominee should insist on a weigh-in before the debates. I'll max out to the Democrat who takes a scale onstage and dares Donald to step onto it. "What's the matter, Donald? Is the IRS auditing that big ol' belly?"

This is a dogfight, and unless America sees "some fight in the dog," as we say down south, Donald Trump will walk all over you. When you start hitting, don't let up.

2020 Debate Fact Check no. 3

During the first of three presidential debates last night at Bryn Mawr College, President Donald Trump made the following claim:

"The Wall is now completed. It is 3,000 miles long and covered in gold leaf. Very classy. The moat is very deep—some people say the best and deepest moat ever—and is filled with robot alligators. We're stopping caravans every day filled with hundreds of thousands of MS-13 terrorists who want to force gay marriage and socialism on America."

FACT CHECK

No new sections of wall have been completed. Approximately 50 miles of fencing has been repaired as of this time.

The U.S.-Mexico border is approximately 1,400 miles, not 3,000.

No moat exists in relation to U.S. border control measures. Medievalists tell us the average moat was less than 16 feet deep, but it is difficult to judge claims about a nonexistent moat.

Robot alligators do not exist, nor could we find any mention of their acquisition and purchase in the *Federal Register.*

So-called migrant caravans have been infrequent, occurring at most a few times a year. There is no evidence of "daily" caravan interceptions.

MS-13 members are estimated to number a few thousand worldwide, according to the FBI and internal law enforcement agencies.

There is no evidence of the ideological preferences of MS-13. No reference to either gay marriage or socialism could be found on their website.

START EARLY

Ronald Reagan won the election of 1984 in the fall of 1983.

George H. W. Bush lost the 1992 election in the spring of 1991.

Bill Clinton won the 1996 election in the spring of 1995.

George W. Bush won the 2004 election in the spring of 2003.

Barack Obama won the 2012 election in the spring of 2011.

The short and sweet explanations of each of those incumbent reelection campaigns come down to a strategic decision to start framing the race early, and clearly, using the awesome power of the White House to drive the news and shape the political battlefield.

Reagan announced his reelection campaign in January 1984, but the groundwork to organize the effort had been undertaken in mid-1983. In those simpler times when propriety was still a thing, the president stayed above politics until the last possible minute. Reagan, ever mindful of staging, imagery, and the chance to use the White House's awesome powers for just that, let his advisors set up the apparatus early and framed the race as a simple referendum: prosperity at home and strength abroad.

Reagan's "Morning in America" campaign was messaging against the Democratic field generically, not specifically. It didn't matter if they pulled Walter Mondale, Gary Hart, or Jesse Jackson in the general; it mattered that their ads, speeches, and surrogates were all-in on economic optimism and national security as the core messages, and early. Mondale's cataclysmic, terrible campaign lost forty-nine states in part because Reagan's team planned ahead.

In 1991, George H. W. Bush was in the catbird seat politically, with the highest approval ratings in presidential history, a successful war under his belt, and an economy that, if not booming, was still coasting along. The campaign, in the hands of Mary Matalin, never quite gelled, and was imbued with 41's sense that it was a little undignified for the White House to be put to work too strenuously in the election effort. Even when Patrick Buchanan, the paleoconservative firebrand who, as it now seems clear, set a path that would lead to Trumpism, entered the race, Bush's campaign was still slow to move, slow to respond, and slow to hit back. Late starts are fatal.

Bill Clinton, for all his personal weaknesses, was one of the greatest political card players in American history. He was and is a voracious consumer of polling data, a data nerd, and a man willing to follow the numbers where they led. In the spring of 1995, with a tenuous grasp on his power at the end of his first term, he followed the numbers to a political messaging strategy that gave him a marked advantage.

Clinton and his campaign manager, Dick Morris, read the surveys and got out of the gate early with the famed triangulation strategy. Triangulation has fallen out of fashion in our current political climate, but Clinton's center-right posture on crime, drugs, and deficits and center-left posture on abortion, healthcare, and education left Bob Dole with little room to maneuver.

Clinton had secretly engaged Morris in the fall of 1994 after the GOP's wholesale slaughter of the Democratic Congress, which led him to understand that the 1996 campaign would be an uphill climb. The rest of Clinton's campaign team were less than enthusiastic about the Morris strategy of leading with anti-crime ads, but when the $2.4 million ad buy began seventeen months before the election, the die was cast; Clinton had defined the 1996 battlefield on his terms. This expensive (for the time) effort at an early framing for the campaign was a massive strategic advantage in his successful reelection effort.

Karl Rove, Ken Mehlman, and the rest of the Bush 43 team knew that after the razor-thin, contentious victory in 2000 the world had been radically altered, but the reelection of George W. Bush was by no means a certainty. Drawing lessons from the 2002 Senate races, Rove and his team crafted a choice for voters, a referendum on national security under Bush and the president's personal likability versus John Kerry. Contrary to Democratic folklore, it wasn't just the swift-boat ads (I get accused of making those more often than you'd believe, but not my work) that took out Kerry. The Bush team understood early that Kerry would be the Democratic nominee, and they executed a rigorously planned, ninety-day messaging campaign against him.[1]

Barack Obama started winning 2012 on Election Day in 2008. He never shut down his campaign machine in the ways some candidates do. The groundbreaking campaign data and digital efforts had been effective, and while they didn't run at the pace of the campaign, they never stopped collecting data. He prepped relentlessly for 2012 well in advance of any serious resolution of the GOP field. The scary analogy is this: Trump's team is in large measure agnostic over which Democrat gets the nomination. He's planning for all of them.

Given the economy, the election models all say that at this point Trump could have already put the 2020 election to bed. But he's a day-trading narcissist with a short attention span, unable to focus on anything but his ego, his Twitter feed, and his dick. His kickoff rally was, for him, good enough. His tweets are, for him, good enough.

Plan ahead, because a plan beats no plan every time.

START ADVERTISING. NOW.

Why are Republicans sticking with Trump? What dark magic makes them reject all principle? What keeps them from understanding he's a bad president, an authoritarian statist, and a raging asshole?

I'm going to tell you a not-so-secret secret. It's advertising.

Donald Trump's campaign has been spending real money on targeted digital advertising since he was elected. From December 2018 until August 2019 his campaign and super PAC spent well over $20 million on Facebook alone.[2] He's not spending money to expand the base, soften his message, or Make America Great Again. He's stoking his followers' worst fears and paranoia. This isn't a shock, but the content is a preview of the future, and an investment in keeping his people fired up and loaded for bear.

Yes, the Democratic candidates are all spending on Facebook as well, but they're talking to the edge in a progressive primary, not to the people who will decide the election.

His spending on Facebook and Google ads ramp up and up over time with estimates that they may exceed $250 million for the general election.

Isn't this chump change in the overall scheme of advertising? Don't all presidential campaigns rely on billion-dollar TV advertising efforts? Sure, at the very end. Hillary Clinton's television spending in the last stretch of the campaign dwarfed Trump's. Trump will have an unlimited ad budget, and spending will likely start much sooner than the Democrats expect; this is the Nixon/Ailes playbook for the 1972 reelection. Spend early, spend often, define the battle-field. One stinging lesson from 2016 came in the advertising pattern in Wisconsin and Michigan, two of the states that cost Hillary the Electoral College: Trump had the advertising field to himself until the closing days of the campaign. That's right. Hillary Clinton was *off the air* in Wisconsin and Michigan until two weeks before Election Day.[3]

Trump loves digital advertising. He loves it like a fat kid loves cake. The rising power of digital advertising is that you know whom you're reaching. TV targeting for cable is wildly improved, but noth-ing rivals digital for delivering a single message to a single person. Expect record spending by Trump on digital, expanding well beyond what you're seeing today.

The Trump campaign knows that with targeting so fine-grained and so cost-effective, it can bombard its core voters with a message that absolutely works for them; they'll be able to keep him at 44 per-cent instead of the organic 40 percent approval number. They under-stand that the Facebook and Google (primarily YouTube) ecosystems are siloed and self-reinforcing, and that the political culture of Trump-ism means sharing with like-minded morons, which amplifies their message over and over. The Trump campaign spends about 3.5 times as much on Facebook as it does on Google, but that gap will close rapidly as the campaign continues and they work to control their message in search and YouTube results.[4]

It took the DNC and its allied groups until the summer of 2019 to start advertising against Trump, even though the utility of a generic Democratic campaign in the targeted swing states of the Electoral College makes eminently good sense. So why didn't they? Who knows?

Oh, wait. I do know. It's because the Democratic Party is holisti-cally bad at politics. That said, the Democratic National Committee is showing some signs of life in the early spending department, and recognition of how a thirty-person field has complicated the money, media, and organizing equations for 2020. As Maggie Severns of *Po-*

litico notes, "Some of the Democratic operatives most focused on Trump worry that by the time Democrats winnow their . . . field to one, the president may have secured himself a hard-to-beat advantage" unless Democrats "mount a sustained push against Trump in a swath of 2020 battleground states." They've already fallen behind. Severns reports that in June 2019 the DNC had raised less than half of what the RNC had.[5]

"I take very seriously the fact that Republicans and Trump are already communicating under the radar to sets of voters they are already in threat of losing," said David Pepper, chairman of the Ohio Democratic Party, who has been working to raise funds and counter the Trump campaign's advertising online in his state. "If Trump has an entire year to be hitting these voters with all sorts of garbage, the mindset will be cemented in with a lot of voters by the time we find them."[6]

Democratic-leaning groups need to get on the air right now. Right. Now. In swing states and in one specific market I'll address in a moment.

Instead of jerking off running impeachment ads or launching a futile run for president, Tom Steyer should be on the air in the swing states, nuking Trump into a glowing crisp on the trade war (for Iowa) and for the lies over new jobs (Wisconsin and Foxconn, for instance).

The DNC, allied groups, and the Democratic billionaire class need to start eroding the Trump base, today. They need to poison the well for soft Trump voters in targeted states, today. What part of "today" is unclear?

Research the audiences you want and need in the target states. Here's a good thought experiment: If the shoe was on the other foot, what do you think some Republican asshole like Rick Wilson would do to spoil your whole day?

Hire pollsters. Hire a lot of pollsters. Get the data you need for targeting. Ask for help. Data scientists, pollsters, researchers, ad developers, and the digital platforms themselves understand this better than most campaign hacks.

You're not looking to merely reinforce your core voters. You're also trying both to identify and grab back every Democratic voter

Trump won and to dig into the soft sectors of the independent and female Republican base. Your ad makers should develop messages and media that move votes from pro-Trump to Trump-questioning. You're not going to flip them all at once, so use the "kick ass or by-pass" rule. Don't spend money trying to persuade the hardest targets.

2020 Debate Fact Check no. 4

During the first of three presidential debates last night at Bryn Mawr College, President Donald Trump made the following claim:

"Since I purchased Greenland, America is safer than ever, and greater than ever. No other president has ever expanded the United States like I have."

FACT CHECK

Greenland is not a U.S. state or territory at this time.

Greenland is, at this time, still an autonomous territory of the Kingdom of Denmark.

President Trump's 2019 attempts to buy Greenland were both rebuked and mocked by Denmark's prime minister, Mette Frederiksen.

Contrary to President Trump's claims, many American presidents have expanded United States territory, including acquisitions such as the Louisiana Purchase by President Thomas Jefferson and the Alaska Purchase by President Andrew Johnson.

Eric Trump's extensive holdings of territories in the MMO Second Life do not, according to legal experts, constitute actual U.S. territorial claims.

NO MORE POTEMKIN CAMPAIGNS

This is the most critical technical chapter in the book. The Democrats must run a real, modern, data-driven campaign from the top down. They must make themselves accountable, including and especially the candidate. This is about operations, not ideology.

Democrats commonly miss the fact that, while politics is often emotional, campaigns are empirical. They are driven by data, by facts on the ground, by budgets and programs. They are not simply deus ex Obama miracles. To paraphrase Arthur C. Clarke, any winning campaign is indistinguishable from magic. Obama's 2008 victory looked like a movement, but it was really a world-class data and targeting operation, optimized digital and television media buys, a highly organized field program, and a tightly disciplined team hunting votes on the Electoral College map.

Charisma, likability, electability, and—for fuck's sake—policy are fool's gold if the campaign doesn't have its shit together.

I'm going to call hard bullshit on the Clinton 2016 campaign because they deserve it. They were lazy, smug, wasteful, insular, arrogant, incompetent, fractured, tone-deaf, sloppy, and worst of all they lost to Donald Fucking Trump. No one was accountable, ever. Hillary Clinton could have taken Florida, Wisconsin, and Michigan but didn't do the work, leaving those prizes wide open for marginal efforts by Trump and his Russian allies to tip the scales.

HIRE THE RIGHT TEAM

Do you know the biggest mistake made first by the sixteen other GOP candidates and then by the Democratic Party and the Clinton campaign in 2016? They built teams without real leaders. They patched together the candidate's friends and brought in people who allegedly had the secret sauce, but at the top of each campaign was a person who was more a manager than a leader.

All national (and statewide) campaigns are filled with factions, alliances, enemies, ass-kissers, and hacks. Some of them are worth their salt. Some of them are just along for the ride. Some of them are going to bust their asses twenty hours a day from the moment they come on board until Election Night.

For the 2020 Democratic nominee, the campaign's national structure needs to be as light, nimble, and smart as possible. Heavy on politics and press, light on policy and favor hires. It needs to avoid the "hire my guy" problem to which too many operations fall victim. "Hire my guy" is that moment at the end of the primary campaign when, in order to make peace, secure an endorsement, or lock in some core demographic of support, the victor agrees to hire some of the loser's campaign staff.

For the love of God, just this once, don't. The nominee needs a disciplined team of people who are honest and direct behind closed doors and who are smart, loyal communicators in front of the cameras and on social media.

REGISTRATION

Talking shit about doing voter registration is the "my Canadian girl-friend" of politics. Democrats keep talking about it, and keep claiming it's going to swamp the Florida, Texas, and other state GOP branches in the next election. Or the next. Or the next.

Voter registration is the key. New voter drives in the swing states should already be well under way, and if they're not, it's grotesque malpractice. All the issue groups Democrats love so much need to be out hustling registrations as though their political lives depend on it, because—spoiler alert!—they do. Planned Parenthood, Moms Demand, the unions, and the rest need to stop driving for policy concessions and bring real, hard voter-registration drives to the fore of their agenda. That's value to a campaign.

The Democratic billionaire class should be directed to push resources into registration as well, since the state parties in the places Democrats need to win in 2020 range from merely competent to utter train wrecks.

TURNOUT

The election isn't fought on Election Day. It's fought for three to six weeks before Election Day as an increasingly meaningful fraction of voters cast early ballots. If Democrats fail to understand this enormous strategic aspect of the 2020 race, it doesn't matter how November 3, 2020, looks. The GOP professionals around Trump will be banking votes early and often.

Early voting is the not-so-secret weapon the GOP has used in Florida and elsewhere for a generation now. Democrats have started to close the gap, but early and absentee voting require a culture shift for the Democrats, and fast. The old model was warm-body turnout on Election Day, moving meat to market. While that's still important, early voting not only banks votes but shows you what's happening on the ground.

Almost every state allows some form of early voting, whether in-person or absentee balloting.[7] Some are more restrictive, but early voting is a powerful strategic indicator and barometer; it lets you focus resources, serves as a kind of live tracking poll, and warns you if the people you're paying to turn out voters are doing their damn jobs. (Often, they aren't.)

Republicans have aggressively sought to close off early-voting programs that disadvantage them in places like Florida. For once in a generation, the Florida Democratic Party seems to have its shit together; by the spring of 2019, they had a team of attorneys working to ensure protections for early-voting access, Spanish-language ballots, and voting access for ex-felons who regained their right to vote after the passage of Amendment 4 in 2018.[8] Democrats complain a lot about voter suppression, for which I can't blame them when it comes to cases like this. Yes, part of "voter suppression" is the way GOP majorities set the rules (elections, famously, have consequences), but much of that "suppression" can be counteracted with a moderate investment in pipe-hitting election lawyers.

Field operations, even in this digital era, still count. They're still where the rubber meets the road, and where the winners and losers diverge. Field operations is the place where Barack Obama stole a march on John McCain in 2008 and Mitt Romney in 2012. To be sure, Obama was a compelling speaker, a charismatic liberal leader, and a media darling with a killer targeting operation, but the Obama campaign also out-worked, out-hustled, and out-organized my side. Twice.

Don't even get me started on the nothingburger of Hillary's field operations. Even against Trump, who had *no* field operations, she lost. Democrats need to track all of those people down and put them on an ice floe. Republicans may bleat about Alinskyite progressive organizing principles, but here's the stark reality: They're investing in them right now, training and prepping field organizers who will be knocking on doors in 2020.

If the first topic on Tom Perez's mind every morning after raising money isn't deploying a fired-up, motivated field army, he's not doing his job.

2020 Debate Fact Check no. 5

During the second of three presidential debates last night in Santa Clarita, California, President Donald Trump made the following claim:

"I have been tougher on Rusher than any president in history. Vladimir Putin sleeps in a different place every night because he's so scared of me. I am now considered by many to be a czar of Rusher, probably the best czar they've ever had."

FACT CHECK

Noted historians and foreign-policy scholars consider the following U.S. presidents of the past decades to have been "tougher" on Russia than Mr. Trump: Obama, Bush, Clinton, Bush, Reagan, Carter, Ford, Nixon, Johnson, Kennedy, Eisenhower, and Truman.

There is no evidence that Russian president Vladimir Putin has adjusted his overnight locations for fear of Mr. Trump.

The title "czar" does not exist today.

It's *Russia,* you dolt.

MAKE THE WORST
OF TRUMP'S BASE
HIS RUNNING MATE

The self-image of the deplorables is that of the honest, hardworkin' people of the Christian American heartland and South who have been screwed by Washington, D.C., and the coastal elites since the dawn of time. I'm sure there are some good folks inside Trump's demographic, but there are also some people who repel the voters you need to get to in 2020. Suburban moms and the alt-right? No bueno.

After decades of fighting back against accusations of racism in the GOP, it's no longer deniable that Donald Trump's remarks after Charlottesville were a reflection of his character as a man and as president. His birtherism, his long, grotesque flirtation with the worst elements in the alt-right, his racial and ethnic animus, his sliming of "shithole countries"—all this is a feature, not a bug. The fact that he surrounded himself with people like Steve Bannon, Seb Gorka, and Stephen Miller—men who don't just flirt with racial superiority theories but take them out for candlelit dinners—is another proof.

Murderous white boys posting their 8chan manifestos that sound like excerpts from Trump speeches or as if they were stolen from Tucker Carlson's teleprompters engaged in mass murder in Poway, California, and El Paso, Texas. By the time this book goes to print, there may have been more such shootings, and the killers may also spout white-nationalist slogans that sprang from Trump's rhetoric on immigration. These people are the worst of Donald Trump's base. Democrats should make them his running mates.

The long arc of Trump's racism is a book of its own, but in terms of his presidency, from Charlottesville forward there was no mistaking the content of his heart. Candace Owens, Paris Dennard, Diamond and Silk, and Ben Carson aren't exactly speaking to the average African American, and Democrats need no more powerful reminder of the message that President Both Sides sent to this nation when he drew a moral equivalency between Nazis, Klansmen, and alt-right anti-Semites chanting "Jews will not replace us!" and counterprotesters.

Trump's team and his media sycophants have tried desperately to retcon the entire event, but it remains a raw wound. Instead of trying to sell African American voters on the hypothetical of reparations, why not sell them on the immediate reality of a referendum on the man in the White House and the long, terrible history of his racial arson?

Democrats need to make alt-right leaders like Richard Spencer, Klan scum like David Duke, and the entire enterprise of alt-reich assholes into Trump's running mates. He needs to be pressured on this from the start for two reasons. First, it really, really bothers him. He knows how badly he blew it with those Charlottesville comments, regardless of his personal beliefs. The second reason is that it prevents another cycle of Trump playing footsie with overt racists. Opportunity costs were low in 2016; he was viewed as a joke, a prank, and a crank.

Make him own the actions and views of the evil men and women who adore him. Make him face the terrible cost in lives and suffering since his inflammatory language poisoned our culture. Donald Trump, almost uniquely in presidential history, is supported and surrounded by people who can be seen as nothing but evil.

There is no "both sides" in this fight. Make him own it. Make him hurt.

2020 Debate Fact Check no. 6

During the second of three presidential debates last night in Santa Clarita, California, President Donald Trump made the following claim:

"If you elect my opponent, she'll unleash a zombie invasion. It's been her plan all along. She wants to feed Americans to the living dead. It's right there on her website. Nothing can stop her evil plan but my iron will. Without me, you'll be chewing on someone's thighbone for lunch. It's me or the shambling flesh eaters."

FACT CHECK

President Trump's reference to Senator Warren's so-called plan to unleash a zombie invasion is, as readers will now easily anticipate, false. Senator Warren has no plan to release zombies, flesh-eating or otherwise, on the American population.

Senator Warren's website has, at this reporting, 431 plans or policy papers, many exceeding 600 pages in length. None of those plans reference zombies or any other form of the undead.

REACHING TRUMP VOTERS, IF YOU MUST—AND SADLY, YOU MUST

People trapped in a cult need special handling, and the Trump cult is no exception. Cult deprogramming is a bit of a high lift for the 2020 race, but because rescuing people from cults is always a good thing, this chapter will offer some helpful hints for how to deal with the victims of Trump misinformation and propaganda, and how to talk to Mom and Dad about getting off the Facebook Trump crack.

I'm not kind to Trump fanatics, but the Democrats need to give some of the people getting nauseous on the Trump train's rough ride a kind, smooth path to acceptance. The actions of Trump have built a sense of disappointment, disquiet, and division that has already pushed many Republicans away from him. The job now is to turn regret and remorse into votes, particularly in swing states.

Trump voters, on paper, seem like implacable members of a cult so rigid and so inflexible that it makes Scientology look like a bunch of free-thinking libertines. You've seen all the Saddam-like stats: "107% of Republicans love Trump, with 102% saying they strongly love Trump!" "87% of Republican women would give their daughters to Trump for his sexual gratification!" When this is over, there will be Trumpers out there in the jungles of some remote suburb, convinced the war never ended and that the God-Emperor Trump still reigns, but the monolith myth of the GOP today is just that.

The reason Trump's number stays so high is that many Republicans have stopped identifying themselves to pollsters as Republicans. They're unwilling to be associated with the behavior and actions of Trump, ideology be damned.

SUBURBAN MOMS AND EDUCATED VOTERS

Let's be honest with ourselves. The number that blew every campaign analysis in the 2016 exit polling was that educated, suburban women voted for Donald "Pussy Grabber" Trump. It was a shock to the system because he was every single thing we were told women hated: a vulgar, abusive bully. And yet, the 2016 exit polls—particularly in the swing states that Trump surprisingly won—told the tale. Trump captured 42 percent of the female vote against Ms. Break the Glass Ceiling herself. *Forty-two percent.* Trump won the suburbs in 2016 by 50 to 45 percent. The suburbs, whence a majority of the votes in the 2020 targeted Electoral College states will come, will need to see Democrats improve that number dramatically.

These groups are falling from the GOP's orbit like a crapped-out Russian space station plunging back to earth, but they're by no means a lock.

They made a conflicted choice in 2016, and one that many clearly regret, judging by the current survey of work and voter data analysis from 2018.

A mild suggestion to Democrats, if I may: Please don't scare the living shit out of them. Telling them things like "We're going to eliminate your private health insurance" isn't a recipe for confidence in these skittish voters. They're from the suburbs. They like normalcy. They like a system that doesn't feel too disruptive. They want a return to sanity, not a different flavor of ideological passion. Many will be divided families in 2020—Mom with the Democrats, Dad with Trump.

Trump is doing a lot of your work for you with these groups, but if you fall into too many of the culture-war traps, there's a meaningful chance these folks will step back out of the fold and either vote for Trump again or simply stay home. You can't afford either outcome.

Please don't think that they're suddenly hardcore progressive Democratic base voters.

You're dating, not sleeping together, but you might get lucky if you play your cards right.

THE J. D. VANCE DEMO

How Democrats approach the vital questions of the economic realities in the key Electoral College states and defuse the idea that only Trump and Trumpism are the solution for their problems is perhaps the fundamental issue of the 2020 campaign. As with everything else in this election, Democrats must make these questions a referendum on Donald Trump.

The conventional wisdom of 2016 was that Trump voters were the hurt children of globalism, international trade agreements, shifting demographics, and the radical arc of technological change. They were angry with Washington and the coastal elites.

In 2016 J. D. Vance wrote an excellent book, *Hillbilly Elegy,* about this world, and a cottage industry of analysts and writers sprang up to discuss the pathologies of the heartland beset by forces beyond their ken and a sense of rage and despair that led them into the arms of Donald Trump. It was an easy story to believe, because there really is pain, dislocation, and fear in the heartland.

But that reason is looking more and more like an excuse. The tribal nature of Trumpism is seated in a host of racial and ethnic hatreds. It's the sloppy permission society writ large, the victim culture of too many liberal clichés from the 1970s turned on its head. Instead of being angry at the corporate world, they've redirected it into being angry at immigrants.

Unlike conservatism, Rust Belt victim culture presumes that market forces must be moderated by the strong hand of the Great Leader. Democrats must not try merely to replace one Big Daddy with another. Promising them government will do for them what Trump didn't is a losing proposition. They like the anger he allows them. They like the idea that the amorphous brown "they" took their jobs and communities, and your promises of job retraining or a panoply of free shit will fall on deaf ears.

The traditional conservative credo of personal responsibility, hard work, and the power of markets doesn't work with them. There is a rising understanding that this demographic never bought into free-market conservatism. They like how Trumpism infantilizes and marginalizes people in ways that would make the heart of any central planner glow. Conservatives once took offense at the belief they were too stupid, provincial, and prone to their various addictive pathologies to succeed. Now they've embraced it.

In some meaningful ways, it's Ronald Reagan's fault. Reagan's ideological instincts were sound on this question: He knew that winning back working-class voters from the Democrats would take more than free-market rhetoric. Reagan talked to union voters as one of them, sounding in many speeches a lot more like Franklin Delano Roosevelt and Friedrich Hayek.

There's a powerful lesson for Democrats from both Trump and Reagan when it comes to winning back white, working-class Democratic voters in the interior oblasts: Stop trying to sell them horseshit. The promise that jobs writing code or making windmill parts are going to replace jobs making auto parts is a cruel lie, whether it comes from Bush, Obama, or Trump. Blue-collar workers have heard this story, and it always ends with a flurry of feel-good press releases and then a big fat nothingburger.

Democrats also need to be deeply aware of the profound cultural trickery my side has used for a generation to steal away your voters, particularly in the Midwest and South. Voters' anger at the elites isn't just because they think the educated coastal Masters of the Universe are richer; it's that the wokeness and politically stifling word games that have come to define far too many in the Democratic political space are tiresome and offensive to them. The idea that a career might be shattered by the incorrect use of a gender pronoun may seem perfectly explicable in New York or San Francisco, but the GOP is really, really good at making voters in the states Democrats must win in 2020 feel like the PC Police will kick down their doors if they wander into the minefield of wokeness.

Reagan understood that these blue-collar Democrats were the soft underbelly of the other side because he was one of them. He didn't roll in with 600-page policy documents (looking at you, Elizabeth Warren); he came to them with a working-class origin story. He came to them as a champion and defender.

Trump took it to another place entirely. The "blue-collar billionaire" element of his story was entertaining but not decisive. Trump channeled their anger and said, both implicitly and explicitly, that hatred was back in style. He told them at rally after rally that his Wall would stop the brown horde from taking their jobs. He told them he'd stop the waves of terrorist Muslims trying to come here from shithole countries. His promise to Make America White Again addressed the darkest cultural space in American politics, and he found willing audiences in the South and Midwest.

Democrats need to understand that this didn't have to be real to be effective.

STOP TALKING TO THE GOD SQUAD

One element of the GOP's coalition is ecstatically, eternally, passionately happy with Donald Trump, and that's the evangelical cohort. In the 2016 exit polls,[9] some 26 percent of Americans identified themselves as evangelicals—you know, born again, saved, forgiven, and allowed to fuck porn stars for money. The traditional definition.

For the 2020 election, the evangelicals are, if you'll pardon a construction they might understand, damned. You cannot reach them. Catholics? Mainline Protestants? Sure. Evangelicals? Nope.

Don't buy into the stories of evangelicals cracking and breaking away because of Trump's potty mouth or Twitter feed. Trump has transformed the evangelical movement into a more cruel and worldly political tool, validating and verifying their two most powerful desires.

First, he empowers them to live in an intolerant society separate from the rest of the United States, one defined and bounded by the Constitution and the rule of law not to protect religious liberty but to achieve their narrowly crafted social policy goals through executive fiat. Their deal with this devil is paying off in spades.

Second, evangelicals have found their golden calf, and they worship him as their new god. The evangelical movement has become a social argument, not a religious calling. Their ability to excuse Trump is the new standard for belief and merit.

For men who usually seek the spotlight to promote the Word, some of Trump's most vocal and visible evangelical enablers haven't come off covered in glory in the Trump era. We'll leave aside Jerry Falwell Jr.'s adventures with Miami pool boys, creepy-eyed airport pastors screaming about how Jesus wants them to have private jets, and the usual high-dollar megachurch grift.

In my first book, I wrote about the compromises evangelicals made in the name of winning this end-times battle in the culture war. Since then, more and more of them have stopped even trying to make excuses. They are swept up in the delights of political power on this mortal plane and, with Trump as their prophet, have transformed into something unrecognizable.

Stop talking to them. You can't move their numbers, and you can't change their minds. Trump has spoken, and for them, that now is the Word of the Lord.

2020 Debate Fact Check no. 7

During the second of three presidential debates last night in Santa Clarita, California, President Donald Trump made the following claim:

"I have run the cleanest administration in history. No scandals. And no collusion. When Hillary Clinton was president, we had scandals every day. Sometimes five or six of them. Also, she murdered people when she was president. Imagine if I hadn't stopped her. It would have been a genocide."

FACT CHECK

From its earliest days, Mr. Trump's administration has been rocked by firings, imprisonments, corruption . . . oh what the hell, people. You know the rest.

Mrs. Clinton never served as president. No, she's not a murderer. For fuck's sake, people.

BE THE PARTY OF MARKETS, FAMILIES, AND SECURITY

Democrats have an opportunity in 2020 to recapture that sweet element of political felicity that elected John F. Kennedy, Bill Clinton, and Barack Obama: optimism. Jimmy Carter depended on the externality of Nixon, and LBJ, well . . . you know.

All three of those men were able to recast Democrats as something other than out-of-touch academics, bureaucratic bossypants, and do-as-I-say hypocrites. Hope may not be a strategy, but in the era of public rage and distrust, it's a start.

The opportunity to recapture that magic is there because Trumpism is a fundamentally negative, reductive, zero-sum political movement. In Trump's reality bubble, the song is always the same: The media, the educated, the elites, the immigrants are coming for the Trump voters. They hear the message, hammered home every day on Fox and its online imitators: We've lost the culture war. They're coming to convert you to Islam. The gays want to force your kids to participate in the school holiday drag shows. Christmas is under attack. We've lost the values that made America white—oh, pardon me, I meant great.

Democrats have a generational opportunity to rebrand as the party of markets, families, and security because the referendum against Trump is a powerful contrast on all those points. They have the chance to talk about hope and freedom and uplift, not by selling endless expansions of government but a return to the character and beliefs that shape America more broadly.

The traditional Republican strengths in all of these categories have been blown apart because of Trump and Trumpism; the party is now defined only by Trump, who believes in nothing but himself, and sells nothing but his cult. If Democrats are smart, they will understand the market opening here is enormous and revolutionary. Since, as I've said, they're usually not good at speaking American, I'll outline it for them.

This is a chance for them to be heroes for the working-class voters Trump snatched up in Wisconsin, Pennsylvania, Ohio, Michigan, and elsewhere. Trump didn't win them with policy; he won them by promising to be a fierce, unrelenting avatar of their anger at the economy and their disaffection with politics, and a back channel for the not-so-hidden racism and xenophobia. The fake billionaire scanned as more working-class than the middle-class-girl-made-good Hillary Clinton.

What do you think sells in western Pennsylvania? Mike Rowe, or some stern-faced, super-woke commissar telling a white working-class guy he's got to give up eating meat, driving a truck, and hunting? You may want him to, but how well do you think that *sells*? The guy who used to make $37 an hour in a union auto-parts manufacturer doesn't give a flip flying fuck about climate change, genderless bathroom mandates, or paper straws. He does care about getting and keeping a real job that can support his family and—stop me if you've heard this one—his guns and religion.

I will continue to beat this message until Democrats understand it: This is a game of the Electoral College, not *Chapo Trap House*. Middle America isn't on the cusp of being Berkeley or the Upper West Side by a long, long shot.

Pennsylvania, Ohio, Wisconsin, and Michigan are states that define the American working-class image. And my vital home state of Florida, king of the swing states? Guess where the majority of all those retirees flooding the Villages, Sun City Center, the exploding population centers of Central Florida and the west coast, from the Big Bend of the Panhandle down to Marco Island, came from?

Yeah. These people are working- and middle-class folks from Pennsylvania, Ohio, Wisconsin, and Michigan, drawn here for the vibrant multicultural . . . oh, who am I kidding? They're here for the low taxes, cheap real estate, and ubiquitous strip clubs. They don't give a half-shit about speeches on diversity, relitigating busing, or trans rights. If the Democratic campaign thinks that educating them into embracing these issues is a winning campaign path, get ready for four more years of Trump.

I know this because we stole these people from you. We spoke their language, in their cadences, and made sure they knew how much Democrats judged them for being insufficiently sophisticated about the latest hot flavor of political correctness. We stole them because they're intensely patriotic, and you rarely praise America without revisiting our sins. Trump got them because they want prosperity and security and for decades the promises from Dems to deliver those things have been hollow.

It's a culture the Democrats have tried to look away from since Bill Clinton. I get it—in your mind's eye, your self-image is the young, hip, diverse party. "We're all like AOC! So telegenic! So social-media hawt!"

Let me share a piece of focus-group wisdom from a Florida voter. In early 2019, we interviewed a group of former Trump voters in the Orlando area who now call themselves undecided. One was an older male, classic Florida swing voter, a union Democrat who moved here ten years ago from Michigan. "I'm 60. I've got two kids just out of college. Same wife for 38 years," he told us. "I voted for him because he was a businessman, not a politician. I just don't want to be told how we should live." I know this is shocking, Democrats, but an awful lot of your target voters in the states you need to win the Electoral College are sixty-year-old white dudes like that guy.

Your almost slavish devotion to the Benetton mosaic of beautiful people is killing you. Maybe consider running ads in places with—wait for it—people who look like the people to whom you're trying to appeal. Shallow? Sure. Have you met the American electorate?

One other danger to winning back voters from the postindustrial heartland is the ongoing debate about socialism. I will tell you from experience in campaigns in Wisconsin, Michigan, and Ohio that a deep part of the self-identity of working-class voters in those states is in the value of hard work and the role that self-reliance plays in the American narrative. It's vital that Democrats fall somewhere between fend-for-yourself harshness and "Free Shit for Everyone!"

Democrats also have the unbelievable luck of being able to win the battle over Obamacare after a decade of screwing it up. As I discussed in *Everything Trump Touches Dies*, the issue of preexisting conditions is one of the most powerful political messages I've seen tested in thirty years of politics . . . but Democrats are on the verge of blowing it. The simple, clean argument over preexisting conditions is a sure winner, which is why the Democrats are talking about single-payer, Medicare for All, and ending private health insurance.

2020 Debate Fact Check no. 8

During the second of three presidential debates last night in Santa Clarita, California, President Donald Trump made the following claim:

"Who stopped the black hole? Me. Who stopped the alien mothership from taking our women for their breeding program? Me. Who killed over 600 ISIS fighters with just a pocketknife? Me."

FACT CHECK

According to astronomers consulted for this fact check, the nearest black hole is over 3,000 light-years away. Under no circumstances could President Trump "stop" a black hole, whatever that means. Like Trump, a black hole is a singularity into which all matter and energy disappear.

No evidence exists of the presence of an alien mothership or breeding program. We believe Mr. Trump may be reading from the erotic science-fiction work of Mr. Stephen K. Bannon, *Sex Slaves of the Lost Planet Trumpbart*.

Bone spurs. Enough said.

THIRD PARTIES AND SPOILERS

I'm going to tell you a dirty little secret.

A meaningful fraction of the Green Party candidates you see in races around the country are creations of people like me. Not all of them, to be sure, but enough. They can break off 3 or 4 percent in the odd race here and there, particularly in swing districts. There are GOP consultants who specialize in finding the local college-age dipshit who wants to sit in his apartment, smoke weed, and play Fortnite in exchange for a check for his "campaign committee."

You know why this happens? Because politics is a shitty business where anything that gets you to the finish line without breaking the law can and will be used.

Cynical? Yeah, have you met me?

I know, you're shocked, shocked someone would cheat at the dignified, serious, and honorable profession of political consulting. The old joke in consulting is that when asked what one does for a living you say, "I'm a piano player in the local whorehouse." After they stare for a moment you reply, "Well, I'm really a political consultant, but being a piano player in a whorehouse sounds more dignified."

People cheat. It's not even illegal. Mostly.

Once the smelling salts kick in and you're able to rise from your fainting couch, hear me out.

Some smart Democratic-leaning billionaires need to dump some real qwan into building out some shiny third-party options for the crazies on the right. The cost is relatively low and the friction they cause is delicious. Since we're looking at states where Donald Trump's margins are already razor-thin, I'm going to outline a few quick real and fake third-party options in which a few million dollars would pump enough randomness into the process to make a difference.

AMPLIFY THE LIBERTARIAN PARTY

The Party of Ayn Rand is a real party, on the ballot in fifty states. Good Lord, I know how fucking irritating they can be, but there's a smart play here. Some smart investments in boosting the LP in key states could have a massive return on investment . . . without having to build a new fake conservative-party infrastructure nationally. Libertarian Party voters are almost exclusively going to draw down from Trump's vote total.

The Libertarians mount campaigns of greater or lesser seriousness depending on the political climate of the moment. There are a little over half a million Libertarians registered across the nation, which comprises about a half a percent of all voters.

Trivial, you say? Hold still, because I need to slap some reality into you.

Donald Trump's margin of victory in the swing states that moved the Electoral College into his column was infinitesimal. Of the 137 million votes cast in 2016's election from hell, just 107,000 votes in three states decided the race.

The ticket of Gary ("What is Aleppo?") Johnson and Bill Weld, which reflected skepticism about Donald Trump's commitment to anything even in the same neighborhood of Libertarian Party commitments to free markets and individual liberty, was, by any third-party standard, a success. Johnson and Weld took in over 4.4 million votes, or 3.24 percent of the popular vote total. It was a high-water mark for Libertarian presidential candidates to date. They raised more money, got more media attention, and drew down more votes than any LP nominee had before.

Given their 2016 performance, the LP also secured ballot access for 2018 and 2020 to a degree that no third party in the past century was able to do, and that's important for the 2020 election in big and small ways.

Best-case scenario? Justin Amash follows his heart, runs for the LP nomination, and gives libertarian conservatives and disaffected Republicans a clean conservative option in 2020. Hell, if Amash got on the debate stage à la Ross Perot in 1992, the game would become much more interesting.

BOOST THE GOP CHALLENGERS TO TRUMP

You may have noticed by now that Donald Trump is a thin-skinned, whiny bitch-boy who has an ego more fragile than an Easter egg. He is also in charge of the Trump Cult, Inc., which is the rebranded name for the Grand Old Party. His command of the GOP is so complete that no one will dare to challenge him . . . right?

Former Massachusetts governor Bill Weld, a wonderful man and a thoughtful public servant, won as a centrist Republican in a deep-blue state. He's building out a campaign for president, and at this writing seems willing to run headlong into the threshing machine of the Trump GOP. Joe Walsh, former Tea Party firebrand and born-again woke anti-Trump warrior, promises to run a scorched-earth campaign from Trump's right.

Weld's climb uphill is so steep as to be perpendicular, but no incumbent, particularly one with an ego as fragile as Trump's, wants a challenger. In Walsh, Trump faces an unfettered opponent.

Mark Sanford, former governor of South Carolina, is running a campaign based on—wait for it—traditional Republican ideas, fiscal discipline, and principled limited-government conservatism.

Will they catch fire? Honestly, probably not, but a boy can dream.

Primary challenges to incumbents are historically rare, but they can blow up the illusion of invulnerability and party unity that helps to ensure most incumbents win reelection.

Donald Trump, as ignorant and blinkered as he is, remembers that in 1992 Pat Buchanan entered the field against George H. W.

Bush. Buchanan was doomed from the start, but the corrosive nature of his candidacy ate at the Bush campaign. Hadn't Bush ended the Cold War, for goodness' sake? Hadn't he ushered Manuel Noriega into a Miami jail cell and dismantled his narco-state? Hadn't we beaten Saddam's ass and skated out of Iraq a few weeks later in a nearly bloodless and militarily perfect campaign?

None of it mattered to the dipshit paleocons around Buchanan. They were the proto–Tea Party purists, the cult kids willing to burn down the GOP for the lulz. Buchanan opened a vein, turning a re-election that could have been about a four-year term of success around the world into an existential fight. He wounded Bush badly, draining resources into having to put down the cur Buchanan in-stead of focusing on the general. That blood brought the sharks. Ross Perot saw how wounded Bush was and entered the race as a third-party economic populist; the rest is history.

The 2020 GOP field's task is much harder. In 1992 there was no Fox News agitprop channel to keep the masses in line, and for all of Buchanan's raw politics, he had a certain rhetorical flair that spoke to the conservative wing of the conservative party. They almost cer-tainly can't beat Donald Trump, but a lesson from the Cold War springs to mind. Charles de Gaulle once said of France's nuclear de-terrent that, though it could never be large enough to defeat the So-viets, with it he could at least "tear off an arm."[10]

The Democratic candidates should start framing every discussion of the general election with a phrase guaranteed to send Trump into a hissy fit: "Whether my opponent is Donald Trump or Bill Weld or Mark Sanford or Joe Walsh . . ." Like all bullies, Trump can't tolerate competition or challenge, and getting him to focus on his primary opponents will heighten the dissension in the GOP. Democrats need his Twitter attention focused on his own challengers for even a little while. Watching him act out his petty resentments over his primary competition is good media and good politics.

The entire legal mechanism of the GOP and the state Republican parties will dedicate millions of dollars and man-hours to keeping challengers off the ballot. A few million dollars to ensure Trump isn't able to legally hack his way to a ballot with no Republican challengers on it would also be a smart investment.

PRANK PARTY LINES

If I was king—a shortcoming I regret on the daily—I'd spin up a few state-specific parties with a focus on immigration.

And before I forget, if some billionaire prankster really wants to have some fun, the creation of the MAGA Trump QAnon Build the Wall Now Party in a handful of states wouldn't take much effort or cash. It would be one more way to drag a few of the loons off the GOP line in the fall.

As Democrats, you're thinking narrowly about how to get your candidate to the finish line. You're looking at the apocalyptic political Thunderdome in which you will battle Trump in the news and social-media space every day between now and Election Day 2020. You're going to try to draw a stark ideological and personal contrast with Trump, because of course you are. But why not muddy the waters? Don't underestimate the political value, and the sheer fun, of fucking with Donald Trump from the right.

KILL YOUR SPOILERS

Making Trump work harder by posting conservative spoiler candidates in the primary—and conservative party spoilers in the general election—is good politics, but Democrats must fear and manage their own spoilers in the 2020 election.

First, the progressive wing of the progressive party is rich with spoilers on the farthest fringes of the far left who can and will try to burn it all down. They're willing to ensure a second term for Trump if they're denied even the smallest items on their road map to ideological nirvana. Some are even convinced that reelecting Trump will hasten the revolution.

Some, like Tulsi Gabbard, look like creations from the 4chan/Putin Center for Candidates Who Just Want to Wreck Shit and Destroy the Republic. If the Democratic Party has any leadership at all, they should dedicate themselves to narrowing the field, fast, and pushing the lower-tier also-rans into Senate, governorship, and house races as quickly as possible. The field remained so large in late 2019 it became a running joke.

The spoilers in the middle lane are the billionaire-class candidates potentially flirting with runs as independents on the left. Howard Schultz and Michael Bloomberg have declined to run, but don't write off some center-left spoiler with too many zeroes in their bank account; they'll doom the Democrats by targeting the same set of voters the Democratic nominee needs to win. Democrats need to work very quickly to neutralize and marginalize these center-lane spoilers. Don't put it past Tom Steyer to leave the Democratic field in the spring of 2020 and run as an independent.

Other spoilers aren't candidates but interest groups. In politics, no one works harder to make you do dumb things than your own political allies. The nominee will need to tamp down hard, and fast, the constellation of Democratic interest groups, activists, and policy goons who will do what they always do—put the cart before the horse and start declaring victory and making demands. From environmentalists to gun-control types to LGBTQ activists, these groups will put pressure on the nominee to announce he or she is all-in on every detail of their agenda. The unspoken and spoken threat is, sign on to our wish list or we'll stay home on Election Day.

Believe me, the GOP has faced this kind of blunt-force blackmail from the evangelicals and other groups for decades. Like all extortion attempts, it deserves a two-word response: Fuck you.

Anyone who doesn't understand that subsuming your own public goals until after the win isn't an ally, they're idiots. It's the dumbest politics, and the nominee and the campaign need to be utterly merciless at telling them to shut the hell up or they get nothing. In the words of Van Jones, "Drop the radical pose to achieve the radical ends."

Sound cynical? I can't tell you the number of times my far-right candidates have wanted to announce some public change of their policy because Group X threatened to stay home. Ask Barack Obama about dealing with Jesse Jackson and Al Sharpton in 2008. If they're going to stay home, you don't have them anyway. As one of my wisest friends in politics says, "Fuck 'em and feed 'em oatmeal."

The biggest possible spoiler of all, of course, is Bernie Sanders, who is a seemingly impossible problem for the mainstream of the Democratic Party. We've covered him elsewhere, but if the nominee doesn't get a handle on Bernie, fast, expect him to bitch and moan loudly, sniping at the Democratic Party's standard-bearer all the way to Election Day.

2020 Debate Fact Check no. 9

During the final presidential debate last night in Tampa, Florida, President Donald Trump made the following claim:

"Many people consider me a god. Some people even say the best god. Some think I'm the king of kings. Others call me Mohammed's spiritual successor."

FACT CHECK

For this fact check, we reached out to a number of leaders of major religious denominations.

His Holiness Pope Francis replied: "I refer you to 1 Peter 5:8—'Be sober, be vigilant; because your adversary the devil, as a roaring lion, walketh about, seeking whom he may devour.'"

The Grand Mufti of Saudi Arabia told us: "I would call him a filthy infidel, but the Koran counsels mercy to the insane."

The Dalai Lama was bodysurfing off Honduras. A number previously known to be associated with him responded to a text message reading, "New phone. Who dis?"

INVESTIGATE +
INTERROGATE > IMPEACH

Y ou want to impeach him. I get it. He deserves it.

Should he be impeached? Fuck, yes.

Can he be? Maybe, but it won't be easy or without complications.

The capture of the House in 2018 is one of the biggest weapons the Democrats have in the effort against Trump. The House GOP bled Hillary with the Benghazi hearings from 2014 to 2016, and the Democrats should now return the favor. Congressional committees should drive and drive hard on corruption by Trump, his cronies, family members (*particularly* his family members), his business interests, and his allies. His cabinet members need to be on the hot seat early and often.

I remain a deep skeptic of impeachment as a political strategy for another reason: He'll raise a quarter of a billion dollars off it. The boob-bait GOP base emails will never end. Convinced of his impending removal from office, Trump would batter down every possible email inbox to scrape the last $5 from Granny's Social Security check for his campaign grift. He's already going to have a hell of a financial advantage; don't make it worse.

I've argued time and again that the smart play is IIABN—impeachment in all but name—but the great beast of Washington shambles ever forward, its ponderous, inexorable tread leading it toward the inevitable impeachment proceedings against Donald John Trump, forty-fifth president of the United States.

For the love of God, don't bet the farm on it unless you can win in the Senate.

Look, I feel your pain and frustration, but unless you convict Trump in the Senate and destroy his political future, you're not fucking anyone; you're just enjoying a masturbatory revenge fantasy. Democrats who make the argument on the impact of impeachment hearings do so based largely on magical political thinking. They're missing the point.

This isn't the Watergate era. Not a single Republican vote beyond Justin Amash can be guaranteed in the House, and the Senate landscape is entirely bleak. Until you can get to two-thirds of the Senate for a conviction, impeachment means nothing. Do you really think Mitch McConnell will do more than laugh? I'd put down 3:2 odds that McConnell could flip two or three Democrats.

The Senate *will* exonerate Trump. He will hang his entire campaign on No Collusion, No Obstruction, No Conviction. You think Trump will be shamed, and you're wrong. He cannot be shamed. Ever. Your people don't need impeachment to win, given how fired up their base is for his removal; they do need to keep up the pain.

The Democrats aren't helpless. They can and should turn 2020 into a spectacle. Let the congressional oversight become a weaponized accountability tool. Open a second front in the war of 2020. Lest you think that the American people would reject such a transparently political ploy, may I remind you of the 2015–2016 Benghazi show trials? How'd those turn out for Hillary Clinton? I'll tell you how: badly.

Constant, always-on, televised torture sessions won't backfire in the way an impeachment would. Show Americans the dregs and scum who work for Trump. Keep beating the drum. Keep dragging Trump's feeble mental process back to Russia, impeachment, corruption, emoluments, his sons, his little friends Cohen, Manafort, and Stone.

The trick is to keep up the pace of investigations and flood the zone. Democrats need to up the tempo and visibility of these hearings. You need cameras, spectacle, vivid moments the public can see and remember. This is playing by the rules of your reality-TV show, not Trump's.

This isn't just about Russia and the 2016 election scheme to help Trump. No, this is also about the rich portfolio of corruption and self-dealing that comprises this entire criminal enterprise masquerading as a White House. So what if they're gone? Bring in Pruitt, Carson, Tillerson, Mattis, Lewandowski, and the rest, both the good and the bad. Get their asses in the chair for public testimony. Drill, baby, drill. You will rivet Trump's attention to the spot.

Here's just one small example of how the House Democrats could drag the administration into a deep mire and frame the 2020 referendum on Trump:

In July 2019 it was revealed that a secret Facebook group of current and former Customs and Border Patrol agents and officers was a revolting sink of raging racism, abuse, and mockery of immigrants, including dead immigrant children who died while being held in detention centers.

Every one of the currently serving CBP officers on that group should be dragged in front of the cameras. Drill down. Get into it with them. These are Stephen Miller's frontline troops in the war on migrants, and they're a lockstep group of Trump supporters. One even posted a meme called "Lucky Illegal Immigrant Glory Hole Special Starring AOC," showing the Bronx congresswoman being forced by President Trump to service him orally.

I'm not a reality-TV producer, but this is the kind of play that is riveting television and will cause Trump to dig deep to defend crooked, sick cops. Adorable moppets telling stories of their time in cages? Call me cynical, but that's good TV, and in the Trumpverse, good TV counts.

Trump's reality is bounded by television. It is defined by cable news. If the Democrats in the House make this an aggressive element in 2019 and 2020, Trump will begin his usual obsessive watch-tweet-sleep cycle and further elevate the stories of his lawless administration.

You want to drag Don Jr. off the campaign trail. You want Hope

Hicks and Michael Cohen and Paul Manafort and Kellyanne Conway and the rest of the parade of his clingers and toadies taking the oath, sitting through the grilling, generating pictures and headlines.

Impeachment may work, but it's likely a bridge to nowhere. Investigations serve a valid accountability purpose, and have the corollary benefit of being a great earned-media and political trap for this president.

Besides, what else are you going to do? Pass an infrastructure bill?

2020 Debate Fact Check no. 10

During the final presidential debate last night in Tampa, Florida, President Donald Trump made the following claim:

"This election is a choice between me, and my satanic opponent. Many evangelicals, who know me and who love me very much, are telling me that the devil himself is behind my opponent. It's a vote for me—your Lord and Savior, the Chosen One—or a devil-worshipping socialist vegan."

FACT CHECK

Satan, when reached for comment on his electoral preferences, said, "Hell no, bro. I've been with the Donald from the very, very start." When asked if he had any recent contact with the 45th president, the Lord of the Eternal Flame responded, "No, but I'll be seeing him very, very soon, and we'll have plenty of time to catch up."

The Democratic nominee is a nonpracticing Catholic.

The Democratic nominee is not a vegan.

THE TARGET LIST

The 2020 battle against Trump has to be waged on every front, and by every stakeholder in the coalition against him. The goal is to deprive Trump of having the singular ability to set the topic of conversation every day. The goal is to drive up the friction in his world, to push him into defensive positions. He's going after your people. Be ready to do the same.

NO CIVILIANS ON TEAM TRUMP

I've tried to live by the "consultants are never the story" rule, but Trump's forward-facing consultants are such a parcel of dead-enders, grifters, scumbags, and wannabes that we would be remiss in not making them part of the story.

I'm not arguing for political attacks on Trump's consultants just because I'm cruel. I'm arguing for making them part of the story because it isolates Trump from people who could help steer his efforts, and it raises the friction inside the machine. These people are a paranoid, ratty clan of backstabbing villains, and the more you focus the hot light of inquiry on them, the more their grubby little deals and scammy actions are exposed.

His more dangerous and effective backroom guys are rich targets for opposition research; most don't want to be seen or known to be working with Trump. Many have separate corporate and lobbying clients. Some are in line for massive paydays by taking their cut of the revenues and expenditures of Trump's 2020 campaign. Many will craft deals structured to cleverly keep them off Trump's personal radar. They'll hide their profits, jack up apparent costs, and play other games with subcontractors and vendors because they don't want the Trump clan to ask for a piece of the action.

A current Republican consultant to the RNC told me that Donald Trump is obsessive about what the people working for the campaign and the national committee are making. As always, it all comes down to whether he and the family are getting their slice of the vig.

The people running scam PACs in Trump's name are also fantastic targets.

With names like the Great America PAC, the American Greatness PAC, the PAC for America PAC, every variation of MAGA-PAC, and the Red Hat PAC for People Who Can't Read Good and Want to Read Good, the gigantic hoovering sound you're hearing is millions of olds eagerly sending their money into the swampy vortex of scam PACS in the Trump era. From the earliest days of the movement on the right, the Howard Phillips and Richard Viguerie types discovered a gold mine was out there in the bank accounts of Middle America's conservative voters, waiting to be tapped one $25 donation at a time.

The advent of email marketing, consumer profiling, and social media turned these appeals into psychologically compelling, laser-focused weapons where Granny couldn't hit CLICK HERE TO SAVE AMERICA FROM GODLESS HOMOSEXERS fast enough.

Conservatives who had made their uneasy peace with Trump were appalled.[11] In the old days, the donations would largely be spread across campaigns; donors were interested in the House, Senate, and presidential races. Today, the GOP small-dollar donors love Trump and almost Trump alone. One email fundraiser for a Senate race told me in 2019 that the reason they mention Trump in every sentence of every email is that it's now the only thing that moves the small-ball donors to click.

When I was in the business, I enjoyed raising my money the old-fashioned way—from pitch meetings with billionaires who could crap out a $5 million media buy and have it not even constitute a rounding error in their smallest bank account. I was never at home with the idea that some lurid, screaming-headline, fundraising mailer to a little old man on Social Security was a moral option.

The worst of Trump's lot on this are David Bossie and Corey Lewandowski. They play an odd role in Trump world: strategists for a man notoriously without a strategy, and advisors to a president who only takes advice from the gibbering demons in his head. Lewandowski, tolerated by Trump for his willingness to get rough with female reporters, his world-class dickishness, and his utter subservience, is a human wrecking ball. His raging anger-management disorder is a weapon and an earned-media opportunity for the Democrats, who should absolutely engineer face-to-face encounters with this guy. Send women. He's not good with women.

Lewandowski is rumored to have had an affair with presidential favorite and former aide Hope Hicks, to which Trump told Hicks, "You're the best piece of tail he'll ever have." Because he's such a gentleman, Lewandowski got into a screaming match with Hicks on the street outside Trump Tower in 2016.[12] Stay classy, Corey.

Long a player in the conservative monetization demimonde, he was yellow-carded in Trump world in May 2019,[13] likely for not cutting the Large Adult Sons or Jared in for a slice of the pie. Bossie's scam PAC used breathless direct-mail pieces featuring pictures of Trump, quotes from and about Trump, and lurid claims that George Soros and Nancy Pelosi are beating down the door to impose full sharia communism and only AN IMMEDIATE DONATION RIGHT NOW will stop them. Sure, the sleaze of direct-mail fundraising has reached new lows in the era of Trump, and the vivid scaremongering now features everything but ISIS werewolves tagging up with MS-13 zombies, but Bossie's was a cut above.

In May 2019, Trump figured out how much money was rolling into Bossie's pockets and realized the scope of the scam. Bossie's "Presidential Coalition" raised $15.4 million and spent just $425,000 on actual campaign activity. Trump snapped, releasing a statement aimed squarely at Bossie's low forehead:

President Trump's campaign condemns any organization that deceptively uses the president's name, likeness, trademarks, or branding and confuses voters. There is no excuse for any group, including ones run by people who claim to be part of our coalition, to suggest they directly support President Trump's reelection or any other candidates, when in fact their actions show they are interested in filling their own pockets with money from innocent Americans' paychecks and, sadly, retirements. We encourage the appropriate authorities to investigate all alleged scam groups for potential illegal activities.[14]

When the Campaign Legal Center broke the Bossie story, it wasn't a shock to anyone inside the campaign world; Bossie's long series of hustles seemed to have a high cost and low impact. In one campaign we helped in the late 2000s, Bossie, Roger Stone, and Dick Morris seemed to pocket roughly ten times more in "consulting fees" than hit the airwaves in the ads we made for the effort. It was a shock to one person, however, and that person was Donald Trump.

"There is a cottage industry of groups targeting vulnerable communities with self-serving borderline scams. What sets the Presidential Coalition apart is that it is explicitly—and successfully—capitalizing on Bossie's connection with the president of the United States."[15]

So powerful was the condemnation of Trump, virtually the only person willing to defend Bossie was Richard Viguerie, another vampire squid who has spent decades bleeding cash away from credulous old folks for various iterations of scammy undertakings.

As in 2016, not every Trump supporter is a vile, cousin-fucking, Jew-hating racist shitbird, but in 2020, all the vile, cousin-fucking, Jew-hating racist shitbirds are Trump supporters. This time, he'll be looking to squeeze out any advantage, and if he sees a path to turn out that faction for him again without opposition, he'll most certainly take it.

THE GREATEST HITS ARE COMING BACK

Trump is like a black hole of sleaze, a singularity of scumbags drawing the worst of the worst into his crappy orbit. Many of these people are, to put it mildly, now long-term guests of the federal government in facilities not known for their turndown service and Pratesi linens. You'd do well to continue to remind the American people just how many of the Best People in Trump's world are, you know, fucking criminals and scumbags. There's no downside in reminding Americans about the people around Trump. The list is long, and distinguished only in their scummy opportunism.

STEVE BANNON

Bannon is the Maximum Leader of the nationalist-populist Wee Fascists Club and, as an apostate to Trump, a rich target to bring back into the dialogue. It won't be hard, and it will vex the hell out of the Donald. Trump was for a time under Bannon's greasy spell but cast Gristle Icarus into the outer darkness for leaking. Because Bannon cannot resist the media, he'll be back from his supervillain lair in Europe to opine, and opine, and opine on Trump, immigration, nationalism, and how to get the blood of Gypsy children out of your Barbour jacket.

PAUL MANAFORT

Paul Manafort is busy right now, mostly in prison, but I'm sure reminding the president of the United States that his former campaign chairman was a mobbed-up Russian money launderer and scumbag now serving a long stretch in the hard yard will go just fine with President Touchy Bastard.

Also, he's still in prison.

MICHAEL COHEN

Michael Cohen is still a dangerous loose cannon, and has the potential to drag Trump's dirty laundry into the 2020 campaign. Someone needs to fill up his commissary account, get his wife a book deal, and get Mike talking. He's angry, Trump fears him, and he's still got tales to tell.

ROGER STONE

Former Trump advisor and a walking example of the Everything Trump Touches Dies rule, Roger Stone has watched his fortune plummet. Abandoned by Trump, his last scam PAC efforts from 2016 are behind him now, and he's reduced to being a sad old man in a one-bedroom apartment shitposting on Instagram for his legal defense fund.

Roger will likely soon be spending more time with Paul Manafort in the custody of the federal correctional system.

PART 6

EPILOGUE

I know not all of this book was easy to read for my Democratic friends. I poked you in some soft spots that generally breed a bit of resentment, because the truths are hard, and my elbows are sharp.

I told you in the beginning I would treat you like a client, and clients don't pay me to be delicate with their feelings. Some of the advice in this book will be heeded, some not.

Do not, as my party did, underestimate the evil, desperate nature of evil, desperate people. Do not come to this fight believing that the Trump team views any action, including outright criminality, as off-limits. This is a battle that decides whether they have an unlimited runway to create a dynastic kleptocracy based on an authoritarian personality cult that makes North Korea look like Sweden, or whether the immune system of the republic kicks in and purges them from the body politic.

If I was facing Trump, knowing what I've learned about him in the past four, long, dark, shitty years, I'd work based off that knowledge. I'd know that there is no bottom. There is no shame. There are no limits. He'll push beyond all norms and boundaries, because losing this race most likely ends up with a trip to prison. Winning means a century of Trumps. I'd know that politics triumphs over policy, and passion triumphs over ideology. I'd lie, and cheat, and fight so dirty that it would barely be on this side of the law.

Well? How about it? You're in a bar fight with bikers, not a fucking

Princeton debating society. You gonna pick up the axe handle and start swinging, or you gonna try to win based on a 600-page health-care plan? Are you going to shut up about the shit you know is political poison in the Rust Belt, or are you afraid of Woke Twitter and Media Matters?

Are you going to—in the words of Winston Churchill—deserve victory?

Trump is surrounded by cowards with frightening and tremendous skills, and they understand you as well as I do. We fought alongside them to destroy you and your party for decades, and they're damn good at it. They will never let you make a mistake without cost. They will take help from any enemy of this nation in order to win, as they proved in 2016.

They will never blink or stop or give you the benefit of the doubt. To rely on their mercy is to beg for your political death. They are smart—smarter than your folks, in many cases. They always had to work with the folks we had, and unlike you, we rarely pulled a magical, generational wunderkind candidate like Obama, JFK, or Bill Clinton.

And they'll burn this country to the fucking ground to win. You'll cry out in horror at what they'll do and how far they'll go. They will ignite a race war, wreck the economy, and abuse their fellow humans to win. They put children in cages for political theater, and laughed about it.

Never, ever underestimate how much they'll do to survive.

Trump is not invulnerable. He is broadly loathed, seen as a liar and a moral failure. He is beset with legal and criminal exposure at every turn. He is a specific flavor that works for a specific set of demographics. He is stupid, but cunning. He is unpredictable, but shallow. He is corrupt, but brazen. He is a reckless, day-trading gambler with the luck of the devil. He is a sign and a symptom of an America in transition from one world to the next, and a rebuke to a broken two-party system. He will always be with us, to the end of our days, either as a warning or as a boot stomping on our faces, forever.

Donald Trump has long avoided the judgment he deserves on every front, and America is at a crossroads so important and so urgent that we are all faced with difficult choices and painful compromises. I beg you: Run the campaign you should rather than the one you want.

2020 will demand much of you.

If I can leave you with one final piece of counsel, it is this: Compromise on everything except your utter commitment to his absolute, crushing defeat.

Do America a favor, OK?

Don't fuck this up.

ELECTION NIGHT, NOVEMBER 3, 2020

It's Election Night, and you feel something familiar in the air. It's a feeling of confidence, of rising joy and anticipation. It's been a long, tough campaign, but victory is in sight.

You're going to win, and you know it. It's a certainty. After four years of Trump, the Democrats are poised to claim a sweeping Electoral College and popular-vote victory.

Finally.

The last few weeks of October were a blissful whirl, with polling numbers looking strong across the board but your candidate joyfully working the crowds in swing states. She's a happy warrior, praised for her political skills and the subject of endless glowing media profiles, but she keeps coming back to the big message: This is a referendum on Donald Trump. Almost every newspaper in America endorsed her in the final week, picking up that message; this is about removing him, at all costs. Your campaign broadened its appeal, not reaching a state of beautiful progressive wokeness but of a sense of common mission and purpose, a promise to restore American norms and values.

After the debates, it was clear your candidate, though occasionally rattled by Trump's in-your-grill debating presence, had triumphed. She was smart, articulate, humble, and when it mattered, she hammered his weak spots. It's everything you've dreamed about since Obama. Trump has been flailing, angrily tweeting a dozen times a day, stoking the MAGA base at an endless series of campaign rallies, but he's punchy and tired, and looks worn-out.

Your campaign has a hard rule against engaging even those elliptical conversations about what role you might play in a Democratic White House. Instead, any time someone starts one, you cut it off, pushing them to focus on their mission, and work harder for the win. You're going to need to rebuild the government from scratch, but there's time for that after you defeat Trump.

A few of your older, wiser hands are grudgingly pleased, smiles slowly spreading on their weathered faces. They see how hard the team is working, down to the door-knockers and phone-bankers, all of whom are tracked to the very limits of technology. Everyone is exhausted, but people are knocking on doors, making calls, and pushing out voters until even after the polls close. The candidate herself insisted on adding events until the last second, her voice shot, her advance team shaky. Your finance people report that the campaign is going to end with just enough money in the bank to pay salaries and expenses, and not a dollar more. Everything else—*everything*—is either on the air in the swing states or in digital advertising to targeted voters.

They keep staring intently at the FiveThirtyEight map and running the same mental calculations over Electoral College numbers they've done a thousand times, but hey, you feel really great about this, not because of anecdotes, but because of data. You spent an eye-popping amount on targeting, data analytics, and digital, more than any campaign in history. You fought only where the battle was, and let the rest take care of itself. You ignored the screams from safe blue states, and kept the candidate and your dollars in the fifteen states you knew were the swing battlegrounds.

The campaign's social-media metrics were weird the last few days, though, and your data and analytics people counterpunched hard against the massive inflows of ads from brand-new Republican super PACs and 501(c)(4) dark-money groups. You couldn't take the chance this was just the last gasp for the Trumpian grifters making a last buck on the Donald. You suspected it was his Russian friends trying an end-run, just like 2016, but you had ads in the can, and a budget to respond. The Trump campaign and the RNC (but I repeat myself) ad buys were scattershot, and on issues that seemed off-kilter.

As the night starts, the ballroom is packed to the gills with eager, happy people ready to put Trump and Trumpism in the rearview mirror of history. The media risers, crowded with the A-talent from every network, are jammed. The results are about to come in, and the army of reporters in the back of the ballroom is in a near-frenzy.

You didn't repeat the Hillary mistake of not visiting the states Trump and his Russian allies scored in 2016. Your candidate made the stops, and your advance and targeting efforts filled the halls and stadiums with big, happy, raucous crowds. Trump's rallies were full, but the 2016 magic was missing from 2020, and it showed. Your state organizers tell you they've got armies of volunteers knocking on doors, making calls, and driving turnout. Your monitoring and data systems confirm it for you.

Still, the final tracking polls were close. You knew you couldn't take your foot off the pedal in Florida, Wisconsin, Arizona, Michigan, Ohio, and the rest. You took absolutely nothing for granted.

The exit polls were closer than you wanted but still looked good. As the first results were about to roll in, the AP, *Washington Post, New York Times,* Decision Desk, and *Politico* analysts started pinging you and the rest of the campaign's senior staff.

"What's going on in Michigan? Do you hear this stuff out of Florida?" Something is moving, something big, and you don't quite know what it is yet.

By 9:30, it's not looking like what you expected. Ohio, where polls showed Trump with a razor-thin lead, is breaking, barely, your way. He's losing Michigan, as record turnout in Detroit rolls up a massive African American turnout, and the expected defection of suburban women means a bloodbath for Trump in Macomb and Oakland counties.

Florida is Florida, and although you had projected a four-point lead, by 10:00 the vote total shows the usual tied ballgame. It's going to be a long night in the Sunshine State, but the exits are showing that you swung the Orlando, Tampa, and even Jacksonville suburbs cleanly enough to offset the blowout in the Panhandle and on the Gold Coast of southwest Florida.

Florida's enormous influx of Puerto Rican voters meant the Democrats were on track for a stunning victory there because someone bothered to register them, communicate with them, and turn them out. *You* did. You fired any consultant who wouldn't produce results.

You post sky-high numbers in South Florida.

"What the hell is happening in Wisconsin?" is your next question. With the Democratic gains in 2018, you expected to do well, but as local results roll in, it seems that 2018 wasn't a fluke; Trump's deep unpopularity is realigning the state. The disastrous scam of Foxconn left Wisconsin workers holding the bag for a failed deal with China. Wisconsin farmers had suffered terribly from Trump's trade war. The Wisconsin GOP is wiped out, top to bottom.

Pennsylvania is a blowout. You focused on calling out Trump's economic bullshit in western PA and rolled up earthshaking female turnout in Philly and its suburbs, and it worked.

Hell, even Texas is closer than you thought, though you still don't win it. You lose New Hampshire by a nose, but Shaheen holds the seat. Taxes are still a thing there, and that's one message you couldn't escape.

In nearly every swing state, you're losing rural areas and taking the most affluent suburbs, just as you planned. Turnout is sky-high everywhere, and you needed it. GOP turnout percentages are just as high, but the party itself isn't what it was. All those newly minted independents in the suburbs used to be Republicans, and you were there to catch them.

That's why, come midnight, your candidate is in the suite, taking the call from Donald Trump to concede the election. There are tears all around. You can hear Trump on the speakerphone, curt and smug. His concession tweet will be late in coming.

———

The next morning, you begin to put together the mosaic of data points in your head from the last few weeks. You start to see the messages and strategies Trump and his campaign used that seemed lurid and absurd at the time, and how easily you could have fallen into his traps in the same way Hillary Clinton did in 2016.

You weren't trying to win big, swing the nation toward a new ideological polarity, or be the next savior. You were animals, trapped in a win-or-die moment, and you used tooth and claw to succeed. You realize as the Electoral College numbers for the Democrat rise and rise that Trump's campaign needed the cliché Democrats to run the cliché campaigns of the past, and you refused to play that game.

Suddenly, you see that your candidate's refusal to be bound to policy proposals and white papers, and her very measured words on climate change, reparations for slavery, Electoral College reform, guns, the Green New Deal, and healthcare policy, were assets. You put electoral realities ahead of progressive fantasies, and as difficult as it was, it paid off. Refusing to give Alexandria Ocasio-Cortez and Bernie Sanders keynote addresses at the convention where they could declare fraternal communist solidarity with the workers of the world was a smart move.

You refused to let the primary race to secure the progressive bleeding ideological edge blind you to the reality of largely center-right states on the Electoral College scoreboard. You refused to hand Trump the weapons he could use to cut off your head. You knew Trump's lowest-common-denominator message was cultish, racist, and blisteringly stupid, and even though it was simple, constant, and repeated, you refused to feed him issues to use against you.

Wall. MAGA. Judges. Socialism. Revenge.

You laughed it off, bringing it back to Trump, over and over. You posited one question, and one question only: "Should this man be president?" You never, ever lost focus on the fact that this election is—I promise, this is almost the last reminder on this point—a referendum on Donald Fucking Trump.

You believe in your progressive message but know it isn't universal, and you know the swing states have a very different political polarity from California, New York, or Massachusetts. You knew you could never shame Trump or Trump voters into listening to the better angels of their nature by talking about diversity, inclusion, and progressive values. You never gave the Trump campaign fodder for the weaponized grievance machine that put him in office in the first place.

You never let them distort, twist, or slander your message, policies, and values. You turned out your base, and added to it, winning back the Obama-Trump voters, consolidating African American and Hispanic support, and appealing to the moderates in both the GOP and the Democratic Party. You destroyed the GOP with Hispanics, winning almost 80 percent of their vote for the first time ever. Kids in cages turned out to be a bad look.

You beat the worst president in history.

You beat him by making the campaign about him; his record, his hideous personal behavior, the reeking cloud of corruption, and his broken economic promises made him unelectable for even a decent campaign, and you ran—shockingly—a decent campaign. His divisive, shitty, be-worst reign was a stain and an embarrassment. He tried to make it a referendum on policy, not a referendum on himself, and you never let him. You went into a reality-television contest understanding the rules, and you beat the master of the genre at his own game.

The sun is rising over America again, and you're exhausted, beaten down, and shaking. For five years, you've greeted every Trump tweet with a sense of dread. Has he conceded?

Does it matter?

At this point you open the Twitter client on your iPhone, enter "@realDonaldTrump" one last time, and do what America just did, and put him on mute, forever.

You send a text message to Kellyanne Conway: "In the words of the poet, sage, and philosopher DJ Khaled, 'You played yourself.'"

ACKNOWLEDGMENTS

I would like to thank Mary Reynics, my editor at Crown Forum, for her consistently excellent insights into how to make *RATD* more relevant, more engaging, and sharper. She's a delight to work with as a friend and as an editor, and doesn't hesitate to whack out large blocks of my text with a cold-eyed efficiency that's slightly terrifying but ultimately makes for a more crisp and illuminating read.

My agent, Christy Fletcher, is, as always, a rock star, and I literally couldn't do this without her. She has the ability to look at five hundred of my random ideas and grab the ones that work, every time.

As always, the love, support, tolerance (*so* much tolerance), and outstanding humor of Molly, Nora, and Andrew are as amazing to me every day as they are unstinting. I'm truly blessed with a family who are all loving, brilliant, and strong as hell.

I also treasure the love, encouragement, and occasional shit-checking of a circle of personal and political friends who keep my head from growing too large (have you *seen* this thing? It's gigantic to start with) and who are all in this fight in their own ways.

NOTES

INTRODUCTION TO THE PAPERBACK EDITION

1. Steve Peoples, "Election Year to Feature Bitter Fights, Deepening Divides," *AP News,* January 6, 2020, apnews.com/b79ca550fa2dca88b3799477b700542e.
2. Karen Hao, "Nearly Half of Twitter Accounts Pushing to Reopen America May Be Bots," *MIT Technology Review,* May 21, 2020, www.technologyreview.com /2020/05/21/1002105/covid-bot-twitter-accounts-push-to-reopen-america.

PART I: THE CASE AGAINST TRUMP, OR FOUR MORE YEARS IN HELL

1. Cristina Maza, "Sanctioned Russian Oligarch's Company to Invest Millions in New Aluminum Plant in Mitch McConnell's State," *Newsweek,* April 15, 2019, www.newsweek.com/company-russian-oligarch-millions-aluminum-plant -mitch-mcconnell-1397061.
2. Paul Kane, "McConnell Defends Blocking Election Security Bill, Rejects Criticism He Is Aiding Russia," *Washington Post,* July 29, 2019, www .washingtonpost.com/politics/mcconnell-defends-blocking-election-security -bill-rejects-criticism-he-is-aiding-russia/2019/07/29/08dca6d4-b239-11e9 -951e-de024209545d_story.html.
3. Donald J. Trump, @realDonaldTrump, Twitter.com, April 14, 2019, twitter .com/realDonaldTrump/status/1117428291227533312.
4. Julie Hirschfeld Davis, "Trump, at Putin's Side, Questions U.S. Intelligence on 2016 Election," *New York Times,* July 16, 2018, www.nytimes.com/2018/07/16/ world/europe/trump-putin-election-intelligence.html.
5. David D. Kirkpatrick, Ben Hubbard, Mark Landler, and Mark Mazzetti, "The Wooing of Jared Kushner: How the Saudis Got a Friend in the White House," *New York Times,* December 8, 2018, www.nytimes.com/2018/12/08/world/ middleeast/saudi-mbs-jared-kushner.html.
6. Nahal Toosi, "U.K. Defends Ambassador After Disparaging Trump Comments Leak," *Politico,* July 6, 2019, politi.co/2NFxFB6.

7. Tom McCarthy, "Pence Acknowledges Tie-Breaker May Be Needed to Confirm Kavanaugh," *The Guardian*, September 9, 2018, www.theguardian.com/law/2018/sep/09/brett-kavanaugh-supreme-court-confirmation-mike-pence-tie-breaker-vote.

8. Dylan Matthews, "How the 9th Circuit Became Conservatives' Least Favorite Court," *Vox*, January 10, 2018, www.vox.com/policy-and-politics/2018/1/10/16873718/ninth-circuit-court-appeals-liberal-conservative-trump-tweet.

9. David Brennan, "Does Windmill Noise Cause Cancer? Donald Trump Renews Campaign Against Wind Power with New Claim," *Newsweek*, April 3, 2019, www.newsweek.com/donald-trump-wind-power-windmills-noise-cancer-renewable-energy-birds-1384338.

10. I was the first Republican consultant to condemn the stupid birther smear in 2008. Relax, people.

11. Julie Bykowicz, "Checking In: Report Lists Dozens of Groups That Used Trump Properties," *Wall Street Journal*, January 16, 2018, www.wsj.com/articles/checking-in-report-lists-dozens-of-groups-that-used-trump-properties-1516078861.

12. Natasha Bertrand and Bryan Bender. "Air Force Crew Made an Odd Stop on a Routine Trip: Trump's Scottish Resort," *Politico*, September 6, 2019, politi.co/2A1XDVG.

13. David Smith, "Trump Nepotism Attacked After 'Out-of-Her-Depth' Ivanka Given Key Summit Role," *The Guardian*, July 1, 2019, www.theguardian.com/us-news/2019/jul/01/donald-trump-ivanka-g20-north-korea-nepotism.

14. "John Bolton Left in Mongolia While Trump Schmoozed in North Korea," *Vanity Fair*. n.d. Web. July 1, 2019, www.vanityfair.com/news/2019/07/john-bolton-mongolia-trump-tucker-carlson-schmoozed-in-north-korea.

15. Garry Kasparov, @Kasparov63, Twitter.com, June 24, 2019, twitter.com/Kasparov63/status/808750564284702720.

16. Martin Matishak and Kyle Cheney, "Senate Intelligence Leaders: Russians Schemed to Help Trump," *Politico*, May 16, 2018, politi.co/2rN6N3T.

17. *The Federalist Papers* No. 10, Avalon.law.yale.edu, n.d., avalon.law.yale.edu/18th_century/fed10.asp.

PART 2: THE MYTHS OF 2020

1. Orion Rummler, "Where Each 2020 Democrat Stands on Abolishing the Electoral College," *Axios*, April 7, 2019, www.axios.com/electoral-college-2020-presidential-election-candidates-94d89ca6-b402-4de3-ae8e-06139592408e.html.

2. Ryan Bort, "What It Would (Really) Take to Abolish the Electoral College," *Rolling Stone*, March 19, 2019, www.rollingstone.com/politics/politics-news/electoral-college-2020-810187.

3. Greg Sargent, "How Democrats Can Defeat Trump and His Ugly Ideas, According to Pete Buttigieg," *Washington Post*, March 19, 2019, www.washingtonpost.com/opinions/2019/03/19/how-democrats-can-defeat-trump-his-ugly-ideas-according-pete-buttigieg.

4. Pew Research Center, U.S. Politics and Policy, "Public's 2019 Priorities: Economy, Health Care, Education and Security All Near Top of List," January 24, 2019, www.people-press.org/2019/01/24/publics-2019-priorities-economy-health-care-education-and-security-all-near-top-of-list.

5. "Cook Partisan Voting Index," Wikipedia, the Free Encyclopedia, Wikimedia Foundation, September 7, 2019, en.wikipedia.org/wiki/Cook_Partisan_Voting_Index.

6. William Cummings, "Obama Warns Democrats That Ideological 'Rigidity' Can Lead to a 'Circular Firing Squad,'" USA Today, April 8, 2019, www.usatoday.com/story/news/politics/elections/2019/04/08/2020-election-barack-obama-warns-democrats-circular-firing-squad/3398051002.

7. Stephen Hawkins, Daniel Yudkin, Míriam Juan-Torres, Tim Dixon, "Profiles of the Hidden Tribes," Hidden Tribes of America project, More in Common, 2018, hiddentribes.us/profiles.

8. Ibid.

9. Ibid.

10. Ibid.

11. Ibid.

12. Aaron Blake, "How Trump Wins in 2020: Americans See His Opponent as a 'Socialist,'" Washington Post, July 8, 2019, www.washingtonpost.com/politics/2019/07/08/how-trump-wins-americans-see-his-opponent-socialist.

13. Neil Newhouse, memorandum, Public Opinion Strategies, February 22, 2019, pos.org/wp-content/uploads/2019/02/National-POS-poll-Socialism.pdf.

14. Hillary Clinton, press release, June 9, 2008, web.archive.org/web/20080609202817/http://www.hillaryclinton.com/news/release/view/?id=7904.

15. Point Taken–Marist Poll, May 2016, maristpoll.marist.edu/wp-content/misc/usapolls/us160502/Point%20Taken/Reparations/Exclusive%20Point%20Taken-Marist%20Poll_Reparations%20Banner%201_May%202016.pdf#page=4.

16. Tom Curry, "Young Voters Not Essential to Obama Triumph," MSNBC.com, November 7, 2008, www.nbcnews.com/id/27582147/ns/politics-decision_08/t/young-voters-not-essential-obama-triumph.

17. Grey Gordon, "Accounting for the Rise in College Tuition," National Bureau of Economic Research, December 12, 2017, www.nber.org/chapters/c13711.

PART 3: ARMY OF DARKNESS: TRUMP'S WAR MACHINE

1. Alan Rappeport, "How Companies Learned to Stop Fearing Trump's Twitter Wrath," New York Times, March 20, 2019, www.nytimes.com/2019/03/20/us/politics/trump-twitter-businesses.html; Neal Rothschild, "Metrics Show Trump's Tweets Are Losing Their Potency," Axios, May 26, 2019, www.axios.com/president-trump-tweets-engagement-4c6067a8-734d-4184-984a-d5c9151aa339.html.

2. Jeff Horwitz, "Trump 2020 Working with Ex-Cambridge Analytica Staffers," AP News, June 15, 2018, apnews.com/96928216bdc341ada659447973a688e4.

3. "The Living Room Candidate—Commercials—1984—Train," Livingroom candidate.org, n.d., www.livingroomcandidate.org/commercials/1984.

4. Tamara Keith, "With Voter Data and a Volunteer Army, a Whole New Trump Campaign for 2020," NPR Politics, June 27, 2019, www.npr.org/2019/06/ 27/735913950/with-voter-data-and-a-volunteer-army-a-whole-new-trump -campaign-for-2020.

5. Peter Baker and Michael Crowley, "Trump Steps into North Korea and Agrees with Kim Jong-un to Resume Talks," New York Times, June 30, 2019, www .nytimes.com/2019/06/30/world/asia/trump-north-korea-dmz.html.

6. Lindsey Graham, @LindseyGrahamSC, Twitter.com, May 3, 2016, twitter.com/ LindseyGrahamSC/status/727604522156228608.

7. "Leading Cable Networks in the United States in August 2019, by Number of Viewers," Statista, updated September 2, 2019, www.statista.com/statistics/ 347040/cable-networks-viewers-usa.

8. Brendan Nyan and Jason Reifler, "When Corrections Fail: The Persistence of Political Misperceptions," Dartmouth.edu, July 12, 2011, www.dartmouth .edu/~nyhan/nyhan-reifler.pdf.

9. Kevin Roose, "Here Come the Fake Videos, Too," New York Times, March 4, 2018, www.nytimes.com/2018/03/04/technology/fake-videos-deepfakes.html.

10. Eric Hoffer, The True Believer: Thoughts on the Nature of Mass Movements (New York: Harper, 1951), 83.

11. Hannah Arendt, The Origins of Totalitarianism (New York: Harcourt, Brace, 1968), 474.

PART 4: HOW TO LOSE

1. Gallup poll, "Abortion," February 1, 2019, news.gallup.com/poll/1576/Abortion .aspx.

2. Donald J. Trump, @realDonaldTrump, Twitter.com, January 31, 2019, twitter .com/realDonaldTrump/status/1090967053689937921.

3. John Cassidy, "James Comey's October Surprise," The New Yorker, October 28, 2016, www.newyorker.com/news/john-cassidy/james-comeys-october -surprise.

4. Kellyanne Conway, @KellyannePolls, Twitter.com, October 28, 2016, twitter.com/ KellyannePolls/status/792055185950515200.

5. Azam Ahmed, Katie Rogers, and Jeff Ernst, "How the Migrant Caravan Became a Trump Election Strategy," New York Times, October 24, 2018, www .nytimes.com/2018/10/24/world/americas/migrant-caravan-trump.html.

6. Donald J. Trump, @realDonaldTrump, Twitter.com, October 24, 2018, twitter .com/realDonaldTrump/status/1055065538890735616.

PART 5: HOW TO WIN

1. Jim Rutenberg, "The 2004 Campaign: The President; 90-Day Strategy by Bush's Aides to Define Kerry," New York Times, March 20, 2004, www.nytimes

.com/2004/03/20/us/the-2004-campaign-the-president-90-day-strategy-by
-bush-s-aides-to-define-kerry.html.

2. Rex Crum, "On Facebook, Trump's Ad Spending Tops Every Democratic Rival," *Mercury News*, May 21, 2019, www.mercurynews.com/2019/05/21/ on-facebook-trumps-ad-spending-tops-every-democratic-rival.

3. Erika Franklin Fowler, Travis N. Ridout, and Michael M. Franz, "Political Advertising in 2016: The Presidential Election as Outlier?," *The Forum* 14, 4 (2017): 445–69, doi:10.1515/for-2016-0040.

4. Issie Lapowsky, "Here's How Facebook *Actually* Won Trump the Presidency," *Wired*, November 15, 2016, www.wired.com/2016/11/facebook-won-trump -election-not-just-fake-news.

5. Maggie Severns, "Dems Prepare 9-Figure Ad Onslaught to Blunt Trump's Head Start," *Politico*, June 16, 2019, politi.co/2WNnYEO.

6. Ibid.

7. Voter Participation Center, "Early Voting by State," updated August 30, 2019, www.voterparticipation.org/voter-hub/early-voting-by-state.

8. Gary Fineout, "Florida Democrats Get an Early Start on the Legal Battle for 2020," *Politico* Florida, May 20, 2019, politi.co/2JqFXKc.

9. Jon Huang, "Election 2016: Exit Polls," *New York Times*, November 8, 2016, www.nytimes.com/interactive/2016/11/08/us/politics/election-exit-polls.html.

10. C. L. Sulzberger, "New Strategy—a Nuclear Maginot Line?" *New York Times*, December 23, 1964, www.nytimes.com/1964/12/23/archives/foreign-affairs -new-strategya-nuclear-maginot-line.html.

11. Jim Geraghty, "The Right's Grifter Problem," *National Review*, June 3, 2019, www.nationalreview.com/the-morning-jolt/the-real-problem-conservatism -faces-today.

12. Emily Smith, "Trump Campaign Staffers Get into Public Screaming Match," *New York Post*, May 19, 2016, pagesix.com/2016/05/19/trump-campaign -staffers-get-into-public-screaming-match.

13. Tina Nguyen, "Trump Buddy David Bossie Accused of Scamming Elderly MAGA Voters," *Vanity Fair*, May 6, 2019, www.vanityfair.com/news/2019/05/ david-bossie-donald-trump-fundraising-scam-accusation.

14. Twitter, "(67) Kayleigh McEnany on Twitter: 'Our @TeamTrump statement on dishonest fundraising groups: "President Trump's campaign condemns any organization that deceptively uses the President's name, likeness, trademarks, or branding and confuses voters," May 7, 2019, twitter.com/i/web/ status/1125842657371144197.

15. Maggie Christ and Brendan Fischer, "'Can I Count on You?' How the Presidential Coalition Has Capitalized on Its Leader's Ties to the President and Misled Donors," Campaign Legal Center with *Axios*, May 5, 2019, campaignlegal .org/document/profiting-proximity-report-presidential-coalitions-misleading -fundraising-practices.

INDEX

PHOTO COURTESY OF THE AUTHOR

ABOUT THE AUTHOR

Rick Wilson is a renowned Republican political strategist, writer, speaker, commentator, and ad-maker. He is editor at large for *The Daily Beast* and also writes for *The Washington Post, Politico, Rolling Stone,* the New York *Daily News, The Hill, The Bulwark,* and *The Spectator.*

Wilson is the author of the 2018 #1 *New York Times* bestselling book *Everything Trump Touches Dies. Running Against the Devil* is his second book.